The Rise of the Alt-Right

The Rise of the Alt-Right

Thomas J. Main

BROOKINGS INSTITUTION PRESS
Washington, D.C.

Copyright © 2018
THE BROOKINGS INSTITUTION
1775 Massachusetts Avenue, N.W., Washington, D.C. 20036
www.brookings.edu

The Brookings Institution is a private nonprofit organization devoted to research, education, and publication on important issues of domestic and foreign policy. Its principal purpose is to bring the highest quality independent research and analysis to bear on current and emerging policy problems. Interpretations or conclusions in Brookings publications should be understood to be solely those of the authors.

Library of Congress Cataloging-in-Publication data are available.
ISBN 9780815732884
ISBN 9780815732907

9 8 7 6 5 4 3 2 1

Typeset in Ehrhardt

Composition by Elliott Beard

To my wife, Carla Main

Contents

Acknowledgments

I wish to thank the following people and institutions for assistance that made this book possible. The Marxe School of Public Affairs at Baruch College, City University of New York, my professional home for more than twenty years, has been a supportive community throughout. Colleagues at Baruch who have been especially supportive as I wrote this book include David Birdsell, Richard Holowczak, Sonia R. Jarvis, Sanders D. Korenman, Jerry Mitchell, Rita Ormsby, Dahlia Remler, Carla Robbins, E.S. Savas, Ryan Alan Smith, Don Waisanen, and Daniel W. Williams. Colleagues at other institutions who were helpful include Danielle Allen, Michael R. Ebner, George Hawley, Sanford Levinson, Mark Lilla, Rose McDermott, Lawrence M. Mead, and Naomi Zack. My indispensable research assistants were Kari Lien, Ryeri Lim, Peter Nasaw, Robert Tulman, and Hui Zong. I received helpful comments as a result of presentations I made at the Faculty Research Seminar of the Marxe School of Public and International Affairs; Oasis New York, an academic discussion group connected to New York University; and the Society for the Study of Africana Philosophy, organized by Alfred Prettyman. Support for writing this book came from the Democracy Fund, whose president, Joe Goldman, and program associate, Chris Crawford, were particularly helpful, and from the PSC CUNY Research Award Program. My analysis of the audiences of online political magazines relied on data provided by the internet traffic monitor SimilarWeb, where Rachel Rembrandt, Yahav Dagan, and Nick Tuchband provided me with invaluable assistance. Important support and guidance were provided by the editorial team at the Brookings Institution Press, which included Carrie Engel, William Finan, Marjorie Pannell, Steven Roman, Janet Walker, and an anonymous reviewer. Juliet Lapidos of the *Los Angeles Times* edited two op-ed articles I wrote for her newspaper and helped me clarify my thinking. I thank Dave Van Zandt of Media Bias/Fact Check for providing useful information and permission to use graphics from his site. Thanks also to Sabrina Monroe and Judy Weinberg of *Newsday* for their help with archival research.

My wife, Carla Main, commented on and edited the full manuscript and provided invaluable advice based on her wide experience in law and journalism. My sons, Henry Main and Joshua Main, being my hope for the future, gave me a reason to keep working. I benefited from brainstorming sessions with my brother, William Main, and supportive conversations with my cousin Margaret Gallacher. I owe my love of learning to my mother, Catherine Main, vital support for my education and much else to my father, George Main, and my Irish sense of humor to my grandmother Catherine Gallacher. All quotes from other sources are provided verbatim unless otherwise indicated. All remaining errors and omissions are my own.

Part I
The Problem of the Alt-Right

1

The Emergence of the Alt-Right

Prior to the 2016 presidential election season, only a handful of political die-hards followed the machinations of a new political ideology called the alternative right, or Alt-Right. So how did this political faction spring from obscurity to occupy center stage in American politics? The conservative movement, the Republican Party, and American politics in general are today in a crisis that is both reflected in and caused by the crystallization of the Alt-Right.

Before the extraordinary presidential election of 2016, the Alt-Right went unnoticed by the general public and was of interest primarily to observers of right-wing extremism. That situation changed when in the heat of the campaign, Donald Trump chose Stephen K. Bannon, former editor of the web outlet *Breitbart News*, as his campaign CEO. Bannon himself described *Breitbart News* as "the platform for the Alt-Right."[1] Hillary Clinton immediately criticized Trump for embracing the "emerging racist ideology known as the 'Alt-Right.' . . . A fringe element has effectively taken over the Republican Party."[2]

Suddenly the Alt-Right went from obscurity to infamy. Many commentators responded to Clinton's speech. Liberals, moderates, and mainstream conservatives praised the speech, while Alt-Right outlets criticized it as irrelevant and low-energy. But public awareness of the new movement shot up, with Google searches of the term "Alt-Right" spiking immediately after Clinton's remarks and then falling but staying at a much higher level than before.[3] The Alt-Right had arrived.

Why is the Alt-Right so widely perceived as a new threat to Republicans and indeed the republic? At first glance, Alt-Rightism seems to be no more than a collection of well-known far-right talking points. It supports the mass deportation of undocumented immigrants and protectionist trade policies. It opposes feminism, diversity, globalism, gun control, and civil rights. Are such positions, which have been staples of the conservative movement for years and about which reasonable people may differ, any more problematic now than they have ever been? Is the Alt-Right's heated rhetoric really more problematic than the conspiracy-mongering and race-baiting found at the fringes of the right for decades?

In fact, the Alt-Right is far more radical and dangerous than the right-wing extremism of past decades. For it is the underlying ideology of the Alt-Right, rather than its controversial policy positions, that merits concern. In the following statements, prominent Alt-Rightists sum up their ideology:

James Kirkpatrick (contributor, *VDARE*): "The Alt Right is . . . a refusal to accept the frame imposed by those who are hostile to us on issues like morality, politics, and culture. . . . Key concepts: A) a critique of egalitarianism; B) a recognition that liberal 'morality' is a tactic to acquire or safeguard power; C) a recognition of HBD [human biodiversity]."[4]

Jared Taylor (editor, *American Renaissance*): "What is the Alt Right? It is a broad, dissident movement that rejects egalitarian orthodoxies. These orthodoxies require us to believe that the sexes are equivalent, that race is meaningless, that all cultures and religions are equally valuable, and that any erotic orientation or identification is healthy. These things we deny. The Alt Right is also skeptical of mass democracy. It opposes foreign aid and foreign intervention—especially for 'nation building.'"[5]

Hateful Heretic (contributor, *The Right Stuff*): "The Alt-Right is the right wing stripped of any superstitious belief in human equality and any admission of the left's moral authority; it is the right in full revolt against the progressive establishment."[6]

Richard Spencer (editor, *Radix Journal*): "The Alt-Right is . . . serious opposition to, not just the left, but also the conservative status quo. . . . The alt-right would agree that . . . race is the foundation for identity. . . . Almost all people in the Alt-Right have an awareness of Jewish influence . . . and . . . [are] skeptical of it."[7]

Kevin MacDonald (editor, *Occidental Observer*): "It's legitimate for white people to identify as white and pursue interests as white Americans."[8]

Mike Enoch (editor, *The Right Stuff*): "The . . . Alt-Right . . . [is about] race realism . . . [and] Jewish power, its affect on our political world geopolitics, United States politics, global politics, everything."[9]

Greg Johnson (editor, *Counter-Currents Publishing*): "The Alternative Right means White Nationalism. . . . White Nationalism['s] . . . self-evident corollary [is] anti-Semitism."[10]

Andrew Anglin, editor of the *Daily Stormer*, an Alt-Right website visited more than 900,000 times each month, gives the basic tenets of the movement as follows:

Anti-Semitism . . . Jews are fundamentally opposed to the White race and Western civilization and so must be confronted and ultimately removed from White societies completely.

    White Countries for White People . . . The end goal of the movement is to establish pure White racial states in all formerly White countries. . . . We believe in mass deportations of all non-White immigrants. . . . This would include, in America, a repatriation to Africa of the descendants of slaves (or an allocation of autonomous territory for them within our current borders).

    Scientific Racism . . . The Alt-Right does not accept the pseudo-scientific claims that "all races are equal. . . ."

    Opposition to Feminism and "Gender Equality," Support for Traditional Families . . . The claim that "men and women are equal" is looked at as entirely ridiculous by the Alt-Right.

    Endorsement of White History . . . We view Whites as the creators and maintainers of Western civilization.

    Cultural Normalization . . . The Alt-Right seeks . . . authoritarian measures to deal with addictive drugs, pornography, crime and other de-generate social ills.

Commonsense Economics . . . Physically remove Jews. . . . Most in the movement would support a type of free market socialism.

White Struggle as a Global Battle. The Alt-Right views the struggle for the continued existence of the White race as a global battle between Whites and the Jews.[11]

Brad Griffin, editor of the website *Occidental Dissent*, who often writes under the pen name Hunter Wallace, describes the Alt-Right's "three hallmark characteristics" as follows:

Realism: I mean that [the] Alt-Right is non-ideological and analyses almost every question from the perspective of whether or not it is true. . . . The Alt-Right looks at the question of racial equality, demands to see the evidence, and draws the conclusion it is just a bunch of bullshit. . . . The evidence for racial equality is less plausible than Medieval alchemists trying to turn lead into gold.

Identity: . . . The Alt-Right's analysis of history and biology has led us to the conclusion that human beings ARE NOT primarily individuals. On the contrary, we are tribal beings who invariably divide the world into in-groups and out-groups, and those tribes have always been in a primor-dial struggle for DOMINANCE. . . . The timeless struggle for DOMI-NANCE between rival groups is why we have POLITICS.

Iconoclasm: Third, the Alt-Right has a strong Nietzchean streak. Even if many of us have studied Nietzsche at one point in our lives and moved on as we grew older, we still tend to relish creating mischief. We enjoy smashing idols.[12]

Peter Brimelow is the founder and editor of *VDARE*, which is named after Virginia Dare, whom he identifies as " 'the first white child of English parents' born in America."[13] He describes himself as a "godfather" of the Alt-Right[14] and offered this definition of the movement:

The Alt Right is the name sometimes given to the group of websites and individuals who have broken with the corrupt, cowardly, intellectually bankrupt, Establishment Right. VDARE.com is often included in it. . . .

The Alt Right surfaces issues that the Establishment Right won't touch—of course most notably, from VDARE.com's point of view, immigration.[15]

Alt-Right leaders, relative to neo-Nazis or Ku Klux Klan supporters, are intellectually and rhetorically sophisticated. Jared Taylor, editor of the *American Renaissance* website, holds degrees from Yale and the Institut d'études politiques, Paris. On his site, Taylor published "An Open Letter to Cuckservatives"—the Alt-Right's insulting term for mainstream conservatives—laying out his beliefs.

In the letter, Taylor denies the notion that "the things you love about America . . . are rooted in certain principles." Rather, "they are rooted in certain people." That is, white people: "Germans, Swedes, Irishmen, and Hungarians could come and contribute to the America you love," Taylor says. "Do you really believe that a future Afro-Hispanic-Caribbean-Asiatic America will be anything like the America your ancestors built?" White nationalism is more important than inalienable rights because "even when they violate your principles, white people build good societies. Even when they abide by your principles, non-whites usually don't."[16]

Richard B. Spencer of the National Policy Institute, who went to the University of Chicago and the University of Virginia, is openly anti-American. In an interview with the *New York Times*, he said, "America as it is currently constituted—and I don't just mean the government; I mean America as constituted spiritually and ideologically—is the fundamental problem. . . . I don't support and agree with much of anything America is doing in the world." He despises "cuckservatives" because "we've recognized the bankruptcy of this ideology, based on 'free markets,' 'values,' and 'American exceptionalism.'"[17]

In short, this new strain of reactionary thought goes beyond the garden-variety racial prejudice of yore—which certainly was bad enough—to a root-and-branch rejection of American political principles. The Alt-Right is a form of radical Gnosticism as fundamental in its rejection of the American democratic tradition as the Communist Party line of the 1930s and the most fevered effusions of New Left radicalism of the 1960s were.

Alt-Rightism is in essence a political ideology rather than a movement, constituency, or interest group. This book is primarily an analysis of Alt-Right ideas—their development, dissemination, and implications for

American political discourse. The movement's history and personalities are taken up in the course of exploring and evaluating its thought. The book's main thesis is that the Alt-Right represents the first new philosophical competitor in the West to democratic liberalism, broadly defined, since the fall of communism. The main challenges to democratic liberalism now come not from the radical left, as was the case in the latter half of the twentieth century, but from the radical right.

The distinctive features of Alt-Right thought can be summed up as the following:

- A rejection of liberal democracy. The Alt-Right holds, in essence, that all men are *not* created equal and concludes that liberal political principles, broadly understood, are obsolete.

- White racialism. A polity can be decent only if the white race is politically dominant.

- Anti-Americanism. As racial equality has displaced white dominance, the United States of America has declined and no longer merits the allegiance of its white citizens; they should transfer their loyalty to the white race.

- Vitriolic rhetoric. The propensity for intemperate language often found at the ends of the political spectrum is taken by the Alt-Right to lengths previously seen only among fringe elements. The movement rejects the standard ethics of controversy and indulges in race-baiting, coarse ethnic humor, prejudicial stereotyping, vituperative criticism, and the flaunting of extremist symbols.

Plan of the Book

Is the Alt-Right big enough to be important? A possible objection to this entire project is that the Alt-Right is so extreme that it is isolated, with no influence on mainstream politics. It is sometimes argued that the Alt-Right has no more connection with mainstream conservative movements than left-wing extremists—communists, for example—have with mainstream liberals. Chapter 2 addresses this concern through an analysis of traffic to web political magazines of various ideological orientations, including the

Alt-Right. The finding is that Alt-Right web magazines have a considerable audience, one comparable in size—as measured by web traffic—to those of established organs of left, right, and centrist opinion. The rise of the Alt-Right is simply this dissemination of its ideas, which is widespread relative to that achieved by other antidemocratic ideologies of the near past and present and represents a toehold gained in American political discourse.

Chapters 3 and 4 concern the intellectual roots of the Alt-Right. Chapter 3 describes the development of what might be called a proto-Alt-Right. The ideological origins of the Alt-Right can be traced back to the appearance of the *National Review* in 1955 and the effort of its founder, William F. Buckley, to define a mainstream conservatism consistent with the American liberal democratic order. Especially early on, those efforts were not always entirely successful. But eventually Buckley cobbled together a rightist ideology that emphasized traditional values, capitalism, and anticommunism, and drove out of the movement anyone to the right of that consensus. But by the early twenty-first century, exiles from conventional conservatism had embraced a more radical rightism than ever before and had organized themselves to make a successful challenge for leadership of the conservative movement. Chapter 4 looks at the crystallization of the Alt-Right as a distinct political ideology during the period 2000–16. How the political shocks of the early twenty-first century and the rise of the new communication medium of the internet contributed to the weakening of traditional gatekeepers of American political discourse is discussed. Some of the Alt-Right intellectuals who took advantage of that new discourse habitat are profiled.

Chapters 5 through 9 look at the ideology of the Alt-Right today. Chapter 5 discusses how to think about political ideologies. Chapter 6 considers the Alt-Right's rejection of American political philosophy as it is expressed in such foundational documents as the Declaration of Independence, the *Federalist Papers*, the Constitution, and other accounts. Chapter 7 looks at the racialism of the Alt-Right, and chapter 8 explores the movement's anti-Americanism. Chapter 9 looks at a variation on Alt-Right ideology that might be called "Alt-Lite," that is, the somewhat watered-down version of the Alt-Right's ideology that is most notably disseminated by *Breitbart News* and that outlet's former editor and former White House adviser, Steve Bannon. Donald Trump is also considered a purveyor of Alt-Lite ideas.

Chapter 10 considers what the rise of the Alt-Right implies for American democratic discourse and sketches a political vision that more effectively responds to some of the concerns the Alt-Right has identified. The Alt-Right is wrong in thinking the nation is dominated by what it calls a "managerial oligarchy," which amounts to saying that America is practically a totalitarian regime. A correct diagnosis is much simpler: American politics is unduly influenced by the very rich. Through constitutional and political reform, America needs to get much better at redistributing the wealth generated by its economy so as to compensate and reintegrate the interests that temporarily lose out in the inevitable processes of globalization and capitalist creative destruction. Better redistribution requires a political system less dominated by gridlocked factions and more responsive to ideas that can override group interests. An American political process in which public ideas are stronger than they are now—stronger relative to other resources, such as money, votes, and organization—would improve democratic accountability and make the system more responsive to nonelite groups in general, including the "Middle American Radicals," or white working class, with whom the Alt-Right is sympathetic.

Absolutely the worst possible response to the challenges of economic restructuring is that forwarded by the Alt-Right: fragmenting still more the already blooming, buzzing confusion of American interest group politics by further subdividing the polity into the windowless, irreconcilable monads of racially defined identity groups. The likely consequences of the radically racialist form of identity politics espoused by the Alt-Right are disorder, violence, and economic shrinkage. Vastly more promising is a political order in which all interests accept a liberal democratic framework, acknowledge each other's legitimate aspirations, and remain open to persuasion by convincing public ideas.

2
How Big Is the Alt-Right?
Analysis of Web Magazines' Visitorship

If the following of the Alt-Right is minuscule, perhaps it is best snubbed, as fringe elements used to be. In November 2016, then Fox News commentator Bill O'Reilly made that argument in a TV segment on the Alt-Right, or the "white power" movement, as he called it.[1] The gist was that the movement was extremely small. O'Reilly pointed out that a recent Washington, D.C., press conference held by Alt-Righter Richard Spencer drew only about 275 participants but fifty journalists, that only a few thousand hate crimes are committed in the United States each year, and that most Trump supporters aren't racists. O'Reilly's conclusion: the white power people were "hapless nuts" but so few in number as to be unimportant; they were getting attention only because the liberal media wanted to discredit Trump.

Alt-Right figures have made suggestions about the size of their audience. In August 2016 Andrew Anglin, editor of the *Daily Stormer*, one of the most radical Alt-Right websites, claimed the movement had a "cohesive constituency" of 4 million to 6 million people, but did not disclose the basis for his estimate.[2] Brad Griffin, who usually writes under the pen name Hunter Wallace, is the founder and editor of another such site, *Oc-*

11

cidental Dissent. He noted the movement was "so anonymous and online based that no one really knows" how large it is, but guessed it had "a core of several hundred thousand and a much wider sphere of sympathizers and fellow travelers."[3] But again, these are mere guesses.

So a better-grounded estimate of the size of the Alt-Right's following is needed if we are to know whether the movement is too small to care about or too large to ignore. But in the context of political movements, size is a relative matter. Whether a movement is "big enough" depends on what it is trying to do and how big the other movements are that are trying to do the same thing. What, then, is the Alt-Right trying to do?

Greg Johnson answered this question when he was asked what the purpose is of his Alt-Right web magazine, *Counter-Currents Publishing*. Johnson responded:

> I'm running a small business, really, and the business is metapolitics. . . . People say that politics is the art of the possible. Well, what determines people's view of possibility? It's their basic ideas about how the world works and about who they are. So, if you change people's ideas about identity, about morality, about the politically possible, you make new things possible in the political realm and that's what we're trying to do. We're trying to make White Nationalism conceivable for people that simply find it inconceivable and absurd at the present time, and I think that we're making some inroads because I keep getting new people tuning in saying, "Hey, you've had a big influence on me. I'm beginning to see the world as you see it. Is there something I can do? I'd like to start writing for you."[4]

Johnson is in the business of "metapolitics"—that is, changing how people *think about* politics—as a preliminary step to changing the political order farther down the line. Most important figures among the Alt-Right say the same thing: for the present, the Alt-Right is about metapolitics, that is, about changing people's basic ideas about how politics works.

The term *metapolitics* was developed by the European New Right (ENR), a political movement that the American Alt-Right knows well and seeks to emulate. One prominent figure of the ENR who has influenced the Alt-Right is Daniel Friberg, a leader of the Swedish New Right and CEO of Arktos Media, a publisher of reactionary literature. According to Friberg:

Metapolitics can be defined as the process of disseminating and anchoring a particular set of cultural ideas, attitudes, and values in a society, which eventually leads to deeper political change. This work need not—and perhaps should not—be linked to a particular party or programme. The point is ultimately to redefine the conditions under which politics is conceived, which the European cultural Left pushed to its extreme.[5]

Just as the ENR seeks to emulate what it sees as the metapolitical success of the European cultural left, so the Alt-Right tries to adopt the metapolitical strategy of the ENR into American politics and challenge the alleged intellectual hegemony of mainstream ideologies, especially mainstream conservatism.

Thus Hunter Wallace explains that "the definition of 'effective metapolitics' would be 'intellectual work' that is successful in *narrowing the gap* between White America and White Nationalists." And Richard Spencer of *Radix Journal* and ALTRIGHT.com has written "The Charlottesville Statement: A Meta-Political Manifesto for the Alt-Right Movement," which defines a cardinal point of the movement's ideology in the following way:

Metapolitics: Spirit is the wellspring of culture, and politics is downstream of that. The Alt-Right wages a situational and ideological war on those deconstructing European history and identity. The decrepit values of Woodstock and Wall Street mean nothing to us.[6]

Spencer made the same point more prosaically at a Washington, D.C., press conference when he said, "I don't think the best way of understanding the alt-right is strictly in terms of policy. I think metapolitics is more important than politics. I think big ideas are more important than policies."[7]

In short, for the present, the Alt-Right is most accurately thought of not as a voting bloc, interest group, demographic constituency, or party organization but as a metapolitical or, to use a more familiar term, an ideological movement. The question then is how large, and by what measure, does an ideological movement have to be to have an impact on the way nonideological actors think about politics? The rest of the chapter attempts to develop such an estimate.

Methodology

First of all, we need to decide what exactly we mean by the following of or audience for the Alt-Right and what data exist to measure it. A poll published by the Pew Research Center in December 2016 found that 54 percent of American adults had heard "nothing at all" about the Alt-Right, while 28 percent had heard "a little" and 17 percent had heard "a lot." The poll, however, did not address how many might be movement followers. There is no way to determine the number of Alt-Right "trolls," that is, anonymous users of various digital media who make rude right-wing comments. However, there are good data on the traffic to Alt-Right websites, so the audience of these movement outlets can be determined. Finding out how many people visit the *Daily Stormer*, *Occidental Dissent*, and similar sites is a feasible first step to gauging the Alt-Right's following.

This study used data provided by the internet traffic monitor Similar-Web. Data were available for both *visits* and *unique visitors*, which are distinguished as follows: if one person accesses a website five separate times in one day, that represents five visits but only one unique visitor (based on ISP address).

But what websites should be counted as Alt-Right? The pitfalls to be avoided here are making entirely subjective judgments about what counts as Alt-Right and then arbitrarily picking a collection of sites to support a predetermined theory. To avoid these traps, I took the following steps:

1. I began not with my own list of Alt-Right sites but with a preexisting list of sites compiled by contributors to an Alt-Right-related forum established at Reddit.com, a network of message boards.[8]

2. I contacted editors of the Alt-Right sites on the Reddit.com list, explained to them my research, and asked what sites they thought should be included in the list.

3. I contacted researchers at the Southern Poverty Law Center and the Center for Right-Wing Studies at the University of California, Berkeley, and asked them for sites to include.

In all cases I was interested in Alt-Right sites only. I did not specifically inquire about sites related to other far-right movements such as neo-Nazism and the Ku Klux Klan (KKK). Thus some sites of potential interest were not listed as Alt-Right. For example, *Stormfront* and David-Duke.com were not included because my sources considered them to be respectively neo-Nazi and KKK in orientation rather than Alt-Right.

I also developed lists of websites of other ideological orientations for a comparative assessment of the size of the Alt-Rite movement: whether a political movement can be considered big depends on its size relative to that of other movements. Thus I sought a list of websites analogous to those of the Alt-Right but associated with other political tendencies.

As to what sort of sites were analogous to the Alt-Right sites, I decided to think of Alt-Right sites as the digital equivalent of hard-copy political magazines. One of the Alt-Right sites, *American Renaissance*, had in fact begun as a print magazine. All of these sites looked very similar to the websites associated with traditional political magazines such as *National Review*, the *New Republic*, *The Nation*, and others.

The next challenge was to find a way of classifying a significant number of political web magazines "objectively," or at least in some systematic manner that reflected more than my personal choice. Fortunately, this task had already been accomplished by the organization Media Bias/Fact Check (MBFC), which describes itself as "an independent online media outlet... dedicated to educating the public on media bias and deceptive news practices . . . [that] follows a strict methodology for determining the biases of sources."[9] MBFC has evaluated hundreds of websites according to its methodology. Figure 2-1 gives a sense of the results of these evaluations.

MBFC News categorized the sites it evaluated according to the following typology: right bias, right-center bias, least biased, left-center bias, left bias. The organization did not have a separate "Alt-Right" category but had evaluated some of the sites I identified as Alt-Right. MBFC evaluated several Alt-Right sites and an Alt-Right-related site. Figure 2-2 shows how MBFC placed the sites on its left-right bias continuum.

In figure 2-2, "National Policy Institute" refers to the website of a think tank established and headed by Richard Spencer, editor of the Alt-Right online magazine *Radix Journal*. That journal was not evaluated by MBFC. The National Policy Institute site evaluation by MBFC is included in figure 2-2 for comparison purposes, to give a sense of how the organization evaluated Alt-Right-related sites. The analysis in this chap-

FIGURE 2-1   **Media Bias/Fact Check Ratings of Selected Sites**

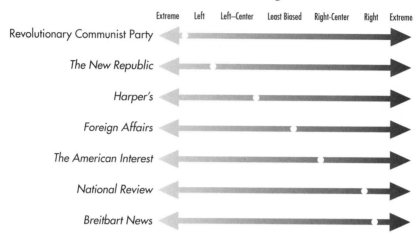

Source: Media Bias/Fact Check (https://mediabiasfactcheck.com).

FIGURE 2-2   **Media Bias/Fact Check Ratings of Alt-Right Sites**

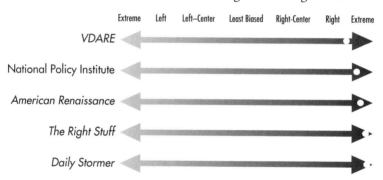

Source: Media Bias/Fact Check (https://mediabiasfactcheck.com).

ter considers the web traffic to the online magazine *Radix Journal* only, not to the site of the associated organization, National Policy Institute.

How much should we rely on the categorizations by MBFC? The organization's owner and editor freely admits that "our methodology is not scientific. . . . We should be viewed more as movie or book critics rather than scientists or researchers."[10] Websites are categorized by volunteers, who adhere to some guidelines and standards but do not have experience as professional journalists. Obviously, a more scientific approach implemented by political scientists or media experts would be preferable. To the best of my knowledge no such scientific or expert classification of a wide range of web political outlets now exists. I relied on MBFC only to provide a rough picture of the types of ideological magazines available on the web and not for an analysis of individual sites. I visited all the websites used in my analysis. The categorizations by MBFC generally agreed with my own intuition, developed from my years of experience in public affairs journalism as an editor, contributor, and reader and my training as a political scientist. The organization's work is probably the best available ratings source of its kind and, despite its limitations, served the purposes of this analysis.

Out of the many sites evaluated by MBFC I selected those of political magazines. Among the sites excluded were those of television networks, newspapers, think tanks, membership organizations, advocacy groups, political parties, and nonpolitical magazines.[11] Only American sites were included. Sites in categories other than Alt-Right sites for which reliable data were not available for every month of the period from October 2015 to February 2018 were not included. In the Alt-Right category there were some sites for which reliable data were not available for every month of that period. Richard Spencer's latest web outlet, ALTRIGHT.com, was not established until January 2017, so there are no data for any month before then. For the month of October 2017, SimilarWeb reported that there were no more than 5,000 visits to two sites established earlier by Spencer, *Alternative Right* and *Radix Journal*. All these sites are of considerable interest and were thus retained in the analysis.[12] In the end, I narrowed the sample to 136 different web magazines (box 2-1).

Findings

Figures 2-3, 2-4, and 2-5 show the number of visits and number of unique visitors each month to the above websites, grouped by ideological category. Table 2-1 shows average visits and unique visitors per month and the percentage change in those variables for the time periods September 2016 to February 2018 and October 2015 to February 2018.

From these data, it is clear that the Alt-Right sites combined have a much smaller audience than the combined sites of all other political orientations. If we look at visits per month between September 2016 and

BOX 2-1 Bias of Political Web Magazines as Categorized by Media Bias/Fact Check (N = 136)

Alt-Right Web Magazines (N=10)

Alternative Right
ALTRIGHT.com
  (01/2017—01/2018
  only)
American Renaissance

Counter-Currents
  Publishing
Daily Stormer
Occidental Dissent
Occidental Observer

Radix Journal
VDARE
The Right Stuff

Right Web Magazines (N = 40)

Accuracy in Media
American Spectator
American Thinker
BizPac Review
Breitbart News Network
Chicks on the Right
Chronicles
City Journal
CNS News
Commentary
Conservative Daily News
Conservative HQ
Conservative Post
Conservative Review

Controversial Times
Daily Signal
FrontPage Magazine
Hot Air
Human Events
Legal Insurrection
Lew Rockwell
Liberty Alliance
Liberty Unyielding
National Review
Newsbusters
PJ Media
Politichicks
Power Line

Red Alert Politics
Red State
Rich Wells
Tea Party Tribune
The Blacksphere
The Federalist
The New American
The Political Insider
The Patriot Post
Townhall
Weekly Standard
WND (World Net Daily)

Right-Center Web Magazines (N = 10)

Anti-War
Cato Institute
Learn Liberty
Naked Capitalism

National Interest
Punching Bag Post
Reason
The American Interest

The American
  Conservative
The Libertarian Republic

Least Biased Web Magazines (N = 14)

Consortium News
Foreign Affairs
Foreign Policy
Harvard Political Review
National Journal

New America Foundation
Open Secrets
Public Integrity
The Conversation
The Humanist

Wilson Quarterly
World News
World Politics Review
World Press Daily

Left-Center Web Magazines (N = 12)

ATTN:
Bill Moyers
Harper's
Mint Press Review
Monthly Review
Ozy

Politico
Propublica
Reveal: Center for
  Investigative
  Journalism
The Fifth Column

TomDispatch.com
World Affairs Journal

Left Web Magazines (N = 50)

Addicting Info
Alternet
AmericaBlog
Bust Magazine
Common Dreams
CounterPunch
Crook and Liars
Daily Kos
Dead State
Democracy Now
Dissent
Drudge Retort
Everyday Feminism
Evonomics
In These Times
Jacobin
Little Green Footballs
Mediaite

Media Matters
Mother Jones
Ms.
Nation of Change
New Republic
News Corpse
News Hounds
OpEdNews (OEN)
PoliticusUSA
Raw Story
Revolutionary
  Communist Party
Reverb Press
Right Wing Watch
Salon
SourceWatch
Talking Points Memo
The American Prospect

The Daily Banter
The Daily Beast
TheGrio
The Nation
The New Civil Rights
  Movement
The Progressive
The Root
Think Progress
Towleroad
Truthdig
Truth Out
Vox
The Washington Monthly
Wonkette
Z Magazine

FIGURE 2-3   **Visits per Month to Web Political Magazines, September 2016–February 2018**

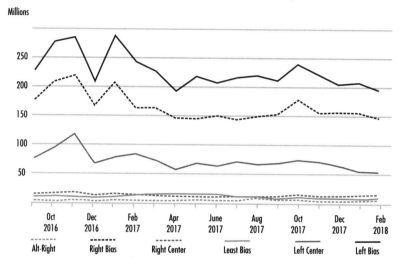

Source: SimilarWeb (www.similarweb.com).

FIGURE 2-4   **Unique Visitors per Month to Web Political Magazines, September 2016–February 2018**

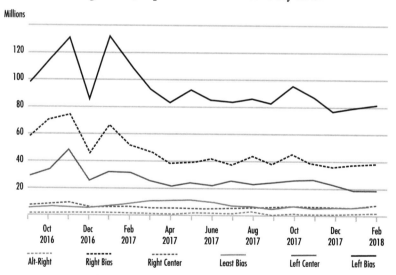

Source: SimilarWeb (www.similarweb.com).

FIGURE 2-5   **Visits per Month to Web Political Magazines, October 2015–February 2018**

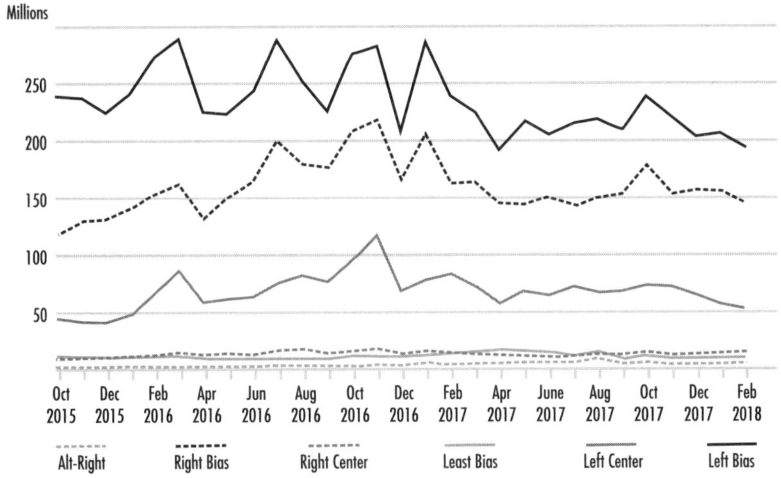

Source: SimilarWeb (www.similarweb.com).

February 2018, the Alt-Right sites combined received a monthly average of 4.4 million visits, compared to 165.5 million visits for right-biased sites and 226.8 million for left-biased sites (center-right and center-left sites are excluded). Visits to Alt-Right sites over this period grew by 33 percent, while visits to right-biased sites and left-biased sites fell by 17 percent and 15 percent, respectively. But this growth for the Alt-Right is not especially impressive, for the Alt-Right sites started from a much lower baseline.

The story is much the same if we look at unique visitors over the September 2016 to February 2018 period. Again, the Alt-Right sites combined had a much smaller audience than the combined sites of all other orientations. Alt-Right sites combined received on average 1.1 million unique visitors a month over that period, compared to 46.9 million and 94.3 million for right- and left-biased sites, respectively. However, unique visitors to Alt-Right, right, and left sites all declined over this period, by 29, 35, and 18 percent, respectively.

The picture changes somewhat and the growth of the Alt-Right looks more noteworthy if we consider the longer time period of October 2015 to February 2018. For this period, data on unique visitors were not available for all websites, so only visits can be considered. Once again, the Alt-

TABLE 2-1   Web Traffic to All Political Magazines

Alt-Right	4.4	+ 33	1.1	− 29	3.6	+ 154
Right	165.5	− 17	46.9	− 35	160.0	+ 23
Right center	13.1	− 1	6.0	+ 10	12.8	+ 60
Least biased	11.1	+ 3	6.9	+ 16	10.5	− 11
Left center	72.7	− 31	26.5	− 34	68.2	+ 21
Left	226.8	− 15	94.3	− 18	235.5	− 19

Source: Data from SimilarWeb (www.similarweb.com).

Right had the least web traffic of all the categories, receiving on average 3.6 million visits per month over this period, compared with 160 million and 235.5 million visits for the right- and left-biased sites, respectively. But over this longer term the Alt-Right showed by far the greatest growth in number of visits, a 154 percent increase, which, however, was achieved from the lowest baseline.

So far the audience of the Alt-Right looks unimpressive. Perhaps, then, we should conclude the Alt-Right is so small that it can safely be ignored, as past fringe movements have been. However, the size of the Alt-Right looks much different when we move from a macro to a micro perspective. Tables 2-2 to 2-4 look at the audiences for selected individual sites.

Tables 2-2 to 2-4 present a different perspective on the size of the Alt-Right's web audience. For the moment, let us consider only the period from September 2016 to February 2018. The coarsely racist *Daily Stormer* received monthly averages of about 956,000 visits and 247,000 unique visitors. In so doing, it drew a larger audience than the sites for such long-standing mainstream magazines as the *Washington Monthly* (853,000 visits, 247,000 unique visitors) and *Commentary* (623,000 visits, 296,000 unique visitors). On the other hand, both monthly visits and unique visitors to the *Daily Stormer* declined by about 95 percent, probably owing to the fact that in recent months the outlet has been kicked off a series of domain registers unwilling to tolerate its obnoxious content.[13]

Also noteworthy was the performance of another very radical site, *The Right Stuff*, at least in terms of visits. During this time period the monthly visits to the site averaged about 1.1 million and grew by 122 percent. The site's performance in terms of unique visitors was less impressive but better than that of some mainstream sites. *American Renaissance* (690,000 visits, 175,000 unique visitors) and *VDARE* (632,000 visits, 170,000 unique visitors) both had larger audiences than the sites of the familiar leftist magazines *Dissent* (196,000 visits, 86,000 unique visitors monthly) and *The Progressive* (145,000 visits, 71,000 unique visitors). Of course, traditional intellectual elites have not been overthrown. The audiences for *The Nation* (3.9 million visits, 2.3 million unique visitors), the *New Republic* (3.8 million visits, 2.2 million unique visitors), and the *National Review* (about 10 million visits, 4.3 million unique visitors), all well-established magazines, were far larger than that of the combined Alt-Right sites.

On the other hand, the Alt-Right's combined web audience com-

TABLE 2-2   **Average Visits per Month and Percent Change for Total Alt-Right Sites and Selected Individual Sites across the Political Spectrum, September 2016–February 2018**

POLITICAL BIAS	MONTHLY AVERAGE	PERCENT CHANGE
ALT-RIGHT		
Total Alt-Right sites (N = 9, 10*)	4,374,282	+ 33
SELECTED ALT-RIGHT SITES		
Daily Stormer	956,355	− 96
The Right Stuff	1,116,563	+ 122
American Renaissance	689,849	+ 25
VDARE	631,963	+ 126
ALT-LITE		
Breitbart	64,084,589	+ 0
RIGHT		
National Review	10,148,826	+ 24
Weekly Standard	2,300,744	− 24
City Journal	642,379	+ 12
Commentary	623,074	− 20
RIGHT CENTER		
Reason	3,759,170	− 4
American Interest	395,672	− 51
LEFT CENTER		
Harper's	531,554	+ 13
LEFT		
The Nation	3,957,667	− 8
New Republic	3,818,861	− 20
American Prospect	616,674	− 26
Washington Monthly	853,068	− 27
Dissent	196,289	+ 85
The Progressive	145,457	+ 101

*ALTRIGHT.com was established in January 2017.

TABLE 2-3 **Average Unique Visitors per Month and Percent Change for Total Alt-Right Sites and Selected Individual Sites, September 2016–February 2018**

POLITICAL BIAS	MONTHLY AVERAGE	PERCENT CHANGE
ALT-RIGHT		
Total Alt-Right sites (N = 9, 10*)	1,079,499	− 29
SELECTED ALT-RIGHT SITES		
Daily Stormer	296,052	− 95
The Right Stuff	103,550	− 13
American Renaissance	175,440	− 59
VDARE	170,244	+ 40
ALT-LITE		
Breitbart	10,376,378	− 26
RIGHT		
National Review	4,297,045	+ 26
Weekly Standard	1,304,148	− 10
City Journal	279,360	+ 28
Commentary	296,175	− 36
RIGHT CENTER		
Reason	1,903,385	+ 14
American Interest	152,818	− 51
LEFT CENTER		
Harper's	237,371	+ 36
LEFT		
The Nation	2,308,791	+ 3
New Republic	2,159,606	− 18
American Prospect	347,721	− 32
Washington Monthly	247,405	− 68
Dissent	85,733	+ 51
The Progressive	70,839	+120

*ALTRIGHT.com was established in January 2017.

TABLE 2-4 **Average Visits per Month and Percent Change for Total Alt-Right Sites and Selected Individual Sites across the Political Spectrum, October 2015–February 2018**

POLITICAL BIAS	MONTHLY AVERAGE	PERCENT CHANGE
ALT-RIGHT		
Total Alt-Right sites (N = 9, 10*)	3,633,731	+154
SELECTED ALT-RIGHT SITES		
Daily Stormer	829,467	– 92
The Right Stuff	825,052	+371
American Renaissance	618,573	+ 69
VDARE	550,388	+332
ALT-LITE		
Breitbart	57,794,889	+ 72
RIGHT		
National Review	9,864,671	+ 9
Weekly Standard	2,671,767	– 30
City Journal	579,471	+ 95
Commentary	625,257	– 29
RIGHT CENTER		
Reason	3,878,218	+ 17
American Interest	390,549	– 16
LEFT CENTER		
Harper's	502,635	+ 31
LEFT		
The Nation	3,919,193	– 5
New Republic	3,712,037	– 7
American Prospect	602,370	+ 12
Washington Monthly	851,246	+ 20
Dissent	180,158	+134
The Progressive	148,850	+ 29

*ALTRIGHT.com was established in January 2017.

pares quite favorably with that of the *Weekly Standard* (2.3 million visits, 1.3 million unique visitors), the well-known, neoconservative flagship where William Kristol, an Alt-Right bête noire, is based. Further, over the period September 2016 to February 2018, visits to the Alt-Right sites rose by 33 percent, while for the *Weekly Standard* they declined by 24 percent. Unique visitors to both the combined Alt-Right sites and the *Weekly Standard* declined, but by much more for the former than for the latter (29 percent as opposed to 10 percent).

If we look at visits to individual sites over the longer time period of October 2015 to February 2018, the audience of the Alt-Right again looks more striking. Average visits per month over this period to the *Daily Stormer* easily surpassed the number of visits to well-established mainstream outlets such as *Commentary*, *Harper's*, *Dissent*, *The Progressive*, the *American Prospect*, and the *Washington Monthly*. However, visits to the *Daily Stormer* declined by 92 percent, again probably for the reasons mentioned above. *American Renaissance*, *VDARE*, and *The Right Stuff* all achieved striking growth in visits, of 69, 332, and 371 percent, respectively. Those three Alt-Right sites all surpassed *Dissent*, *The Progressive*, and *American Interest* in average visits per month. Further, average monthly visits to all Alt-Right sites combined (3.6 million visits) were more than those to the *Weekly Standard* (2.7 million visits) and grew by 154 percent, while visits to the *Weekly Standard* fell by 30 percent.

The picture changes substantially, however, if we stretch the definition of an Alt-Right site to include *Breitbart News*. My sources did not classify it as such and the site does not explicitly reject political equality as the Alt-Right does. But former *Breitbart* editor Stephen K. Bannon once declared that his publication was "the platform for the alt-right," and its incendiary populism is very much in the movement's style. Some Alt-Rightists describe *Breitbart* and similar outlets as "Alt-Lite," which is an apt term.[14] At about 64 million visits and 10.3 million unique visitors on average per month from September 2016 to February 2018, and 57.8 million visits on average per month from October 2015 to February 2018, *Breitbart* operates in a different league not only from Alt-Right and right sites but also from all other web magazines of any ideological orientation.

Comment

The size of the Alt-Right and whether it is big enough to be of concern depend on the movement's objective. The Alt-Rightists I interviewed described their movement as metapolitical rather than political. That is, the Alt-Right seeks to influence how others think about politics rather than provide input to immediate policy decisions. In this respect the Alt-Right consciously emulates the neoconservatives and the New Left of the 1960s and 1970s. To use a more conventional term, the Alt-Right is an ideological movement rather than a political party, a social movement, a lobbying group, or a constituency seeking immediate electoral or policy goals. Of course, the Alt-Right has characteristic policy concerns. The New Left sought an end to the Vietnam War, neoconservatives wanted welfare reform and tax cuts, and the Alt-Right seeks immigration restrictions and the reversal of civil rights laws. But a primary goal of all these movements was and is ideological: to change the way party operatives, media figures, political activists, other notables, and the public think about politics. Particular policy objectives are a reflection of a broader ideological agenda.

Ideological movements are often led by an elite. Here the term simply refers to a relatively small group of people with a disproportionate amount of influence over the thinking and actions of a larger group. That disproportionate influence may be derived from status, resources, or skills. In the case of an ideological movement, people whose education, training, and talents enable them to understand, develop, and communicate ideas with facility will influence others in a way those without such abilities cannot. Such an ideological elite group does not have to be particularly large for the ideas it develops to trickle down to larger audiences and have an influence. For example, from the mid-1960s through the end of the twentieth century, the *Public Interest*, a particularly influential neoconservative journal, never had more than about 10,000 subscribers. The sum total of editors and contributors to the *Public Interest* and similar journals was even smaller.

The point is that the Alt-Right leaders and their immediate audience may be few in number compared with influential voting blocs, membership organizations, and demographic constituencies, but the core of an intellectual movement is always small. Bill O'Reilly's observations about the smallness of the Alt-Right relative to the total body politic are correct as far as they go, but are not to the point. What counts is not the absolute size of a given elite and its immediate followers but rather the depth of the penetration of that core group's production into mainstream political culture relative to the penetration of rival groups.

By these standards, the web traffic evidence suggests that the Alt-Right has developed an intellectual elite that bears comparison with that of traditional ideologies. The findings presented above are sometimes quite striking in this regard. That the *Daily Stormer, The Right Stuff,* and *American Renaissance* have, by some measures, audiences larger than those of the *Washington Monthly, Harper's,* and *Dissent* respectively is unexpected and gives one pause. The same could be said of the finding that the combined Alt-Right audience is by some standards comparable to and by other standards greater than the audience for the *Weekly Standard.* Admittedly, this is a comparison of a collection of Alt-Right sites to a single mainstream conservative site. Nonetheless, the juxtaposition is revealing. The Alt-Right sites are very extreme, as we shall see. And the *Weekly Standard,* home to Irving Kristol's son, William Kristol, who is a leader of the Never Trump forces, has an impeccable neoconservative pedigree and center-right orientation that make it a hate object of the Alt-Right. Perhaps the fact that the virulently anti-Semitic *Daily Stormer* has an audience significantly larger than that of *Commentary* is not as startling as it first seems, insofar as most of *Commentary*'s content is behind a pay wall, whereas the *Daily Stormer* is accessible for free. But for a publication featuring Nazi memes and grotesque caricatures of Jews to surpass the distinguished and Jewish-oriented *Commentary* is a matter of concern.

Also remarkable is the size of the audience for the Alt-Lite outlet *Breitbart News. Breitbart*'s audience dwarfs that of *National Review,* the flagship conservative publication so hated by the Alt-Right for its ongoing purges of right-wing fringe elements. It is an understatement to say that with *Breitbart*'s success, right-wing extremism achieves its fantasy goal of eclipsing the respectable right, for Steve Bannon's former outlet surpasses not only the *National Review* but *every* web-based political magazine across the entire spectrum of opinion. In *Breitbart,* the far right has dramatically turned the tables on the respectable right and achieved, one could say, riches beyond the dreams of avarice.

Conclusion

Though banishment from traditional conservative news outlets used to consign extreme rightists to obscurity, that tactic has not stopped the Alt-Right from reaching a considerable audience, one comparable in size—as measured by website visits—to those of established organs of left, right, and centrist opinion. If the Alt-Right is understood as an ideological movement, it is not minuscule. Rather, the Alt-Right is a significant phenomenon in American political culture, and its ideology merits attention and concern.

Part II
Intellectual Roots of the Alt-Right

3

From Right-Wing Extremism to the Postpaleos

The ideological origins of the Alt-Right trace back to the appearance of the *National Review* in 1955 and the effort of its founder, William F. Buckley, to define a mainstream conservatism. Buckley and his associates cobbled together a rightist ideology that emphasized traditional values, capitalism, and anticommunism, and drove out of the movement anyone to the right of that consensus.

This self-cleansing process was very imperfect at first and, with regard to racism, perhaps never entirely satisfactory. The magazine defended segregation in a notorious 1957 article titled "Why the South Must Prevail,"[1] supported Senator Goldwater for president even though he voted against the Civil Rights Act of 1964, and as late as 1985 was making excuses for South Africa's apartheid government.[2] But by 1965 Buckley was supporting various antidiscrimination policies, and in 1969 he predicted that an African American would be elected president, a development he thought would be "welcome tonic" for the American soul.[3] The *National Review* would always be critical of many civil rights policies, especially affirmative action, but by the mid-1960s its repudiation of open racists was clear. Other elements denied access to the magazine by then included the John Birch Society, anti-Semites, and followers of Ayn Rand. Ostracism from the *National Review* effectively marginalized these tendencies from the re-

33

spectable conservative movement and mainstream political discourse generally. There were few other national outlets for conservative opinion and, because of the costs of pre-digital-era publishing, the ousted movements that came to be termed "right-wing extremists" lacked the resources to compete effectively with the conservative mainstream.

This process of self-policing continued as the conservative movement broke through to the mainstream during the Reagan era. The fortunes of the extremists reached a low ebb, with membership in the John Birch Society dramatically declining. The ideology and demographics of the conservative movement's intellectual leaders began to change as centrist anticommunists, Great Society skeptics, and critics of the New Left began to move rightward. This group, which came to be known as the neoconservatives, pushed the movement to accept the welfare state and the Civil Rights Act. Many of the neoconservatives were Jewish; Irving Kristol and Norman Podhoretz are famous examples. They were aware of their immigrant backgrounds and Jewish identity and so were more sympathetic to immigration, civil rights, and ethnic pride than past conservatives. This position had been articulated by the neoconservatives Nathan Glazer and Daniel Moynihan in their 1963 book, *Beyond the Melting Pot*. Neoconservative publications, such as the *Public Interest* and *Commentary*, took their place next to the *National Review* as outlets of conservative ideas.

By the mid-1980s, thinkers to the right of this consensus were being dubbed "paleoconservatives" rather than "extremists." They did not take kindly to their continued exile, by then deepened by the rise of the neoconservatives, whom they saw as usurpers. At a 1986 conference of the paleoconservative Philadelphia Society, one speaker expressed that tendency's resentment of the neoconservatives as follows: "It is splendid when the town whore gets religion and joins the church . . . but when she begins to tell the minister what he ought to say in his Sunday sermons, matters have been carried too far."[4]

Thus, from the mid-1980s until the turn of the millennium, paleoconservatives had a need to articulate a coherent political ideology that could drive the neoconservative usurpers from leadership of the conservative movement and sketch out a far-right vision of what America should be. This ideology would develop four major themes: (1) a radical rejection of liberal democracy, (2) anti-Semitism, (3) racialism, and (4) anti-Americanism. The rejection of liberal democracy was worked out by Samuel Francis—a journalist and intellectual who based his critique on classical elite theory—and the academic Paul Gottfried. A new brand of anti-Semitism that incorporated themes from Darwinism into old-fashioned conspiracy theory was developed by Kevin MacDonald, a retired professor of psychology at California State University, Long Beach. Michael Levin—a philosophy professor at City College of New York—extended a form of sociobiology into a racialist account of nonwhite populations. A deep alienation from contemporary America was implicit in all this thought, but the virulent anti-Americanism of the Alt-Right developed later, as detailed in chapter 8.

Rejection of Liberal Democracy

Samuel Francis and His Mentor, James Burnham

One of the first detailed responses of the paleoconservatives to what they saw as the leftward shift of the conservative movement was "Neoconservatism and the Managerial Revolution," by Samuel Francis. The article appeared in 1986 in *The World & I*, a magazine supported by the Unification Church. Here and in later works, Francis developed an extraordinary argument that eventually went beyond the immediate controversy with neoconservatism and crystallized into a radical critique of American politics that would strongly influence Alt-Right thinkers. Francis developed this analysis in detail in his lengthy work, *Leviathan & Its Enemies*, which was completed in 1995 but not published until 2016, eleven years after its author's death in 2005. The eventual publisher of Francis's magnum opus was Washington Summit Publishers, a division of the National Policy Institute, an Alt-Right organization that was founded by Richard Spencer, whose *Radix Journal* became a principal node in the web network of Alt-Right thought. Another such website has described *Leviathan & Its Enemies* as "the Alt-Right's *Das Kapital*."[5] *Leviathan & Its Enemies* is the most comprehensive statement of Alt-Right thought and for that reason, rather than for intrinsic merits, warrants close consideration.

Francis's case against the neoconservatives in *Leviathan & Its Enemies* is built on two premises: that the neoconservatives are really defenders of liberalism and that what passes for "cosmopolitan liberal democracy, in fact constitutes a form of totalitarianism" and thus deserves no defense.[6]

Leviathan & Its Enemies tries at length to back up that characterization of liberal democracy.

The intellectual progenitor of this argument was James Burnham, one of five senior editors identified on the masthead of the first issue of the *National Review*, to which he was a regular contributor until the late 1960s. Burnham is best known as the author of *The Managerial Revolution*, first published in 1941, and is the subject of Francis's first book, *Power and History*, published in 1984 and updated in 1999. Burnham occupied an unusual place in the respectable conservative community Buckley had gathered around his magazine. The classic account of that community, developed by George Nash in *The Conservative Intellectual Movement in America since 1945*, is that it represented a somewhat unstable fusion of free-market-oriented economists, defenders of traditional values, and anticommunists. Burnham, a former Trotskyite turned conservative, fitted into that fusion as an anticommunist, but was very different from the anticommunists who also defended traditional values, such as Whittaker Chambers, or the liberal Cold Warriors, such as Sidney Hook, who, over the years, would increasingly ally themselves with conservatives. Burnham's conservatism derived from a school of thought not otherwise represented in the respectable right coalition: the elite theorists of the late nineteenth and early twentieth centuries, such as Vilfredo Pareto, Gaetano Mosca, and Robert Michels.

In *The Rhetoric of Reaction*, Albert O. Hirschman discusses the elite theorists and provides another way the parties to the conservative fusion and Burnham's place among them might be described. Hirschman identifies three types of conservative arguments. The perversity argument holds that liberal reforms, however well intended, will produce the opposite of their admittedly desirable goals. For example, rent control is held to reduce the supply of affordable apartments, and minimum wage laws are said to increase unemployment. The jeopardy argument maintains that new progressive institutions—again, however desirable their ends—will endanger the social progress already made. Thus, economic planning and the welfare state are said to undermine liberty. And the futility argument claims that efforts at social improvement will simply have no effect. Income redistribution, this argument goes, is fruitless because individual differences and social positions will inevitably reassert themselves and leave income inequality unchanged.[7]

If we apply Hirschman's typology to the coalition of the respectable right, the defenders of the free market might be said to specialize in applying the perversity argument to a wide range of progressive schemes. And perhaps traditionalists and anticommunists—whom Hirschman does not discuss—are proponents of the jeopardy argument in that they claim, for example, that social liberation will undermine old aristocratic or bourgeois virtues, or that radical change will derail incremental progress. But among the respectable right of the late 1950s and 1960s the main, perhaps the only, consistent proponent of a version of the futility argument was Burnham.

Burnham and the Elite Theorists

In 1911, Robert Michels's book, *Political Parties: A Sociological Study of the Oligarchical Tendencies of Modern Democracy*, laid out the elite theorists' critique of liberal democracy that would be taken up by Burnham and later applied to turn-of-the-millennium America by Francis and the Alt-Right. However, Francis and the Alt-Rightists give a twist to this school of thought such that their analysis of the prospects for modern democracy is even darker than that of the elite theorists and Burnham.

Michels begins his version of the elite theorists' argument with the observation that in the modern era, "democracy is inconceivable without organization."[8] Any class, group, or party that seeks a given aim requires organization, and because the scale of operations made possible by modern technology involves massive amounts of people and money, those organizations will be large and complex. But in practice it is impossible for such large organizations to be run by direct, mass discussion. Very few decisions of a large business, agency, or party can be put to a vote by all concerned. And the tasks to be executed by large organizations require specialized skills and knowledge that cannot be mastered by everyone. Thus the large organizations of modern society, democratic political parties included, require leadership by a relatively small fraction of their members who possess the necessary abilities. For technical and managerial reasons, then, leadership by a minority is inevitable in modern mass organizations. Moreover, being relatively small in number and unusual in their attributes, the leaders develop their own class consciousness: eventually they realize that their interests are not necessarily congruent with those they represent. Therefore the leaders reinforce their natural indispensability by ensconcing themselves in power however they can. According to Michels, "At the outset, leaders arise spontaneously; their functions are ACCESSORY AND GRATUITOUS. Soon, however, they become PROFESSIONAL leaders, and in this second stage of development they are STABLE and IRREMOVABLE."[9] That is, leaders are irremovable not in the sense that individual leaders cannot be removed but in the sense that the leadership class cannot be dispensed with. Thus, in modern large-scale societies, democracy requires organization, organization requires leadership, and leadership necessarily become oligarchical. This is Michels's famous iron law of oligarchy.[10]

Hirschman classifies Michels's iron law and similar formulations of the elite theorists as expressions of the futility argument because they assume that as a result of invincible laws of social science, liberal reforms are doomed to be ineffectual. With Michels, it is oligarchy that is presumed to be a universal, invariant social reality and democracy the liberal initiative that is bound to fail. Pareto and Mosca make essentially the same argument for the inevitability of domination by an elite group, although based on different social science analyses.

In *The Machiavellians: Defenders of Freedom*, published in 1943, Burnham provides the first detailed account by an American of the thought of the elite theorists, which he sees as an extension of the political philosophy of Machiavelli, whom he presents as the first thinker to truly develop "the science of power."[11] Burnham's summary of this supposed science was to have an enormous impact on Francis and, through him, on Alt-Right thought.[12]

When Burnham applies this science of power to modern societies, he concludes, as the elite theorists generally do, that democracy is futile:

"Democracy" is usually defined in some such terms as "self-government" or "government by the people." Historical experience forces us to conclude that democracy, in this sense, is impossible. The Machiavellians have shown that the practical impossibility of democracy depends upon a variety of factors: upon psychological tendencies which are apparently constant in social life, and, most of all, upon the necessary technical conditions of social organization. . . .

The theory of democracy must, therefore, be understood as myth, formula, or derivation. Debates over the merits of the theory are almost wholly valueless in throwing light on social facts.[13]

Burnham's Application of Elite Theory: The Managerial Revolution

In *The Machiavellians*, Burnham mostly recapitulates the elite theory of his mentors. But in his 1941 book, *The Managerial Revolution*, Burnham makes a distinctive contribution when he applies that general approach to the era of World War II. Burnham's contribution was to identify a new class that was successfully struggling to occupy the position of the ruling elite. This was the managers, that is, not the people who formally owned the means of production—they made up the old ruling class of the capitalist bourgeoisie—but rather the people who, on the basis of their technical skills, actually managed the corporatized means of production and so had effective control of them. In the early days of capitalism, Burnham writes, the capitalists who owned the means of production also managed them. But with the growth in production made possible by continuing technological progress, the tasks of managing the great industrial enterprises became increasingly complex and ownership and management became increasingly differentiated until, in the end, the giant organizations of the modern economy were controlled by the managers who directed them rather than by the capitalists, who were their owners in only a purely formal sense.

In this analysis, large, private corporations, generally thought to be the embodiment of capitalism and the institutional counterbalances to public sector agencies, in fact fulfill neither role. Large organizations, whether public or private, are complex bureaucracies controlled by managers, whose class interest in perpetuating their rule is the same whether they work for corporations or for government agencies. And once ensconced in either the public or the private sector, the managers have the social resources necessary to direct the economy independent of market forces.[14]

According to Burnham, by World War II an international social revolution had commenced in which the old ruling class of the bourgeois capitalists was being replaced by the new ruling class of the managers. As this revolution took its course, the old ideology of the bourgeois capitalist— that is, democracy—was being replaced by new ideologies that legitimated the rule of the managerial elite. The punchline of Burnham's analysis is that these managerial ideologies were expressed "from several different but similar directions, by for example: Leninism-Stalinism; fascism-Nazism; and, at a more primitive level by New Dealism."[15]

There are many problems with this analysis. For one, it is simply untrue that the Stalinist Soviet Union was ruled by managers. The Soviet Union from the 1917 revolution to its final days was ruled not by managers but by the Communist Party.[16]

Another problem is that Burnham's comparison of the New Deal to Stalinism and Nazism was and is extremely strained. Yet in 1941 Burnham was quite serious about that analogy. Toward the end of *The Managerial Revolution*, he asks whether that transference of power in the United States would be accompanied by "terror and purges" as it was in Communist Russia and Nazi Germany. Burnham acknowledges that it was "even possible" the managerial revolution could be accomplished in the United States "in a comparatively democratic fashion." But that was not the way to bet.[17]

According to Burnham, in light of what the science of power tells us about politics and history, New Dealism—what would later be called liberalism or progressivism—might, but probably would not, end up being more democratic than Stalinism and Nazism. This was a somewhat more optimistic analysis of the prospects of modern democracy than Burnham's elite theory mentors are known for, but it does suggest that in the early formulation of his thought, Burnham was entirely serious about analogizing New Deal liberalism with Stalinism and fascism. In later works Burnham would back off from the prediction that the United States would degenerate into sheer despotism. In the introduction to a 1960 edition of *The Managerial Revolution* Burnham admitted that were he to rewrite that book, he "would allow for a greater range of variation within the form of managerial society," but he stood by his analysis that fascism, liberalism, and communism were all fundamentally nondemocratic managerial regimes. This broad-brush comparison of American liberalism with totalitarianism was to be repeated, with both caveats and embellishments, by Francis and the Alt-Right.

Francis's Applications of Elite Theory

In "Neoconservatism and the Managerial Revolution," Francis applies elite theory as interpreted by Burnham against the usurpers who had displaced the paleoconservatives as leaders of American conservatism. According to Francis, the neoconservatives passed as a rightist movement because they defended corporate capitalism, rejected the New Left critique of modern democracy, and accused the Great Society of overextending the reforms of the New Deal. But Francis held that corporate capitalism, modern democracy, and the New Deal amounted to no more than an Americanized version of managerialism. That ideology had already been articulated by the consensus liberals and postwar pluralists of the late 1950s and early 1960s, some of whom—including Daniel Bell, Nathan Glazer, and Seymour Lipset—went on to be identified with neoconservatism. Such relatively conservative managerial liberalism had nothing in common with conservatism rightly understood, according to Francis.[18]

"Neoconservatism," Francis tells us, "was thus the heir of the consensus liberalism of the 1950s and 1960s and served the same stabilizing and legitimating functions of the managerial regime," and so "leaves open the possibility of the continuing expansion of central government and its resumption of social engineering functions, and it thus supports a principal pillar of the managerial regime and agenda."[19] Therefore, Francis concludes, an authentic right, a New Right, that breaks decisively with consensus liberalism is needed. In his magnum opus, *Leviathan & Its Enemies*, Francis develops this managerial analysis into not merely a polemic against his neoconservative adversaries but a critique of modern liberal democracy much more thoroughgoing than that of his Machiavellian mentors.

In its more than 700 pages, *Leviathan & Its Enemies* mostly recapitulates the ideas of the elite theorists, especially Pareto's, and updates Burnham's analysis of world politics through the mid-1990s. But Francis also introduces several variations on this mode of thought. First of all, he formalizes Burnham's eventual acknowledgment of the striking differences between the managerial regimes of New Dealism or liberalism, on the one hand, and fascism and communism on the other. Francis distinguishes between "soft" and "hard" managerial regimes, as follows:

> In the one type—the soft managerial regime that prevails in the Western world—the elite depends mainly upon manipulation of the mass population by means of managerial skills to retain power. The ideologies of the soft managerial regimes reflect this reliance on manipulation in their emphasis on hedonistic and cosmopolitan values and ideas, the promotion of which enable[s] the elite to homogenize the tastes and values of the mass population and to discipline it with mass consumption, leisure,

and entertainment—managerial or "post-industrial" versions of *panem et circenses*. The behavior and policies of the soft managerial elites incline toward resolving problems and challenges by means of manipulation. . . . Because the elite depends so much on manipulation, the mass organizations of culture and communication, which perform their disciplinary and integrative functions principally through verbal and psychic manipulation, become unusually important instruments of power in the soft managerial regime.

In the other type, the hard managerial regime, which has prevailed in the Soviet Union and until recently in the other communist states of Eastern Europe and once prevailed in Germany under National Socialism, the elite depends mainly upon force or coercion of the mass population by means of managerial skills applied to the instruments of force (principally the armed services and the police forces). Their ideologies reflect their reliance on force in their emphasis on ascetic values or a "sacrifice ethic" and on "solidarism"—ideas and values that emphasize group solidarity . . . the party, *Volk*, or "Fatherland." In their behavior and policies, the hard managerial elites tend toward resolving all problems and challenges by means of force.[20]

One might expect that the difference between regimes that rely primarily on "verbal and psychic manipulation"—also known as persuasion[21]—and regimes that rely primarily on "force or coercion" will turn out to be all the difference in the world, and that the author's point is to emphasize how preferable the soft managerial regimes are to the hard managerial regimes. But that expectation would be naïve, and nowhere in his book does Francis express any preference for soft managerial regimes.

An obvious weakness of *The Managerial Revolution* was its unconvincing conflation of New Deal liberalism with National Socialism and Stalinism, a slip that Burnham backed away from in his later writings. Francis, however, thinks Burnham was making a deep point. Francis elsewhere claims that "Roosevelt was in fact a figure of the same kidney as other Leviathan-creating forces of the era, Hitler and Stalin."[22] *Leviathan & Its Enemies* acknowledges that "the character and behavior of the Nazi and Soviet managerial elites were radically different from those of Western managers,"[23] but also insists there is a deeper parallelism:

While the ideological differences between soft and hard managerialism indicate significant differences in the functioning of the respective regimes and in the psychic and behavioral patterns that characterize soft and hard managerial elites, they do *not* point to any significant structural differentiation between the two kinds of managerialism. Both the hard and soft regimes are apparatuses of power in which mass organizations in state, economy, and culture predominate and replace the simpler and smaller organizations of the bourgeois and prescriptive orders. . . .

The differences between the two kinds of managerial regime consist primarily in how power is acquired, preserved, and utilized and not in the real goals of power.[24]

But don't the democratic institutions of liberal regimes represent a "significant structural differentiation" from Nazism and Stalinism? No, Francis insists, because the democracy of the soft regimes is an illusion:

The formal mechanisms of mass liberal democracy—regular elections, competing political parties, universal suffrage, and legal and political rights—do not significantly mitigate the monolithic and uniform concentrations of managerial power. While legal rights of expression provide formal protection for anti-managerial movements, the manipulation of information, images, and symbols by the managerial organizations of culture and communication and their elite tends to neutralize the political and propaganda efforts of most anti-managerial forces. . . .

The formal and constitutional procedures of liberal democracy are thus largely irrelevant to the concentrated social power of the managerial elite. The late Herbert Marcuse noted that . . . "Democracy would appear to be the most efficient system of domination."[25]

Francis asserts the phoniness of soft managerial democracy in several different iterations. We have already seen how he maintains that liberal democracy is a form of totalitarianism.[26] He also writes of

the "despotic" character of the soft managerial regime . . . its tendency toward the monopolization of political, economic, and cultural power by a single social and political force of managerial and technical skills and the expansive, uniform, and centralized nature of its power. . . . The soft managerial regime thus constitutes a "soft despotism" (or . . . a "friendly fascism") that encourages the destruction of the social order and deracinates and alienates the social forces subjected to its manipulative regimes.[27]

These, then, are the descriptions Francis provides of the liberal democracy of the West: "the most efficient system of domination," "despotic," "totalitarianism," and "friendly fascism." Thus, Francis is quite serious about the essential equivalence of contemporary America with communist and fascist regimes.

In short, to quote George Wallace, the populist-segregationist presidential candidate of 1968, whom Francis sometimes praises, "There's not a dime's worth of difference" between soft and hard managerial regimes so far as real liberty is concerned. But if the rule of a managerial elite is inevitable, and if neither style of managerialism offers any prospect of liberty, doesn't it follow that the only political option available to the nonelites is resignation to domination?

To avoid painting himself into this corner, Francis has two options. He could argue that the various managerial elites can be made to check and balance each other and so provide a certain amount of freedom for each other and for nonelites.[28] In an essay on Burnham published in 1987, Francis briefly suggests that Machiavellianism results in a "theory of 'balance,'" and points to Montesquieu, Madison, and the other American framers as exponents of this approach.[29]

But in his later writing, Francis does not follow up on this suggestion, and by the time of completion of *Leviathan & Its Enemies* in 1995, Francis has explicitly rejected the idea that soft managerial regimes have preserved a degree of liberty by balancing a multiplicity of elites. For the idea of liberty preserved by counterbalancing elites amounts to embracing the pluralism of Robert Dahl and other American scholars of the 1960s, which, from Francis's point of view, amounts to a form of corporate liberalism and is a precursor of the neoconservatism that he wants to avoid. Thus, a section of *Leviathan & Its Enemies* titled "The Pluralist Argument: Are the Managers Unified?" answers that, contrary to pluralist theory, the modern elite is indeed unified: "In sum, then, there are no fundamental antagonisms within the managerial elite or among its sectors in state, economy, and media, though there are, as in any elite, disagreements and sometimes rivalries."[30]

Therefore, instead of reconciling with liberal pluralism, and in need of an account of fundamental change that can challenge the all-encompassing domination of the soft managerial elite, Francis makes a move toward Critical Theory and New Leftism, particularly the thinking of Marcuse in *One-Dimensional Man* and other late works. From those sources, Francis pieces together a strategy whereby those outcast from the soft managerial elite can overcome the democratic system of domination and achieve . . . well, what exactly will be achieved is not clear. But Francis sees a chance for the nonelites of the soft regime to oust the managers and make themselves into a new ruling class.

Francis and Marcuse on Radical Change

Marcuse and Francis face a similar challenge: they have to identify some social group capable of overthrowing the unified elite, but since they have described the status quo of the democratic West as a totalitarian system of domination that incorporates, co-opts, or diffuses all challengers, where is such an independent social force to be found?

Marcuse's response to this problem is to identify a group utterly alienated from and with no stake in society and therefore free from the forces of domination and potentially capable of revolutionary action. The traditional Marxian proletariat is not such a group because it has been bought off by the welfare state, accommodationist labor unions, and the consumer economy, Marcuse says. Thus, if the proletariat has been co-opted, the uncompromised, down-and-out lumpenproletariat is the last hope for revolution, under Marcuse's theory.[31]

Just as Marcuse, to find a change agent, had to turn not to the proletariat but to the lumpenproletariat, Francis pins his hopes not on the once revolutionary bourgeoisie but on what he calls the "post-bourgeois resistance," or what one might think of as the lumpenbourgeoisie. Francis describes this force as

> emerging social groups that were neither bourgeois nor managerial and harbored increasingly bitter frustrations with the soft managerial regime. . . . These new forces, the post-bourgeois groups that originated in the collapse of the bourgeois order under the revolution of mass and scale in the early part of the 20th century . . . are separate from the managerial

elite because they lack the advanced technical and managerial skills . . .
that yield control of the mass organizations of the regime and social and
political dominance. . . . Post-bourgeois groups constitute for the most
part the working and lower middle classes . . . dislocated and declining
bourgeois elements of rural or urban background as well as of equally
dislocated but ascending working class elements of European or native
origin. . . . The post-bourgeois strata, despite their relative affluence, constitute a proletariat within the soft managerial regime that the regime has
been unable to assimilate socially or psychologically.[32]

Francis usually refers to this stratum as "Middle American Radicals"
(or MARs), a term coined by the sociologist Donald Warren in his 1976
book, *The Radical Center: Middle Americans and the Politics of Alienation*.
Francis explicitly identifies MARs with the postbourgeois and sees their
ideologies as identical:

The MAR worldview is thus consistent with and indeed is an articulation
of the post-bourgeois consciousness that accepts the mass organizations of
the managerial regime on which post-bourgeois groups are materially dependent but simultaneously rejects the elite that controls and directs these
organizations, the ideology by which the elite rationalizes its dominance,
and the manipulative skills and techniques by which the dominance of the
elite is maintained.[33]

Later in *Leviathan & Its Enemies* Francis expands on the political ideology that expresses the consciousness of the postbourgeois MARs, whom
he sometimes describes as a "post-bourgeois proletariat":

Hence, the post-bourgeois proletariat displays little attachment to the
hard property capable of generating wealth, to the entrepreneurial firm
or the market economy of entrepreneurial capitalism, or to the classical
liberal ideology that offered formulas of rationalization for these institutions of bourgeois order. Nor does the post-bourgeois proletariat ex-
hibit significant attachment to the "night watchman" or constitutionally
limited, decentralized, neutralist, minimal state of the bourgeois order,
or to the "rule of law" formulas that rationalized it. Both post-bourgeois
needs for economic security as well as post-bourgeois attraction to coer-

cive mental and behavioral patterns and to ideological formulas of racial, national, and cultural solidarism point toward a political organization that is colossal, centralized, and active in the protection and enforcement of post-bourgeois economic incentives and cultural aspirations.[34]

This passage makes clear that the political agenda of the MARs will be not only antiprogressive but also anticonservative, at least as regards the mainstream conservatism of postwar America. MAR or postbourgeois political ideology will disdain property rights, economic growth, capitalism, classical liberalism, constitutionalism, limited government, and the rule of law. MAR ideology will embrace economic security (as provided by the programs of the welfare state, it turns out),[35] "solidarism" (a.k.a. collectivism), and a "colossal, centralized" political party. In short, MAR political ideology has little in common with the conservative fusionism of postwar America, or with any form of liberal democracy. In fact, MAR ideology very much resembles the ideology of one-party communist states. (A one-party state is implied because if the colossal, centralized party spurns limited government, constitutionalism, and the rule of law, what will stop it from establishing a monopoly on political organization once it comes to power?) But insofar as postbourgeois ideology features a collectivism based on race and nation rather than on class and displays an attraction for coercive behavior patterns—that is, the use of force—it is more apt to compare that brand of politics with fascist, rather than communist, one-party states.

Francis's thought has been laid out here in so much detail because otherwise the radicalism of his utopian—or dystopian—vision might be hard to believe. Moreover, it is precisely his radicalism that accounts for much of his appeal to the Alt-Right.

A Critique of Leviathan & Its Enemies

In an essay published in 1946, George Orwell put his finger on a problem in Burnham's thought that Francis tries to remedy—with striking consequences. Orwell notes, "It is curious that in all his talk about the struggle for power, Burnham never stops to ask why people want power."[36] The response that people want power to stay in power only pushes the question off a step.[37] *Leviathan & Its Enemies* sets out to correct Burnham's vagueness on precisely what elite groups want to do with their power.

The question is, what will elites finally do with power once they assuredly have it? Some account of the psychology of elite groups that goes beyond simply saying they desire power is needed. Francis finds such an account in Pareto's theory of "residues," by which Pareto means something like a fixed sentiment or psychological propensity of a social class.[38] According to Pareto, there are six classes of residues that drive human action, but Francis simplifies this classification to just Class I and Class II types, which are characteristic of two very different social groups. According to Francis, "These two types of residues give rise to distinctive behavioral and mental patterns that appear to conform to the types that are predominate in the two types of managerial elite."[39]

Class I residues are an "instinct for combinations," that is, an inclination to innovate by recombining known ideas and things into new discoveries. Francis tells us that Class I residues predominate in intellectuals, scientists, and reformers, who "tend to be adverse to the use of force and to rely on various forms of intelligence and cunning (deception, persuasion, manipulation) in the pursuit and retention of power."[40]

Class II residues are an instinct for "group preferences," for the "persistence of aggregates," and are reflected in the tendency to hold together the patterns of thought and action that Class I residues seek to break apart and recombine. Francis approvingly quotes the following characterization of people who are mainly driven by Class II residues: "They are aggressive, authoritarian, reliant on force and the threats of force, and contemptuous of manoeuver, persuasion, and compromise."[41]

Different elites, according to Francis, are characterized by different combinations of Class I and Class II residues. Class II residues were predominant in the aristocratic elites of pre- and early mass societies. Class II residues also dominate in the postbourgeois resistance of the MARs, whose attachment to local communities and relative lack of skills and education keep them from rising into the managerial elite. Class I residues prevailed in the elite managers of the soft managerial regime. The bourgeois elite of the heyday of capitalism featured a mix of both classes of residues.

The elite managers of the hard managerial regimes represent a consequential variation on their counterparts in the soft managerial regimes. In *Leviathan & Its Enemies*, Francis argues that the twentieth-century shift toward gigantism of organizations and societies that brought the managers to power developed very differently in Germany and Russia as compared with Western nations. In those countries the development of mass organizations took place not under the auspices of the bourgeois capitalists but under those of the traditional aristocracy and the bureaucracy of the monarchical state, institutions that did not exist in the United States. Therefore, in the United States, the managers of the new mass organizations originally worked for the bourgeois capitalists, whose preferences for at least the appearance of democratic norms the managers partly incorporated into their worldview even as, eventually, they came to displace the bourgeois as the new ruling elite. But in Germany and Russia the managers originally worked for the aristocracy and the monarchy and so incorporated into their worldview the preferences for collectivism, authoritarianism, and violence characteristic of the Class II residues that dominated among those old elites. It is these differences in the social psychology of the managerial elites that account for the differences in the soft and hard managerial regimes. The Class I residues characteristic of all managerial elites are, in the soft regimes, shaped by the political and ideological references of bourgeois liberalism. In the hard regimes, Class I residues are strongly influenced by the Class II residues that predominated in the old aristocratic elites, with their authoritarian and militaristic political ideologies.

We now understand the social and psychological differences between the managerial elites of the soft and hard regimes. The question now is, how do those different psychologies affect the goals of these two regimes? Francis thinks he has established that elites of both regimes primarily seek power, but now he should be able to say to what uses these elites will put their power.

It turns out that managerial elites of all types seek power not just for power's sake but in order to ameliorate social conditions. Thus, Francis acknowledges, "The ideas that human society can be significantly ameliorated or perfected and that this amelioration is possible through the application of scientific managerial skills to human beings and social institutions and processes are essential to the legitimatization of mass organizations and the managerial elites that control and direct them."[42]

However, two hitches present themselves. First, Francis is unclear about whether managerial skills are scientific or, as he often writes, "scientistic," that is to say, pseudoscientific. If managerial skills are based on pseudoscience, presumably they are not effective, and therefore mastery of them should confer no power, in which case, how do the managers stay in charge? On the other hand, if managerial skills are truly scientific, presumably they are effective and can produce a real improvement in social conditions that would legitimate managerial rule. But this problem seems not to occur to Francis and will not be pursued here.

The second hitch is that social groups in which distinct residues predominate have entirely different conceptions of what constitutes "amelioration." In particular, there is a very sharp contrast between the point of view of the soft managerial elite and that of the postbourgeois resistance as to what counts as a more perfect society.

Soft regimes, Francis writes, "depict amelioration in the hedonistic, eudemonian, and cosmopolitan terms appropriate to an economy of mass consumption and 'liberation' from a 'repressive' social and historical environment."[43] Earlier in *Leviathan & Its Enemies*, Francis has specified the goals of soft amelioration as "abolition or significant reduction of war, crime, poverty, inequality, corruption, disease, hunger and ignorance."[44]

Amelioration from the point of view of the hard regime elites and the postbourgeois is something quite different. Francis writes:

Post-bourgeois rejection of manipulation thus involves . . . the reformulation of the meliorist and scientistic formulas of the soft regime in terms compatible with the hard regime toward which post-bourgeois forces point. Post-bourgeois ideology must express a solidarism that postulates a collective identity, synthesizing the elements of class, race, nation, and culture . . . [and] a formula and ethic of asceticism that rationalizes deferral of gratification, acceptance of sacrifice for the solidarist identity. . . . Post-bourgeois ideology also would postulate reliance on coercion rather than manipulation as a means of responding to challenges and resolving problems.[45]

The above passages are highly illuminating. Soft and hard managerial elites both use their power to stay in power, but also seek to ameliorate social conditions. Soft elites aim at "liberation," "mass consumption," and "reduction of war, crime, poverty, inequality, corruption, disease, hunger, and ignorance." Hard elites aim at reinforcing racial, national, cultural, and class identity, inculcating asceticism, and promoting the effective use of coercion, which is to say violence.

Leviathan & Its Enemies ends with a statement that shows Francis is endorsing the overthrow of the soft managerial regime and its replacement with a hard managerial regime:

> The metamorphosis of the managerial regime may therefore represent the future of modern society and, despite the peculiar vulnerabilities that a hard managerial regime would exhibit, it may offer an opportunity for a more enduring and effective mobilization of mass loyalties and energies in a new managerial civilization than has been possible under the liberal and humanist formulas of its stillborn predecessors.[46]

This passage confirms the thrust of *Leviathan & Its Enemies* and the rest of Francis's work: a hard managerial regime based on coercion, collectivism, and asceticism is to be preferred to a soft managerial regime with its democratic institutions and reformist aspirations.

What would the transformation of the soft managerial regime into a hard managerial regime led by the MARs be like? Francis says of the post-bourgeois that "its emergence as a new elite would probably be attended by violence and physical conflict."[47] He also writes that there is hardly any real prospect for the transformation of the soft regime until its managerial functions are seriously interrupted "by economic depression, for example, war, insurrection, or the extreme disintegration of discipline."[48] Paul Gottfried, a fellow paleoconservative thinker, Alt-Right precursor, and personal friend of Francis, notes in his afterword to *Leviathan & Its Enemies* that Francis "made no secret of his belief that if a change in the power structure favoring his side was still possible, it would take little short of the Apocalypse to allow that to happen."[49]

At the end of *One-Dimensional Man*, Marcuse speculates about the prospects for an end to the "totalitarian tendencies of the one-dimensional society" and gloomily observes, "Nothing indicates it will be a good end."[50] But Marcuse looks like a cockeyed optimist compared with Francis and the future he outlines for humankind. Either there will be world-wide catastrophe and civilizational collapse, followed by a Stalinist- or fascist-style tyranny—which is the rosy scenario—or the despotism of a soft but totalitarian regime will go on unchecked indefinitely. That is,

Francis offers us a choice between the dystopias of Orwell and Huxley and suggests Orwell's is preferable.

Conclusions on Francis and His Critique of Liberal Democracy

The radicalism of Francis's antidemocratic ideology can hardly be over-stated. He wants to replace what he calls the soft managerial regimes of contemporary liberal democracies with hard managerial regimes pat-terned after National Socialism and Stalinism. Further, this transforma-tion is to be accomplished through a series of world-historical cataclysms next to which the troubles of the 1930s and 1940s will look like a walk in the park.

The mystery is why Francis thinks overthrowing liberal democracy in favor of a Soviet- or Nazi-style despotism will be so wonderful as to make a near Apocalypse worthwhile. The hard regime will be authori-tarian, ascetic, coercive, collectivistic, aggressive, and violent. All these features will be purchased with the abandonment of humanism, demo-cratic institutions, individualism, tolerance, prosperity, progress, and the free pursuit of happiness. Most readers will have their minds made up for them merely by realizing the nature of the choice Francis presents. But apparently Francis sees something in the hard regime that makes its high cost worthwhile. One wishes Francis would tell us what he sees that most of us do not. There will be no greater political freedom under the hard regime than under the soft regime, for both regimes are dominated by a managerial elite. So there will be no compensation for all the pains of the hard regime in the form of more real freedom. In the hard regime the new ruling elite will claim to represent a new social class, the MARs or postbourgeois proletariat. But Francis's Machiavellianism holds that no elite truly represents its followers, so it is unclear what the benefit of the hard regime will be to the MARs, let alone any other class. In an essay published in 1982 Francis suggests a MAR regime may have something to recommend it. Then he wrote that MARs offer "a discipline, a code of sacrifice for something larger than themselves, and a new purpose," but ventured only to conclude that "the objective interests of their own formation *appear to* dictate a social order quite different from, and *probably* better than, that designed, manipulated, and misruled by the manage-rial class and its cohorts."[51] This is not a convincing endorsement for the rule of a class whose path to power runs straight through hell on earth. *Leviathan & Its Enemies*, completed in 1995, offers no such suggestion that MAR rule *"may be* beneficial to America as well."[52] Apparently Francis simply prefers the harshness of the hard regime to the mildness of the soft regime, but this is a mere matter of taste, not backed up by a positive argument in favor of hard managerialism.

In the end, it seems the only thing the hard regime has to recommend it is that it is not a soft regime. If one feels as embittered toward America's liberal democratic order as Francis does, perhaps Soviet- or Nazi-style regimes start looking good. No doubt the neoconservatives will at last get their comeuppance under hard managerialism, as will all dissenters. But anyone without such axes to grind will find the chaos followed by brutality recommended by Francis extremely unappealing.

Gottfried's Critique of Liberal Democracy

Leviathan & Its Enemies is followed by an afterword by Paul Gottfried, an academic political theorist formerly at Elizabethtown College. Gottfried is the premier theoretician of paleoconservatism and is perhaps best known for his role in coining the term "Alt-Right." Gottfried is a key figure in the transition from paleoconservatism to Alt-Rightism. He is the most academic of the Alt-Right precursors discussed here. His main contribution to the rise of the new movement has been to develop a right-wing critique of liberal democracy that softens, complexifies, and apologizes for the gross excesses of his colleagues but retains their radical core.

We saw that Francis cites Marcuse and makes use of his theory of revolution. Gottfried not only cites and makes use of Marcuse but, as a Yale graduate student in the early 1960s, he studied under Marcuse and, in the 1980s, went on to make a sort of intellectual alliance with disciples of Marcuse and other Critical Theorists associated with the journal of radical political theory, *Telos*. It would be entirely wrong to say that Francis and Gottfried are disciples of the Frankfurt School who merely apply that form of analysis for right-wing purposes. In political studies, analytical means and political ends interpenetrate and cannot be sharply distinguished. Yet it remains true that the paleoconservative thinkers discussed here have been strongly influenced by the Critical Theorists and do arrive at conclusions that, while right wing, share some of the desire for the radical and even revolutionary transformation of liberal democracy displayed by Marcuse and other thinkers of his school. Thus Gottfried writes:

> To think of myself now as a disciple of Marcuse or of the broader Frankfurt School movement to which he belonged has become difficult but not impossible. . . . I have borrowed from the interwar Left a particular strategy for unmasking contemporary Leftists. Such borrowing is different from membership in the tradition whose ideas one is adapting. . . . Intention is integral to our understanding of social and political positions. What may be argued, however, is that intellectual traditions bind people in spite of their obvious differences. . . . It seems to me . . . correct to underscore the possibility of a far-ranging agreement about certain premises among thinkers who would not otherwise have much in common.[53]

As we now see, these influential paleoconservative precursors of the Alt-Right consciously borrowed from radical left-wing thinkers, and therefore there is quite a bit of overlap in those schools of thought. Particularly interesting is how these right-wing thinkers have "borrowed from the interwar Left a particular strategy for unmasking contemporary Leftists." It should be noted that this strategy involves not engaging the arguments of one's adversaries but rather "unmasking" them as artifacts of power bloc interests. This approach of overlooking ideas and focusing on the political forces behind them will be emulated, though often in a vulgar and juvenile style, by the Alt-Right.

Gottfried has criticized that rhetorical style of the Alt-Right. A 2016 article in the *American Spectator* reported that Gottfried said of the Alt-Right, "I don't take them all that seriously as a political or intellectual force. There's a lot of childishness in what they do. . . . They don't seem to be able to control their own excesses. . . . Any responsible conservative movement has to practice discretion. It's the indiscretion that bothers me."[54] But Gottfried nonetheless has some degree of affinity with the Alt-Right. An interviewer writing about Gottfried in 2016 reported, "'I view it as a partial vindication,' he [Gottfried] told me just over a month before the presidential election, about the rise of the alt-right." So there is an intellectual continuity between the paleoconservative movement and the postpaleo Alt-Right, but also a considerable generational difference in tone.

The careers and thought of Francis and Gottfried overlapped to a considerable extent. Both detested the neoconservatives, who they believed
had damaged their careers.[55] In fact, it was Gottfried who commissioned
Francis's early attack on neoconservatism, "Neoconservatism and the
Managerial Revolution," in 1986 for the *The World & I*.[56] Gottfried writes
of his intellectual relation to Francis that "the two of us were mostly in
agreement in our views. . . . I was indelibly influenced by Sam's views
about interlocking managerial elites and by his insistence that 'disagreement' within our ruling class is more apparent than real."[57]

There are, however, some important differences in Gottfried's thought
compared with that of Francis. Francis denied that the ruling elites believe their own ideology, while Gottfried was willing to acknowledge that
the elites' beliefs, though false, were "deeply held."[58] Francis believed that
corporate and public sector managers were co-equals in the essentially
homogeneous ruling elite. Gottfried sees more variation in the ruling
elite as "not all members of the presumed managerial class swing equally
large clubs," with big business being "at the mercy of government and the
media priesthood."[59] Gottfried also acknowledges that he is "much less
of a Burnhamite" than is Francis but offers the qualification that "while
I do not embrace *The Managerial Revolution* as the final key to modern
historical change, Burnham's conception of managerial rule has nonetheless affected my thinking deeply."[60] Gottfried also specifies that "it goes
without saying that Sam is more of a populist democrat and less of a bourgeois conservative or liberal than I."[61] Perhaps the biggest intellectual difference between these two thinkers is that Gottfried is unconvinced by
Francis's vision of the transformation of the soft managerial regime into
a hard regime. Thus Gottfried writes, "As for the possibility of making
over the managerial state into a conservative force . . . he [Francis] thinks
it's possible but I don't."[62]

Much of the difference between these two progenitors of the Alt-Right
stems from the fact that Francis was mainly a journalist while Gottfried
is an academic. Francis did most of his writing for newspapers and magazines. Gottfried has produced plenty of journalism too, but as a professor
of humanities he also wrote for scholarly journals and academic presses.
Much of Gottfried's academic writing focuses on German philosophy and
its influence on American conservative thought. Other themes include
the conservative tradition in general and a critique of liberalism. In his

academic writing Gottfried displays considerable erudition and can sometimes add nuance to arguments expressed more bombastically by other
paleoconservatives. On the other hand, his scholarly work sometimes
complexifies matters so much and skips so rapidly from one author or
source to another that his point becomes unclear.

What is abundantly clear is Gottfried's detestation of the mainstream
of postwar American conservatism, especially the fusionism developed
under William Buckley, and, even more so, neoconservatism, whose followers he excoriates repeatedly. Gottfried identifies with the "Right,"
which he distinguishes sharply from classical European conservatism—as
exemplified by Burke, for example, who defended a living tradition against
revolutionary forces—and the American conservatism nostalgic for that
earlier tradition. The Right arose in countries where there was no such
traditional base to serve as a bulwark against convulsive change. According to Gottfried:

> The Right . . . is a predominantly bourgeois reaction, explicitly against
> social and political radicalization, that has taken many forms. But these
> forms arose in societies in which the *ancient regime*, to which classical
> conservativism had rallied, was already tottering or had never existed.
> Whether one is discussing Italy on the eve of Mussolini's march on Rome
> in 1922 or the resistance to the New Deal, one is looking at post conserva-
> tive reactions to unwelcome changes or the threat of disruption.[63]

One might say the Right would like to defend a stable social base
against destabilizing change but finds it has no such base to defend. The
Right Gottfried finds attractive is a conservative movement without a
social base to conserve.

As Gottfried sees things, such hanging, order-seeking interests without a base to defend have two options. One is to accommodate themselves
to whatever regime the forces of change throw up—which in the United
States is the liberal welfare state—and then pretend to be fighting off
social disruption by invoking conservative traditions that are no longer
relevant because their aristocratic or bourgeois social bases have been destroyed. According to Gottfried, both the conservative fusionists around
Buckley and later the neoconservatives grasped at this straw. In the *National Review* circle, traditionalists like Russell Kirk latched on to Burke

and other defenders of social orders that no longer existed; free-market economists did the same with another deceased social institution, the free market and the classical liberal ideas associated with it. Neoconservatives, using the approach of Leo Strauss, claim to see a long tradition of political thought stretching back to ancient times that culminated in modern liberalism. But according to Gottfried, such a tradition is mere illusion. Vital political philosophies grow out of social forces embodied in existing regimes. When those forces and regimes pass on, the ideas they threw off are no longer relevant to future situations. To claim otherwise is to endorse mere "happy talk" that serves only to legitimate the contemporary liberal regime by giving it a false appearance of continuity.[64] Contemporary American conservatism amounts to no more than such window dressing, in Gottfried's opinion.

At this point, like other paleoconservatives, Gottfried seems to have painted himself into a corner. If the stable regimes of the past are dead, if the ideas associated with them are irrelevant to the present search for order, how is it possible to offer any opposition to the disruptive social change instigated by revolutionary or progressive forces? In particular, what social groups will oppose the soft managerial regime and the uprooting of order that its scientistic social engineering provokes? In fact, Gottfried is very pessimistic. In a phrase that prefigured the coinage of the term "alternative right," Gottfried suggests that "historical circumstances, namely the establishment of a popular, expanding and highly centralized public administration, may have foredoomed any attempt to keep alive an alternative American Right."[65] But if there are any possible sources of resistance, what are they? It seems the Right will have to patch together on a catch-as-catch-can basis whatever shards of opposition to liberal democracy are present at hand and not be too choosy about its bedfellows. At this point Gottfried develops his account of different types of fascism and suggests there are certain elements of that force the Right can make use of.

Two Alternative Rights, "Mainstream" and "Generic Fascist"

Sometimes the alternative American Right Gottfried envisions seems relatively mild, something well short of the proto-revolutionary social base that Francis sees overthrowing the soft managerial regime in a cataclysmic upheaval. In *Conservatism in America: Making Sense of the American Right* from 2007 Gottfried cites as representatives of the "mainstream version of the Right" Phyllis Schlafly, Pat Buchanan, and George Wallace, none of whom is a revolutionary figure, whatever one thinks of them.[66] But as Gottfried provides more details, the alternative Right he describes becomes more radical. It turns out, for example, the alternative Right embraces racialism. Thus Gottfried writes that "the current Right . . . exemplified by contributors to *American Renaissance* and *The Occidental Quarterly* . . . offers an identitarian or explicitly racialist defense of the majority white Christian population, whose culture and self-respect the Right sees under attack."[67]

Gottfried claims that these racial nationalists of the Right, such as Jared Taylor and Michael Levin, are for the most part libertarian. It is hard to see how the individualism of libertarianism can be squared with the rightist collectivism of racialism. Doing so is really impossible when, as we shall see, and *pace* what Gottfried has to say, Taylor's racialism leads to nostalgia for the segregationist Old South. But the key point here is that the Right Gottfried is so enthusiastic about ends up rejecting not merely centrist Republicanism but racial egalitarianism.

The more one reads Gottfried, the more apparent it becomes that what he conceives of as the Right involves a clean break with liberal democracy. In fact, Gottfried's Right ends up looking a great deal like what Gottfried calls "generic fascism," which, he tells us, is exemplified by Mussolini's Italy.

In *Fascism: The Career of a Concept*, Gottfried develops two arguments. One concerns "the inadmissibility of applying 'fascist' to whatever the speaker finds viscerally repulsive."[68] Certainly the word "fascist" is highly charged and not to be used lightly.[69] So here Gottfried makes a fair but obvious point, one that is not much advanced by his book-length account of various forms of fascism, none of which is attractive.

Out of his taxonomy of the meanings of fascism comes another key claim of Gottfried's book: that there is a sharp distinction between the "radical fascism" of Nazi Germany and the "generic fascism" of Italy under Mussolini. "The moral and theoretical gulf between them was at one time truly immense," Gottfried writes of these variations on the fascist theme.[70] He argues:

> There is a generic fascism, which resembles the Italian fascist movement and, to a lesser extent, the Italian fascist government. This form of fascism shaped the interwar revolutionary Right. . . . Moreover, fascism has a distant family relation to traditional conservativism but less ideological connection to German Nazism. It became perhaps inevitably linked in the popular mind to Nazism because of the (hardly predestined) alliance between Hitler and Mussolini.[71]

Throughout his writings, Gottfried is at pains to distinguish "far less destructive forms of right-wing authoritarianism such as Mussolini's Italy" from Nazism.[72] Gottfried tells us that "Nazis, who have been falsely turned into the quintessential fascists, were far more revolutionary and more totalitarian than generic fascists," and notes with approval recent scholarship that claims "the Italian fascist regime before it was taken over by Nazi Germany killed 'no more than a few dozen' opponents, and those were mostly assassinations that occurred outside Italy, probably without Mussolini's knowledge."[73]

The quotation about the paltry number of Mussolini's murders comes from an interview Zev Sternhell, a controversial but distinguished Israeli scholar of fascism, gave to the newspaper *Haaretz*.[74] Gottfried's citations from Sternhell's *Haaretz* interview are taken out of context,[75] but the important point is that the relatively nonviolent picture of Mussolini's regime Gottfried paints is distorted. It is true that Mussolini's regime was much less murderous than those of Hitler and Stalin, but that is not saying much. Michael R. Ebner documents the brutality of Italian fascism in his authoritative book, *Ordinary Violence in Mussolini's Italy*, which Gottfried nowhere cites.[76]

According to Ebner, in coming to power, Italian fascists killed around 3,000 opponents. Mussolini was a dictator who used violence, murder, and executions to stay in power. Fascists beat and tortured tens of thousands of people, and major political opponents were arrested and put in jail. The regime's Special Tribunal had dozens of opponents executed. The Italian fascist regime was a dictatorship with no liberal democratic protections of any sort and persecution of ethnic, religious, and racial minorities, including Slavs, evangelicals, Jews, and gays. And, of course, under Mussolini, Italy launched wars of conquest in which many thousands of civilians were massacred. This all occurred before Italy was "taken over" by Germany in 1943.[77] Such was the record of Mussolini's regime, which Gottfried characterizes as "a comic opera affair" whose "totalitarian qualities ha[ve] been much exaggerated."[78]

Gottfried places much emphasis on the distinction between the radical fascism of National Socialist Germany and the generic fascism of Mussolini, so much so that a review of his book on the Alt-Right website *VDARE* overstates only a bit when it sums up his thesis as "Nazism, in other words, isn't a species of fascism at all."[79] But if Nazism has so little to do with fascism, then perhaps there is something to say for the milder, generic fascism that is Gottfried's focus. Italian fascism in particular deserves a second look, Gottfried suggests, and, if its Nazi-inspired excesses are factored out, compares favorably with today's oppressive liberal regimes. Thus Gottfried has written that "the fascist state was an Italian variation on the democratic managerial regime which succeeded liberal or quasi-liberal states elsewhere. . . . Italian fascists were engaged in building a modern administrative state— one based on a mixed economy and social services."[80] And further, "For at least two generations the 'new liberals' . . . have trampled on liberty as well as popular government . . . more decisively than Benito Mussolini, who did more boasting than long term damage in *his* war against freedom."[81]

Moreover, just as Gottfried makes a sharp distinction between radical fascism and generic fascism, with the latter looking not so bad, so he distinguishes between the "liberal heritage" and "liberal democracy" (Gottfried often puts the term in quotes), with the latter looking not so good. Nineteenth-century or traditional liberalism, for which Gottfried feels "profound affinity," embraces market economics and academic freedom. But liberal democracy is "flagrantly undemocratic . . . [and] its liberal record has been even worse."[82]

Gottfried's strategy of minimizing the evils of fascism while grossly exaggerating the shortcomings of liberal democracy is particularly apparent in the following passage, in which he compares the present-day Federal Republic of Germany to Mussolini's Italy: "Alas my memory may be failing. But I can't recall that 'monstrous regime,' as opposed to an incompetent, authoritarian one, that Mussolini established in Italy. And I'm also unable to discover the 'liberal' regime toward which we have helped the Germans ascend."[83]

Gottfried goes on to denounce the "precarious" state of civil liberties in, and the "jackboot" repressions of, twenty-first-century Germany and concludes that "neither tolerance nor freedom seems to have benefited from our terror-bombing and subsequent re-educational efforts in that part of the world."[84] In this extraordinary passage, Gottfried not only denies the monstrous nature of the Italian fascist regime but comes within a hair's breadth of saying tolerance and freedom are no better off in today's liberal democratic Germany than they were under the Third Reich. Thus Gottfried strives to get fascism a new hearing by redefining it as something not so objectionable and liberal democracy as something altogether repellent.

However, to his credit, Gottfried acknowledges "the most serious defect of fascism," which is: "Fascists viewed violence positively, as a cathartic agent." So here Gottfried avoids Francis's glorification of transformative violence. In general, despite his admiration for and acknowledged debt to Francis, Gottfried softens and qualifies his friend's analysis and backs it up with better scholarship. Nonetheless, the bottom line of these thinkers is the same: modern liberal democratic regimes are practically systems of domination; rightist authoritarian regimes are much to be preferred.

Again, both Francis and Gottfried seek to unmask liberal democracy as a mere disguise for elite power interests, but their analytical and rhetorical strategies for doing so differ markedly. Francis launches a frontal assault on the concept, brands it a sheer lie, and straightforwardly offers the hard managerial regime as a preferable alternative. Gottfried's approach is more subtle. He traces the history of the concept of liberal democracy and declares it is so obviously devoid of meaning that no one who uses it can possibly be serious. Therefore those who do endorse the idea must have ulterior motives.

Gottfried makes this case against liberal democracy in his 2014 essay, "What Is Liberal Democracy? Exploring a Problematic Term." Gottfried concludes the phrase is "of fairly recent origin,"[85] dating back only about 100 years. Gottfried seems to think the recent origin of liberal democracy is suspicious insofar as its supporters wish "the entire world to accept as a deity" the concept.[86]

So much, then, for the notion that liberal democracy is a serious idea. For the rest of the essay Gottfried merely repeats in several formulations that liberal democracy is just rhetorical cover for the power interests of the elite. The two reasons for the term's current popularity are "its vagueness: it can be made to mean what the speaker wants it to mean," and "it expresses a value judgment for what certain people are praising and the implementation of which is equivalent to political salvation." Gottfried considers two recent defenses of liberal democracy, both of which, we are told, suffer from the same fatal flaw: they are made by professionally successful neoconservatives,[87] and therefore such talk must be rejected out of hand: "'The West,' 'human rights,' and the defense of 'liberal democracy' all fit into this peculiar mode of discourse—and invariably into a context of unending struggle shaped by a particular segment of the socio-political elite."[88]

But Gottfried's opinion is not backed up with a persuasive argument. All he has to offer are hyperbolic and unconvincing accounts of the feeble state of civil liberties in Western democracies. Beyond that his case against liberal democracy is mainly that the elite is for it and therefore it must be pernicious. On the other hand, there may be something to be said for fascism—the generic version, of course—so hated by that same pseudoconservative elite. Gottfried concludes his book on fascism with an account of generic fascism that sounds strikingly like the Alt-Rightism he helped give birth to:

> Finally, the reader should focus one last time on the rightist gestalt that generic fascism exhibited. . . . In their emphasis on particularity, identitarian politics and hierarchy fascists expressed recognizably right-wing attitudes. These may not be the attitudes of American libertarians or Republicans trying to reach out to minorities, but they are the historic attitudes of the Right extending back entire centuries.[89]

That is, the attitudes of the alternative Right that Gottfried has been recommending to us are identical with the views of generic fascism. "Saying this," Gottfried immediately writes, "neither glorifies not discredits the views in question."[90] But why *not* discredit the views in question, which Gottfried acknowledges are fascist? Answer: because the contemptible Republicans reaching out to minorities reject these attitudes; therefore there must be something to them.

Thus Gottfried dusts off certain tenets of fascism and makes them ready again for wider circulation. How these ideas got picked up by the Alt-Right is discussed next.

Gottfried and the Transition to Alt-Rightism

Gottfried can be thought of as the thinker who led the transition of paleo-conservatism to Alt-Rightism. Gottfried announced the start of that transition, and in the process helped coin the name of the new movement, in a 2008 address to the H. L. Mencken Club titled "The Decline and Rise of the Alternative Right." In December 2008 the address was published on the right-wing website *Taki's Magazine*, of which Richard Spencer was an editor. Spencer now claims to have given the piece its title.[91] The phrase "alternative right" does not appear in the printed text of the speech, but Spencer has said to me that his choice of title was inspired by an earlier article in *Taki's* in which Gottfried wrote, "Even now an alternative is coming into existence as a counterforce to neoconservative dominance."[92] Gottfried asserts he and Spencer "co-created" the name "alternative right."[93]

In "The Decline and Rise of the Alternative Right," Gottfried observes that "what is now called paleoconservatism . . . assumed its current form about thirty years ago as a diffuse reaction to the neoconservative ascendancy."[94] Then he describes the decline of the "paleos," the rise of the "post-paleos," and the strategies by which this new "Alternative Right" could oust the neoconservatives and "ultimately do to them what they have done to us":

> I would also stress the possibility for positive change represented by this organization [the H. L. Mencken Club]. We have youth and exuberance on our side, and a membership that is largely in its twenties and thirties. We have attracted beside[s] old-timers like me, as I noted in my introductory paragraph, well-educated young professionals, who consider themselves to be on the right, but not of the current conservative movement. These "post-paleos," to whom I have alluded in Internet commentaries, are out in force here tonight. . . . And when I speak about the postpaleos, it goes without saying that I'm referring to a growing communion beyond this organization. It is one that now includes Takimag, VDARE.com, and other websites that are willing to engage sensitive, timely subjects. . . .
>
> What we can hope to achieve in the near term as opposed [to] what we might able to do in the fullness of time is to gain recognition as an intellectual Right—and one that is critical of the neoconservative-controlled conservative establishment. . . .

If we wish to advance our cause, we must meditate on the successes of our most implacable enemies. . . . But as much as I might rage over neocon mendacity and movement conservative gullibility and cowardice, I can also understand the magnitude of the domination achieved. And as painful as it may be for us, we must try to grasp that in Machiavelli's language, it was not just Fortuna but also virtu that was at work in making possible our enemies' spectacular achievements. Their opponents failed not only because they were obviously outgunned but also because we were less well organized, less able to network, and less capable of burying internal grievances. . . . Their indubitable successes have much to teach anyone who hopes to supplant them.[95]

This article is important for a number of reasons. First, as noted, its title coined the term "alternative right," later shortened to "Alt-Right." Second, it shows that paleoconservatism was a major precursor of the Alt-Right. Indeed, another article by Gottfried published soon after his 2008 address to the H. L. Menken Club refers to "paleoconservatism—what TakiMag's Richard Spencer now calls the 'Alternative Right.'"[96] Gottfried is in effect acknowledging that the Alt-Right is to a considerable degree a twenty-first-century extension of paleoconservatism. Third, this address mentions the development of a set of websites that includes *VDARE* and that would become the major platforms for dissemination of Alt-Right thought. And fourth, the address acknowledges that the new movement would seek to emulate its adversaries, the neoconservatives. The alternative right would be not a mass political movement but an intellectual movement, or what Richard Spencer would come to call a "metapolitical" movement. The alternative right would replace the neoconservatives as the suppliers of ideas and arguments for a broader political force. That is, just as the paleoconservatives saw the neoconservatives as the intellectual vanguard of the managerial elite, the Alt-Right would seek to be the intellectual vanguard of a movement striving to take its place as a new ruling class: the MARs or the postbourgeois resistance.

The radical critique of liberal democracy developed by paleoconservatives such as Francis and Gottfried was picked up and fleshed out by their epigone, the Alt-Right. How paleoconservatives and other extreme right thinkers developed two other themes that would be incorporated into Alt-Rightism—anti-Semitism and racialism—is discussed next.

Anti-Semitism and Racialism

The Critique of Liberal Democracy and the
Transition to Anti-Semitism and Racialism

Leviathan & Its Enemies, completed in 1995, does not take up the theme of race in great detail. But before he died in 2005, Francis developed the implications of his analysis for racial questions and made clear that racialism was central to his thought.

Francis's last book project was editing the volume titled *Race and the American Prospect: Essays on the Racial Realities of Our Nation and Our Time*, to which he contributed the introduction and the chapter "Why the American Ruling Class Betrays Its Race and Civilization." That essay, in sections titled "The Classical Theory of Elites" and "The Theory of the Managerial Revolution," reiterates the brand of Machiavellian analysis he clung to throughout his career. Because of the soft managerial elite's commitment to social environmentalism and social engineering, the elite's power is actually increased when the turmoil precipitated by reformist or liberationist social policy undermines old bases of community founded on region, ethnicity, and race. Blacks and other traditional targets of prejudice are beneficiaries of such policies and so form an alliance with the soft elite in opposition to the interests of the postbourgeois or the MARs, who are mostly gentile and white.

Francis's conclusion on the matter of race is as follows:

> The rise to power of the new managerial elite in the United States (and in other Western states as well) in the early and mid-twentieth century and the need of the new elite to formulate a new ideology or political formula and reconstruct society around it provides an explanation of why the dominant authorities in these countries today continue to support the dispossession of whites and the cultural and political destruction of the older American and Western civilization centered on whites and of why they not only fail to resist the anti-white demands of non-whites but actively support and subsidize them…. It is in the interests of the new elite, in other words, to destroy and eradicate the older society and the racial and cultural identities and consciousness associated with it (not race alone, but also virtually any distinctive traditional group identity or bond, cultural, biological, or political). . . . The interests of the managerial elite, in

other words, are antagonistic to the survival of the traditional racial and institutional identity of the society it dominates. . . . The emergence of the managerial elite promotes the dispossession and even the destruction of whites in the United States.[97]

Besides blacks, another minority group turns out to be a hidden ally of the elite and enemy of white, middle-class American interests, Francis writes. Then he reaches for an ancient scapegoat:

Because the new managerial elite rejects and destroys the mechanisms of the old elite that excluded other ethnic, racial, and religious groups, such groups are often able to permeate the managerial power structure and acquire levels of power unavailable to them in pre-managerial society . . . excluding whites and rejecting and dismantling the institutional fabric of their society. Kevin MacDonald has documented in immense detail how Jewish groups seeking to advance their own ethnically based agendas have accomplished this, and . . . *it is fair to say that Jews within the managerial elite serve as the cultural vanguard of the managerial class.* . . . Thus the emergence of "neo-conservatism" in recent decades reflects not only the Jewish interests and identities of its principal formulators and exponents but also, unlike the older conservatism of the pre-managerial elite, the interests of the managerial class as a whole in conserving the new political and cultural order that class has created but rejecting and dismantling the pre-managerial order the older conservatism sought to defend.[98]

Actually, the above quotation may understate Francis's commitment to anti-Semitism. In an email exchange now available on *Vanguard Network News*, a neo-Nazi website, Francis responded to charges from a white nationalist who complained that Francis had not been explicit enough in his criticism of Jews. Francis's interlocutor was Victor Gerhard, a member of another neo-Nazi organization, the National Alliance.[99] In these posts, Francis tells Gerhard that "I don't agree with your view of the Jews, that the Jews and the Jews alone are solely responsible for everything bad that has happened and is going on Here." But Francis also suggests that his published writings do not fully reflect his radicalism on Jewish and racial issues:

What more do you want? . . . You simply cannot go much further than I have already gone and expect to be published at all in anything like mainstream media. . . . What I have tried to do—explicitly at the [Washington] Times and later as well—has been to make explicit and serious discussion of race respectable. That means picking your shots and not saying everything you'd like to say because you know it will simply baffle or alarm many readers, but it does mean that you can tell many, many people a lot of things they didn't know or hadn't thought about.[100]

One way, then, to think about the Alt-Right is as an alternative to mainstream media in which all the baffling and alarming things about race, anti-Semitism, and much else that its paleoconservative predecessors dared not put into print could at last be disseminated beyond a purely fringe audience.

Thus it is that Francis starts off with elite theory and Burnham's Machiavellianism and ends up with racialism and anti-Semitism. His entire intellectual and rhetorical strategy is to delegitimate the usurping neoconservatism and liberal democracy in general by unmasking rather than answering their arguments and revealing them as motivated not only by elite but also by ethnic interests, those of nonwhites and Jews.

However, Francis is not up to the task of developing an apparently sophisticated account of anti-Semitism or racialism. His thoughts on these matters, compared to his critique of liberal democracy, are primitive. Francis developed his racialism at greatest length in an essay first published by *American Renaissance* in 1996, "The Roots of the White Man," which in 2015 was reposted by *Radix Journal* with an introduction by Richard Spencer describing it as "Francis's definitive statement on the distinctive, fundamental characteristics of Occidental civilization and the White race."[101] Interestingly, Francis first published this essay under the pseudonym "Edwin Clark," which is entirely understandable. "The Roots of the White Man" is a stitched-together collection of themes mostly from outdated and refuted racial theories about the "Aryans," a.k.a. "Indo-Europeans." The quotation below gives a sense of the general tone of the discussion:

One of the principal characteristics of early Indo-European societies is a hierarchical, three-tiered or "tripartite" class structure of priests, warriors, and herder-cultivators. . . . One of the more obvious symbols of social tripartition is colour . . . white to priests and red to the warrior. The third would appear to have been marked by a darker colour such as black or blue. The racial symbolism of such caste colors is obvious, with the higher ranks of society being symbolized by the color associated with the lighter-skinned Aryans and the lower ranks symbolized by the darker hues of the conquered non-Aryan races. . . . The tripartite structure of Indo-European society . . . may also be reflected in the division of political functions into executive, judicial, and legislative in the U.S. Constitution, and even in the Christian idea of the Trinity.[102]

Mercifully, Francis does not offer any thoughts on the racial coloration of the branches of the American federal government or the personalities of the Holy Trinity. A more specious account of racialism and anti-Semitism better suited for wide dissemination would be needed.

Such accounts come from other precursors of the Alt-Right. An updated version of anti-Semitism is offered in the work of another proto-Alt-Right thinker sometimes cited by Francis, Kevin MacDonald, whose voluminous pseudo-Darwinian analyses of Judaism have earned him the moniker "the Marx of the Anti-Semites."[103] The theme of racialism is developed by Michael Levin in his book, *Why Race Matters: Race Differences and What They Mean.* The main works of MacDonald and Levin were published during the mid- and late 1990s, so that by the beginning of the new millennium these authors, along with Francis and other paleoconservatives, had already laid the theoretical foundations of Alt-Right ideology.

Kevin MacDonald's Evolutionary Anti-Semitism

Perhaps in reaction to the incorporation of Jewish intellectuals into mainstream conservatism, paleoconservatism during the 1990s reverted to the anti-Semitic roots of earlier right-wing extremism. Two *National Review* contributors who moved in that direction, Patrick Buchanan and Joseph Sobran, were banned from the magazine. Indeed, Buckley continued his struggle to keep conservatism mainstream by devoting an entire issue of his magazine—titled *In Search of Anti-Semitism*—to the Buchanan affair. Buchanan and Sobran both found homes in paleoconservative magazines.

The thrust of this renewed anti-Semitism was that Jews were hardly Americans at all. Buchanan, in two separate columns against the first Gulf War, first focused on supporters of the war with Jewish-sounding names—Abe Rosenthal, Richard Perle, Charles Krauthammer, and Henry Kissinger—and then contrasted them to the "American kids with names like McAllister, Murphy, Gonzales, and Leroy Brown" who would fight the war.[104] The implication here is that Jews were not Americans at all but a group distinct from Americans. The paleoconservative challenge was to prove that Jews were a group distinct from and antithetical toward Americans generally.

Here the turn toward racialism that would eventually distinguish the Alt-Right from some right-wing extremists of the past began. The distinctiveness of the Jews and their supposed hostility toward Americans was to be "proven" by giving exploded anti-Semitic conspiracy theories a patina of respectability by recasting them in the vocabulary of modern genetic research. Crucial to this task was the work of former University of California at Long Beach psychology professor Kevin B. MacDonald, laid out in copious detail in a trilogy of books: A People That Shall Dwell Alone: Judaism as a Group Evolutionary Strategy (1994), Separation and Its Discontents: Toward an Evolutionary Theory of Anti-Semitism (1998), and The Culture of Critique: An Evolutionary Analysis of Jewish Involvement in Twentieth-Century Intellectual and Political Movements (1998).

Briefly put, MacDonald's theory is that Jewish culture and marriage and childrearing practices produce offspring of high intelligence and a collectivistic personality.[105] These traits are genetically based and thus not easily changed, and they allow Jews to compete effectively with gentiles for scarce resources. Indeed, Judaism overall is nothing more than an extraordinarily successful evolutionary strategy by which its followers thrive in their ecological niche, MacDonald theorizes. The following passages illustrate MacDonald's approach:

> The basic thesis of this book can be summarized by the proposition that Judaism must be conceptualized as a group strategy characterized by cultural and genetic segregation from gentile societies combined with resource competition and conflicts of interest with segments of gentile societies. This cultural and genetic separatism combined with resource competition and other conflicts of interest tend to result in division and hatred within the society.[106]

In a very illuminating 2006 interview with a contributor to the Journal of Church and State, MacDonald was asked whether "your research provides a sort of intellectual legitimacy to anti-Semitism," and responded as follows:

> My logic is as follows: I see conflicts of interest between ethnic groups as part of the natural world. The only difference between conflicts between Jews and non-Jews compared to garden variety ethnic conflict stems from the fact that for over a century, Jews have formed an elite in various European and European-derived societies, an elite with a peculiar profile: deeply ethnocentric and adept at ethnic networking; wealthy and intelligent, aggressive in pursuit of their interests, prone to media ownership and the production of culture, and hostile to the traditional peoples and cultures of the societies in which they form an elite. As an elite, Jews have wielded power that is vastly disproportionate to their numbers, so that anti-Jewish attitudes and behavior are to be expected when Jewish power conflicts with the interests of others. The various themes of modern anti-Semitism all boil down to the Jewish role as a hostile elite whose attitudes and behavior are in conflict with the interests of others. . . . Since I believe that these propositions are intellectually defensible, and since these propositions, if believed by non-Jews, would cause them to attempt to lessen Jewish power and thereby further their own interests, it is indeed the case that my work could be said to provide intellectual legitimacy to anti-Jewish attitudes and behavior. . . . At the end of the day, what counts is whether indeed my writings are intellectually defensible.[107]

This passage is significant for several reasons. First, MacDonald does not deny that his "research provides a sort of intellectual legitimacy to anti-Semitism," and indeed acknowledges that his work does exactly that for what he politely terms "anti-Jewish attitudes and behavior." Generally, although MacDonald never describes himself as anti-Semitic, in his later works he is quite open about his hostility to Jews and his determination to frustrate their interests. MacDonald describes how his hostility developed over the course of writing his trilogy in the following passage from *The Culture of Critique:*

> To be perfectly frank, I did not have a general animus for organized Jewry when I got into this project. . . . By the time I wrote *C of C* I had changed greatly from the person who wrote the first book. . . . Jews have indeed made positive contributions to western culture in the last 200 years. . . .

On the other hand, I am persuaded that Jews have also had some important negative influences. . . . In fact, if one wants to date when I dared cross the line into what some see as proof that I am an "anti-Semite," the best guess would probably be when I started reading on the involvement of all powerful Jewish organizations in advocating massive non-European immigration. . . . In the end, does it really matter if my motivation at this point is less than pristine? Isn't the only question whether I am right?[108]

Shortly we will consider whether MacDonald is "right," but for now it should be pointed out that motivation may indeed be relevant in judging whether a social scientist's work is legitimate. It is entirely possible to string together a series of claims, some of which are individually "right" in some sense, that is mendacious in its overall impression. Such a writer's motivations are indeed relevant in deciding the truth value of his general argument. But the point here is that the above passage is notable for MacDonald's very nearly explicit admission of anti-Semitism.

Second, the above quotations show that MacDonald conceptualizes Jews as an elite. Although the elite theorists and their contemporary followers receive no significant mention in MacDonald's trilogy, his understanding of Jews as an elite group dovetails nicely with Francis's Machiavellianism and allowed paleoconservative critics of liberal democracy to easily incorporate MacDonald's thinking into theirs. MacDonald's account of the Jewish elite locked in a conflict of interests with traditional ethnic elites similarly fits in with the elite theorists' vision of politics as essentially a struggle for power among competing elites. What MacDonald offered to the paleoconservative Machiavellians is an extension of their theory of elite struggle that supported their animus against Jews.

The Machiavellians held that ideas are tools that elites use to advance their power interests, and therefore that such ideas are almost always lies. MacDonald essentially applies this premise to Jewish intellectual history and concludes that virtually all schools of thought whose proponents disproportionately have identified as Jewish are mere projections of Jewish interests and are therefore bogus. Propagating such phony ideas is part of the Jewish evolutionary strategy, MacDonald theorizes. Jews disseminate ideas among gentiles that, when acted on, move gentile society in a pluralist, individualist direction. However, Jews do not practice what they preach, according to MacDonald, and by retaining their collectivist, ethnocentric culture, they achieve an advantage over gentiles in the struggle for power.

The Culture of Critique focuses on a number of twentieth-century intellectual movements whose proponents were disproportionately Jewish: Boasian anthropology, leftist radicalism, psychoanalysis, the Frankfurt School, the New York intellectuals, and advocacy of the 1965 Immigration Act. According to MacDonald:

> I argue that these movements are attempts to alter Western societies in a manner that could neutralize or end anti-Semitism and enhance the prospects for Jewish group continuity either in an overt or semi-cryptic manner. . . . Ultimately, these movements are viewed as the expression of a group evolutionary strategy by Jews in their competition for social, political, and cultural dominance with non-Jews.[109]

For example, MacDonald tells us "neoconservatism is an excellent illustration of the key traits behind the success of Jewish activism: ethnocentrism, intelligence and wealth, psychological intensity, and aggressiveness."[110] These adaptive traits allow Jews to advance their interests by promoting more open immigration policy, which makes for a more diverse society in which Jews can better thrive. Part of the neoconservative strategy is that "non-Jews have been welcomed into the movement. . . . It makes excellent psychological sense to have the spokespersons for any movement resemble the people they are trying to convince."

In developing his argument that ideas are merely tools of group interest MacDonald runs into the same problem that Burnham did: if that is true, aren't MacDonald's ideas masks for some elite's power interest and therefore no better than the falsehoods of his adversaries? At one point, MacDonald admits he has no answer to this objection: "No evolutionist should be surprised at the implicit theory in all this, namely that intellectual activities of all types may at bottom involve ethnic warfare. . . . The truly doubtful proposition for an evolutionist is whether real social science as a disinterested attempt to understand human behavior is at all possible."[111]

Thus MacDonald cannot rebut the charge he has fallen headlong into the same pitfall that supposedly invalidated the philosophies he criticizes. In the face of such doubts, why not admit that evolutionism has clear limitations and that the theories MacDonald dislikes will have to be faced on their own terms? But instead, MacDonald plows on with his analysis.

MacDonald therefore runs into a problem that all thinkers who deploy an unmasking or debunking strategy against their adversaries must face. His arguments are often self-defeating or circular. An example of his self-defeating arguments is when he charges that "skepticism in the interest of combating scientific theories one dislikes for deeper reasons has been a prominent aspect of twentieth-century Jewish intellectual activity."[112] Exactly the same charge can be made of MacDonald's deployment of evolutionism against the "Jewish" theories he denigrates. In fact, the charge applies a fortiori against MacDonald because he has already admitted that his motivations are "less than pristine." So, in legitimating the hunt for the "deeper reasons" behind his adversaries' arguments, all MacDonald has done is stipulate that motivations are indeed relevant to the question of whether one is "right" and that therefore, given his admitted hostility, he is probably wrong.

For an example of MacDonald's circular arguments, we need only consider the following from his book *Separation and Its Discontents*:

> The charge that this is an anti-Semitic book is . . . expectable and completely in keeping with the thesis of this essay. A major theme of this volume . . . is that . . . Jewish theories of anti-Semitism have throughout history played a critical role in maintaining Judaism as a group evolutionary strategy. . . . Parts of the book read as a sort of extended discourse on the role of Jewish self-interest, deception, and self-deception . . . in Jewish conceptualizations of their . . . relations with outgroups. This is therefore first and foremost a book that confidently predicts its own irrelevance to those about whom it is written.[113]

So MacDonald's argument is that the accusations of anti-Semitism lodged against him prove he is right; he predicted that his unflattering account of supposed Jewish self-deception would elicit charges of anti-Semitism, which is just what happened. Thus it is confirmed, claims Mac-Donald, that the Jews are masters of deceit. Of course, the problem is that what has been confirmed is not the whole bolus of MacDonald's thought but only his expectation that he will be charged—quite fairly—with anti-Semitism.

The point is that MacDonald often falls into the contradictions to which all unmasking or debunking strategies are prone. Some account of how ideas can rise above deception and objectively represent the world is necessary; otherwise the unmasking strategy refutes itself. And further, it must be shown that the ideas one wants to refute do not agree with that account while one's own ideas do. MacDonald tries to provide such an account but ultimately fails.

Let us assume for the moment, as MacDonald would have it, that Freudian psychoanalysis, Boasian anthropology, Critical Theory, neoconservatism, and so forth are all intellectual constructs deployed by the Jewish elite to remake their host societies into ecological niches more favorable to their ethnic interests. This strategy will work *only if the members of the host society actually believe those constructs are true.* If the ideas disseminated by the Jews are unconvincing, they will not achieve their intended purpose of remaking the host society in a way favorable to the Jews. Why, then, do the host societies accept the "Jewish" ideas that are inimical to their interests? MacDonald's theory is implausible unless one assumes that the ideas developed by the Jews are, to a considerable extent, "intellectually defensible" to disinterested or even hostile audiences. But his point is that these "Jewish" ideas are false. Therefore, he has to explain how it is that Jews are adept at developing ideas so specious they entirely fool skeptical gentile audiences but are nonetheless demonstrably false. All exponents of elite theory believe that elite groups must lie; MacDonald's contribution to this line of thought is that the Jews are the lying elite par excellence. What, then, is their extraordinary rhetorical strategy that has hoodwinked hostile host societies over the centuries, and how is it that MacDonald, unlike many past generations of gullible gentiles, has at last seen through this deception?

Jews have developed several strategies to pull off their deceptions, according to MacDonald. First of all, Jewish culture has selected for collectivistic personality traits that give Jews an advantage in all walks of life, including science and scholarship, he maintains. According to MacDonald, "Intellectual activity is like any other human endeavor: Cohesive groups outcompete individualist strategies. Indeed, the fundamental truth of this axiom has been central to the success of Judaism throughout its history."[114] Intellectual networks, MacDonald says, in which Jews are disproportionately represented are just such cohesive groups and there-

fore are highly effective at advancing merely specious work at the expense
of true science:

> Yet because of their collective, highly focused efforts and energy, these
> groups can be much more influential than the atomized, fragmented ef-
> forts of individuals. The efforts of individualists can easily be ignored,
> marginalized, or placed under anathema. . . . Judaism has resulted in col-
> lectivistic enterprises that have systematically impeded inquiry in the
> social sciences in the interests of developing and disseminating theories
> directed at achieving specific political and social interests.[115]

Besides cohesive networks, Jews deploy other strategies to advance
their self-interested theories in the face of true science, MacDonald
writes. They cloak their ideas with a "scientific veneer," "center around
a charismatic leader (Boas, Freud, or Horkheimer)," employ "Jewish
crypsis and semi-crypsis" to hide their real origins and interests, and
seek prestige to make them harder to criticize.[116] Thus Jewish thinkers,
by MacDonald's account, are convincing to gentile society not because
of the inherent plausibility of their work but because of superior lobbying efforts. Acceptance of "Jewish" ideas represents not freely given
conviction after due deliberation but rather "an act of authoritarian
submission."[117] In other words, Jewish ideas persuade not because they
are true but because they are backed up by a powerful elite, according
to MacDonald.

Let us be polite and say that this account of Jewish intellectual success
is highly unpersuasive at best. MacDonald admits that even when Freudian psychotherapy, Boasian anthropology, and Critical Theory were at
the height of their influence, Jews were a minority in the relevant scholarly networks and institutions. Even if that minority were the cohesive,
well-organized bloc MacDonald says it was, academic discourse was quite
open during the period described. Scholarly journals, book publication,
and promotion were all largely peer-reviewed. Was it the case that every
convincing critic of Freud, Boas, and the Frankfurt School had his good
work batted down by the Jewish elite and its stooges in their prestigious
positions? If so, wouldn't those critics simply take their work to another,
perhaps less prestigious, forum until they got a hearing? And if the critics were demonstrably correct, wouldn't some ambitious members of the

nonelite take up their ideas and so make professional headway with them? In essence, MacDonald argues that Truth, crushed to Earth, shall *not* rise again—except, of course, until he came along and inexplicably saw through all the Jewish deceits that had tricked the best minds of gentile society for many decades.

At no point did Freudians, Boasians, or Critical Theorists achieve total hegemony over their fields. The Freudians perhaps approached doing so, but other schools of psychology, such as behaviorism, survived. Critical Theory never caught on in American departments of sociology or philosophy the way that, say, functionalism and analytic philosophy did. MacDonald does manage to show that infighting among different academic schools of thought can be bitter, and that some critics of dominant theories suffered setbacks. And it seems that the followers of the philosophies he criticizes were disproportionately Jewish. At no point does he show that a Jewish elite had such a stranglehold on academic life that all legitimate criticism was crushed and the entire gentile world was gulled. Nowhere does he review the contemporary academic literature and show that the critics of Freud, Boas, and the Critical Theorists clearly had the better of the scientific debate but were marginalized by the maneuvers of an alleged Jewish power bloc. But if these ideas have any prima facie appearance of objective truth, pointing out the Jewish background of (some of) their proponents is merely an ad hominem argument. In short, MacDonald's attempt to unmask ideas he dislikes as covers for Jewish elite interests succumbs to a pitfall of unmasking arguments in general. One *first* has to prove that the masking ideas are flawed on their own terms before one can convincingly argue that they are no more than covers for ethnic—or class or gender or partisan—interest.

MacDonald also falls into the pitfalls of another dubious methodology, conspiracy theory, by which I mean much more than that he recycles the ancient stereotypes of Jewish scheming, although that he does. Popper identifies the conspiracy theory of society as "the view that an explanation of a social phenomenon consists in the discovery of the men or groups who are interested in the occurrence of this phenomenon . . . and who have planned or conspired to bring it about." Then he points out the obvious weakness in this approach:

Conspiracies occur, it must be admitted. But the striking fact which, in spite of their occurrence, disapproves the conspiracy theory is that . . . *Conspirators rarely consummate their conspiracy.*

Why is this so? . . . Because this is usually the case in social life, conspiracy or no conspiracy. Social life is not only a trial of strength between opposing groups: It is action within a more or less resilient or brittle framework of institutions and tradition and it creates—apart from any conscious counter-action—many unforeseen reactions in this framework, some of them perhaps even unforeseeable.[118]

The Culture of Critique analyzes modernist schools of thought as attempts by an alleged Jewish elite "to alter Western societies....These movements are viewed as the outcome of conflicts of interest between Jews and non-Jews in the construction of culture and in various public policy issues."[119] The simplistic assumption here is that societies are altered, cultures are constructed, and politics is made precisely in a straightforward trial of strength between groups—and just two of them at that. But the transition of Western polities from the early modernism of 1900 to the post-modernism of today is the result of an immensely tangled knot of multifarious intersecting vectors. These are not only of two ethnic-group interests but of many groups of many different sorts and of many different forces: economic, scientific, technological, cultural, social, political, environmental, philosophical, etc. In MacDonald's telling the essential trend of the last 120 years is largely explained by the amazingly successful efforts of a tiny Jewish elite to remake society in its interests. Indeed he writes that "*CofC* is really an attempt to understand the 20th century as a Jewish century—a century in which Jews and Jewish organizations were deeply involved in all the pivotal events."[120] This attribution of a century of world historical development to the preternaturally effective machinations of a single tiny cabal is intellectually bankrupt. MacDonald never grasps the essential insight of modern social science: social development is the unintended and usually unforeseen net resultant of multiple interacting forces.

The most immediate political payoff of MacDonald's pseudo-Darwinian anti-Semitism comes in his attack on the neoconservatives so detested by the paleoconservatives. MacDonald presents neoconservatism not as a set of ideas to be debated but rather as the evolutionary strategy of an invasive subspecies—the Jews—that must be suppressed lest it come to dominate the ecological niche of the United States at the expense of its other inhabitants. In this view, Jewish influence in the mostly gentile conservative movement serves as a kind of reproductive mechanism as non-Jewish conservatives will be better able to convince the host society to produce a more diverse environment that is supposedly conducive to Jewish advancement but antithetical to earlier niche species. In MacDonald's anti-Semitism, the long-frustrated extremists, now termed paleo-conservatives, believed they had at last found an argument with which to reclaim their rightful position in the conservative movement and American society generally.

Michael Levin's Racialism

Deformed Darwinism was put to many other uses by the precursors of the Alt-Right. It provided a more specious response to the civil rights movement than the John Birch Society's absurd charge of a communist conspiracy. The new argument would be that blacks were disadvantaged not because of discrimination but because their genetic endowments were maladaptive in the ecological niche of American society. In 1997 City College philosophy professor Michael Levin developed this line of argument at length in his book, *Why Race Matters: Race Differences and What They Mean*. One sympathetic reviewer summed up Levin's position as follows:

> Racial groups differ in ability and temperament as they differ in skin color, physiognomy, susceptibility to high blood pressure, and other traits. Thus, Levin notes in studied agreement with the usual stereotypes, there are proportionately more blacks with athletic ability and fewer with intellectual ability; more with an inclination for violent behavior and fewer with the capacity for self-control. Furthermore, Levin doubts that these differences are entirely artifacts of racial discrimination. Instead, he believes . . . that much racial discrimination is a realistic response to differences, which are not only real but also in part hereditary. If he is right, governmentally enforced preference by race is both unjustified and ill-advised.[121]

And here is Levin in his own words. He had

reviewed evidence that blacks are typically less intelligent and inclined to follow rules, and more aggressive, self-assertive, and impulsive than whites. . . . These differences may be summarized by saying that blacks are typically less Kantian. Since Kantianism is the principal Caucasoid measure of personal worth, it follows that, *by ordinary Caucasoid standards, the average white is a better person than the average black. . . . A greater proportion of black than white behavior also falls below the ordinary thresholds of decency, and of tolerability.*[122]

Thus, while once the John Birch Society itself stipulated that "a huge majority of the American people, of both races . . . are good people,"[123] the racialism that would spread through the extreme right by the early twenty-first century asserted that "the average white is a better person than the average black [person]." These two statements are not logically incompatible, but they are polar opposites as axioms of political ideology and public rhetoric. The first was compatible with a racially egalitarian polity; the second implied that a decent society required white political dominance.

Levin's racialism has three distinctive aspects: First, he maintains that the races—black, white, and Asian—differ, on average, from each other in terms of various psychological traits and social behaviors. Levin points to data that show average black IQ scores are lower than those of whites, and white average scores are lower than those of Asians. He also points to statistics that show the average rate of criminal behavior among young black men is much higher than that for comparable whites.

Second, Levin argues that it is legitimate for private citizens and the government, in some circumstances, to judge individuals on the basis of these average racial differences rather than as individuals. He maintains that police may stop and search black, but not white, men driving fancy cars because such blacks are more likely to be drug dealers, and that white pedestrians may legitimately flee from a black rather than a white stranger, again because the black is more likely to be a criminal. Levin also argues that since "blacks *are* more likely to commit crimes than whites . . . more severe punishment might be warranted for convicted black offenders." Perhaps his most infamous suggestions were for "requiring black males to ride in special police-patrolled subway cars," and that "curfews imposed on young black males are also defensible."[124]

Such is Levin's racialist thought in outline; what are we to make of it? Every aspect of it—the data it relies on, the empirical conclusions drawn from them, and the rhetoric with which Levin expresses himself—raises problems. But perhaps the rhetoric, or more exactly the ideological zeal behind it, is most disturbing, for it implies a cavalier attitude toward the rule of law and an obliviousness to the costs of political extremism.

First, let's consider the data Levin uses to back up his racialism. It is important to note that the *existence* of much of these data is not open to question. For example, it is simply a fact that average black scores on IQ tests are lower than average white scores on IQ tests. The controversy comes down to how one interprets these data. Are the IQ tests meaningful or invalid, fair or biased? Is the differential caused by environment, or heredity, or some combination? The fact is that on all these issues, there is a very wide range of opinion among professional psychologists. *Some* serious psychologists believe that IQ data establish the reality of a black-white difference in intelligence, and *some* believe that this difference is *partly* rooted in genetics. Some vigorously disagree. In 1975 the authors of the standard reference work on this issue, *Race Differences in Intelligence*, summed up what was then and now the professional consensus of opinion as follows:

> Observed average differences in the scores of members of different US racial-ethnic groups in intelligence-ability tests probably reflect in part inadequacies and biases in the tests themselves, in part differences in the environmental conditions among the groups, and in part genetic differences among the groups. . . . A rather wide range of positions concerning the relative weight to be given to these three factors can reasonably be taken on the basis of current evidence.[125]

Now, what a lay reader will probably notice in this statement, and in the general consensus among psychologists, is the implication that some of the black-white differential is real and may be genetically based. Levin notices it too, harps on it, uses it as the first stepping-stone in his argument, and baits some observers into attacking him for mentioning it. But the other implication, which Levin ignores, should also be noted: the consensus of current scholarship is that bias and environmental factors probably *also* account for part of the average black-white IQ test score differences. No one should object to serious scholars researching these issues and letting the facts fall out where they may. It is objectionable, however, when nonprofessionals make a raid on this research, grab hold of its most controversial aspects, and use them in a game of race-baiting.

The next problem is with the empirical conclusions Levin draws from the data. Assuming for the sake of argument that various differences between blacks and whites exist, and that these differences are partly based on genetic factors, do those facts justify Levin's policy proposals? Generally, they do not.

Let's consider Levin's suggestion that high black crime rates justify whites' fear of blacks. The issue involves what statisticians call conditional probability: Given that someone met on the street is black, how likely is he to mug you? This is something statistically distinct from the difference in black and white incarceration rates, or any of the other figures that Levin leans on. It does not follow statistically that if black crime rates are higher than white crime rates, then blackness is necessarily the best predictor of whether in a particular situation a given individual will mug you. Levin makes no effort to work out the mathematics of this problem, which would present formidable methodological challenges. In any given situation an infinite barrage of factors besides race—sex, dress, demeanor, location, time of day—could be more or less probable predictors of danger. Sorting them out on the fly is impossible. Simply fleeing every time one encounters a black person is unlikely to be an optimal strategy. A more effective criminal justice system and a lower crime rate overall, both of which have been achieved since Levin made his inflammatory proposals, represent a better approach.

Average differences in intellectual traits between the races—alleged or real—are utterly irrelevant to the question of whether everyone, regardless of race, deserves equal treatment before the law. Those commentators who allow themselves to be sucked into endless debate over the reality of these differences and who assume that, should they prove real, then the case for political equality will be lost, are simply rising to the racialists' bait. As will be discussed in chapters 6 and 7 in connection with later developments in Alt-Right ideology, liberal democratic theory does not base the case for political equality on the factual equality of all humankind for fear that the findings of modern biology provide far too unstable a ground for this cornerstone of free society.

Conclusion

Such, then, was the political analysis that the proto-Alt-Rightist paleo-conservatives bequeathed to the early twenty-first century. Liberal democracy, they argued, is totalitarian, despotic, illiberal, and in reality undemocratic. Hard regimes on the model of fascist Italy, the Soviet Union, and Nazi Germany are alternatives worth considering, they said. Political ideas are mere tools of elite domination, with the sole exception of far-right ideas, which are pure science and mere realism. Racial and ethnic differences trump human rights and the rule of law. Politics is no more than an unending power struggle in which values count for nothing and victory for everything.

The embrace of Burnham, elite theory, and the futility thesis by Francis and other paleoconservatives was highly consequential. The futility argument is the most problematic of the conservative rhetorical strategies identified by Hirschman. To successfully deploy the perversity and jeopardy strategies a speaker must assume, at least for the sake of the argument, that the goals of his progressive interlocutor are desirable. These approaches focus objections only on the proposed means for achieving those legitimate ends. Thus conservatives and progressives are assumed to share common ground, and rational discussion between them is facilitated. The futility argument, however, makes no such concession. Progressive policies are held to be utterly unavailing and mere wastes of resources, so they are not even in principle desirable. No common ground with progressives is assumed, and therefore no rational argument with them is possible within the terms of the futility thesis. The proper response to a progressive thus becomes not critiquing his arguments but impugning his motives. For if sophisticated observers know that progressive measures are futile, then those who advocate them must be either fools or, more likely, knaves. The futility argument, as Hirschman points out, thus leads to the charge that progressive ideas are just masks, veils, or disguises for hidden interests.[126] The irrationalism inherent in much of postpaleo thought was to be picked up and magnified by the Alt-Right and lead to a scorn for ideas, an embrace of vituperative rhetoric, and a decline in the quality of conservative political discourse.

Another consequence of the postpaleo embrace of the futility thesis was a high tolerance for fanaticism. The elite theorists, like all exponents of the futility argument, stressed how impervious to change fundamental social structures are. This position will serve the purposes of conservatives who wish to preserve the status quo. But what about right-wing elements like Gottfried's alternative Right or Francis's MAR-led New Right, who see no status quo they want to preserve? If social structures are invincible, then the status quo is impregnable, and everyone seeking real change—whether right or left—ought to resign themselves to the inevitable. But despair soon gets quite boring, and so would-be revolutionaries must then search for a change agent utterly beyond the pale of ordinary political reality. This impulse explains why, as Hirschman notes, right-wing adherents of the futility thesis have no trouble allying themselves with left-wing radicals, as Gottfried did with the *Telos* circle. Reactionaries suffering from a longing for total revolution can sympathize with similarly disposed leftists. But if alternative Rightists in search of an apocalypse can make peace with even the ultraradical left, how easy they find it to get in bed with the ultraradical right. Thus did the proto Alt-Right open the doors to all of the formerly exiled forces that wanted to get their licks in against liberal democracy: neofascists, racialists, anti-Semites, neo-Confederates, reactionary Russophiles, and so on.

Before 2000 the proto-Alt-Rightism of paleoconservative thought found a relatively small audience. Pat Buchanan was the only political actor of the late twentieth century who displayed real paleoconservative propensities. A 1996 article by Francis for the paleoconservative journal *Chronicles* praised Buchanan highly in the course of an analysis that broaches most of the themes found in *Leviathan & Its Enemies*. Just before Buchanan began his 1992 run for the Republican presidential nomination Francis offered him some advice and got a disappointing response:

I told him . . . "Go to New Hampshire and call yourself a patriot, a nationalist, an America Firster, but don't even use the word 'conservative.' It doesn't mean anything any more."

Pat listened, but I can't say he took my advice. By making his bed with the Republicans . . . he only dilutes and deflects the radicalism of the message he and his Middle American Revolution have to offer.[127]

Before the twenty-first century, any political figure who adumbrated postpaleo thought had to "dilute and deflect" the radicalism of that message, just as Buchanan was careful to do, if he wanted his ideas to receive anything like wide dissemination. But after the turn of the millennium, technological and social developments would allow the Alt-Right's florid variation of that ideology to find a much larger audience than previous extremisms had.

4
Crystallization of the Alt-Right
from 2000 to 2016

After the turn of the millennium, Alt-Right ideas gained a toehold in the American political discourse that the right-wing extremists of the 1960s and the paleoconservatives of the 1980s and 1990s never obtained for their ideas. There were several reasons for this relative success. But before we look at particulars, we need a model that helps explain how ideas come to have an impact on American politics. We can then see how well the model fits the case of the Alt-Right and make whatever modifications are necessary.

The Production of Public Ideas around 2000

First, what is an idea, and what types of ideas have an impact on political life? Mark Moore has described such "public ideas" as follows:

> Most such ideas are not very complex or differentiated. There is no clear separation of ends from means, of diagnosis from interventions, of assumptions from demonstrated facts, or blame from causal effect. . . . Moreover, it is not clear reasoning or carefully developed and interpreted

facts that make ideas convincing. Rather ideas seem to become anchored in people's minds through illustrative anecdotes, simple diagrams and pictures, or connections with broad common-sense ideologies that define human nature and social responsibility.[1]

That is, ideas that have an immediate impact in public life are atheoretical. They are simple, are couched in terms almost sloganlike, and can be immediately grasped by nonexperts. Examples of such public ideas include those phrased as "Broaden the base, lower the rates," in the tax reform debates of the 1980s; "End welfare as we know it," from the overhaul of welfare policy in the 1990s; and perhaps "Build the wall!" from Trump's anti-immigration rhetoric of the 2016 presidential campaign, which replaced an earlier public idea related to immigration, "Close the back door to open the front door."

But where do such ideas come from, and how it is possible for such simplistic phrases to have any validity at all? *The New Politics of Public Policy* (1995) and *Seeking the Center: Politics and Policymaking at the New Century* (2001) are anthologies that tried to answer these questions by developing what might be called the "food chain" account of how public ideas are developed.[2]

At the top of the chain are experts working on problems related to public affairs, but at high levels of abstraction. Such experts are usually professional scholars working at academic institutions. Thus the basic research and theoretical groundwork for the slogans of the tax reformers of the 1980s had been developed decades earlier by academic economists such as Robert M. Haig, Henry C. Simons, and Joseph A. Pechman. By the 1980s a strong consensus had emerged among professional economists in favor of horizontal equity, investment neutrality, and administrative efficiency in the tax code. "Broaden the base, lower the rates" was the (over)simplified public idea that expressed that consensus and derived such power as it had from that fact. *The New Politics of Public Policy* provides similar accounts of how influential public ideas had their roots in a consensus among relevant experts in the areas of environmental policy, welfare, special education, and immigration.[3]

One level down in the food chain are people who usually are not experts themselves but have the education or resources necessary to understand at least the outlines of the thought developed by experts and then communicate them to a wider audience. These are the people whom Hayek famously dubbed "professional secondhand dealers in ideas," that is, intellectuals.[4] It is at this level that abstract academic ideas are rendered into the slogans of public ideas. As Hayek noted, a much broader range of professionals than is often understood qualify as intellectuals in this sense. Journalists of all kinds, editors, broadcast media professionals, writers, teachers, and activists all count as intellectuals. Indeed, anyone with a "wide range of subjects on which he can readily talk and write, and a position or habits through which he becomes acquainted with new ideas sooner than those to whom he addresses himself"[5] counts as an intellectual in this sense.

At the next level down in the food chain are policy entrepreneurs. Anyone who seeks to influence politics by marketing a new policy idea counts as a policy entrepreneur. Policy entrepreneurs can be politicians seeking to achieve recognition by identifying themselves with potentially popular policy ideas and applying them to immediate public affairs issues. In the case of tax reform, Bill Bradley and Jack Kemp functioned as effective policy entrepreneurs, and in the area of welfare reform Bill Clinton and Newt Gingrich filled that role. But policy entrepreneurs need not be elected politicians, as the example of Ralph Nader makes clear.

Institutions too can be policy entrepreneurs. The EPA functioned as such when it became interested in toxic waste amelioration and sold the idea of the Superfund to Congress. Think tanks may also sometimes act as policy entrepreneurs. Such organizations occupy a space between strictly academic experts and political actors with more immediate concerns. Think tank staffers, even when they have academic training, usually focus on applied policy issues and often work in communication rather than analysis, and so are adept at transforming academic expertise into public ideas. A good example of a think tank that was a successful policy entrepreneur is the American Enterprise Institute in its role in the deregulatory movement of the late 1970s through the mid-1980s. Mass media organizations may also function as policy entrepreneurs when they independently develop and disseminate public ideas rather than "objectively" report news. An example is the editorial and op-ed section of the *Wall Street Journal* during the debates on immigration reform in the 1980s.[6]

At the next level down in the food chain of public ideas are the mass media when they are functioning primarily as transmitters rather than developers of ideas. From the mid-1960s until very recently, the most important medium for the dissemination of public ideas was television. When television began to play this role, it had several profound impacts on American politics.

Television was a much more effective way of communicating with the public than the old infrastructure of party machines and operatives. The rise of television therefore weakened the power of political parties.

Also, television broadcasters, because they were in principle making use of the public good of the electromagnetic spectrum, were federally regulated and so were required to maintain at least the appearance of objectivity and nonpartisanship. Under the former federal policy known as the fairness doctrine, expressions of opinion had to be balanced and therefore were usually clearly presented as such and did not have much airtime devoted to them. Of course, the objectivity of broadcast television news was hotly debated then just as it is now. But appearances had to be maintained, and so news departments were professionalized and tried to follow the canons of serious journalism. And, of course, the public nature of broadcasting and federal regulation meant that coarse vulgarity was impossible. So communication of political information to the public was now handled by professional, objective, and well-spoken broadcast journalists rather than by ward heelers, party bosses, and local notables. Journalists working at other important media outlets besides television were also professionalized and followed similar standards and practices.

Further, getting the word out through television, if airtime had to be paid for, was much more expensive than using party machinery, which meant that getting free coverage from news departments was critical for politicians and policy entrepreneurs generally. Candidates had to somehow become newsworthy in the eyes of professional journalists, which meant they had to have something to say that seemed to merit coverage. Politicians who found a place in the food chain of public ideas, who could become at least conversant with the thoughts of experts and policy entrepreneurs, could gain an advantage. Thus ideas became more valuable relative to traditional political resources—such as money, organization, and votes—than they had been before the rise of television. Of course, this is not to say that ideas became *more* important than money or other resources, only that ideas became more important than they had once been, and could be crucial.

Finally, because television emphasized image over substance, expert discourse had to be vastly, even overly, simplified to get coverage. Ideas had to be boiled down nearly to slogans, that is, public ideas, suitable for television and other forms of mass media. Policy entrepreneurs became adept at this distillation process. For example, think tanks began to devote nearly as many resources to repackaging and marketing ideas as they did to the experts who developed them.

At the bottom of the ideational food chain were the consumers of television and mass media, that is, the public. But why should the public, confronting the many distractions of a consumerist economy and private life, pay any attention to public ideas about political affairs, even if they are greatly simplified for mass consumption? The American public is notoriously uninterested in ideas and politics and will pay attention only when circumstances force it to do so. As long as public affairs seem to be unfolding in a way that does not dramatically undermine the conventional wisdom about political life, the public will in fact not be much interested in new ideas. The key elements of the food chain were all in place by about 1960, but public ideas had little impact on politics until the public was shaken up enough to entertain new ideas. According to David M. Ricci in *The Transformation of American Politics*, that shake-up was provided by the pivotal year of 1968. As a result of such events as the Tet Offensive, the decision of incumbent President Johnson not to run for reelection, the King and Robert Kennedy assassinations, the disturbances at the Democratic National Convention, and the Soviet invasion of Czechoslovakia, Americans were "shocked by a trip-hammer progression of widely publicized events that challenged traditional standards of credibility and trust in major political institutions," Ricci writes.[7]

Such was the ideational food chain through which, from about the early 1970s to 2000, public ideas were developed and had an impact on politics: experts, intellectuals, policy entrepreneurs, mass media, and a public more receptive to new ideas than previous publics had been. Of course, a great deal of the discourse generated by this system had little intellectual content. But the system allowed for a certain number of serious public ideas to get a hearing and be influential. When a community of experts had reached a consensus, when intellectuals picked up on that climate of thought, when policy entrepreneurs looking for new wares to sell and mass media in constant need of new content took notice, and when the public was shaken enough to listen, a public idea that could trace its lineage back to real experts had a certain degree of intellectual legitimacy and could be considered serious. Not all such public ideas were intellectually unimpeachable or represented the best possible responses to the challenges of political life. Nor did all intellectual currents have equal access to the system. Among the types that did not get a hearing were schools of thought that failed to achieve a toehold among experts, as well as those that did not catch on among intellectuals. There were also some that pointed to political options unattractive to policy entrepreneurs and others that mass media professionals thought unfit for wide dissemination; those that challenged public sentiment too radically did not get a hearing. Both left-wing and right-wing tendencies that could not get past these gatekeepers had trouble reaching an audience. Nonetheless, in describing this process as it functioned through the 1990s, Ricci found the spectrum of ideas that did manage to get heard was fairly wide: "The range of people who market ideas in Washington today seems quite impressive. Indeed, pluralism is apparently the rule. Among the various policy specialists one finds liberals and conservatives, radicals and libertarians."[8]

This model for understanding how ideas interface with politics was developed to describe the policymaking process and needs some modification when it is used to illuminate broader ideological tendencies. But it provides a useful preliminary framework for understanding the sociology of political knowledge as it existed at the time the Alt-Right began to develop.

Restructuring the Production of Public Ideas in the Twenty-First Century

For several reasons, conservatives in the late twentieth century became especially adept at working this system to their advantage. The transformation of American politics that brought the ideational food chain into existence started in the late 1960s, when for the most part liberalism was ascendant, and so the relatively marginalized conservatives had the most to gain by adapting to a new reality. Moreover, the tumult of the sixties hit university campuses particularly hard and moved a significant part of their faculties rightward, thus creating a larger community of conservative academic experts than had existed before. The counterculture of the 1960s also pushed to the right some nonacademic intellectuals, particularly those based in New York who would become known as the neo-conservatives. These intellectuals and others oriented toward the right developed a network of think tanks and publications that could tap into the community of newly conservative scholars and interpret their work to a wider range of policy entrepreneurs. It may also be the case that since conservatives often emphasized the importance of such intangible forces as tradition, culture, and values, they felt more at home in adjusting to the new ideational politics than liberals, who traditionally emphasized means of production and material interests. However that may be, new conservative public ideas found their way into television and other media and conservatives became known, for a while, as the "party of ideas."

Thus by the late 1970s conservatives had adjusted themselves thoroughly to the new ideational politics, and went on to score many successes under that system up through the end of the century. Insofar as the conservative idea network had strongly pushed for a more forceful foreign policy, perhaps the most dramatic developments conservatives could plausibly claim credit for were the collapse of communism and the victory in the First Gulf War. Mainstream conservatives were well satisfied with their success within the new politics of ideas and therefore had much to lose when that model was shaken up.

It may be, however, that the most salient conservative success had already set the stage for a new ideational politics. By 1990 the Berlin Wall had come down and the collapse of communism was in full swing. The delegitimization of liberal democracy's main ideological rival changed the intellectual climate in the West in ways that were both obvious and subtle. The obvious change was the apparent vindication of liberal democracy and capitalism that was most convincingly articulated in Fukuyama's End of History thesis. But communism's end had implications for a policy area that had been on the back burner in America for much of the postwar period: immigration. The Immigration and Nationality Act of 1965 had ended the country-based immigration quotas that had been in force up till then and that had been specifically designed to preserve the country's ethnic demography by disfavoring immigration from everywhere except Western Europe. That discriminatory policy looked bad in the context of the Cold War, in which the United States was competing with communist countries for influence in the third world and elsewhere. For example, Senator Philip Hart, co-sponsor of the 1965 act, had a few years earlier argued that "until those provisions of our immigration laws which discriminate against certain national and racial groups are eliminated, our laws needlessly provide grist for the propaganda mills of Moscow and Peiping."[9] Thus the perceived need to compete effectively with communism was an important force behind support for immigration reform in the 1960s. The same has been said of support for civil rights, the limited welfare state of the New Deal, and a globalist foreign policy.[10] That is, many of the causes eventually embraced to some degree by mainstream conservatives were easier to sell to more right-wing elements when they could be interpreted as strategic maneuvers against communism. One might speculate that liberal democracy and even capitalism—understood as competitive markets rather than protection of national business interests—found support on the right that they might not have absent their anticommunist utility. With the end of the Cold War all of these relatively centrist impulses lost much of their appeal to American rightists. When American politics no longer had to defend its left flank, the possibility of shifting its entire center of gravity to the right opened up. But that possibility did not begin to be actualized until the twenty-first century brought with it certain technological and political developments.

A Twenty-First-Century Version of 1968

That shake-up came with the start of the millennium. To the public at the bottom of the ideational food chain, the early twenty-first century was like a drawn-out version of 1968. A series of traumatic developments since 2000—the events of 9/11, the Iraq War, the fiscal crisis of 2008, the global recession, economic dislocation, and visible demographic change—shook public confidence in the status quo even more dramatically than did the crises of 1968. Public trust in Washington to do what is right dropped from 49 percent of the public immediately after the 9/11 attacks to 18 percent in October 2015.[11]

The biggest single shock to the ideational environment was the 9/11 attacks. At first the attacks prompted the public to rally round the flag and support the president, as such crises usually do. Neoconservatives associated with the George W. Bush administration sought to take advantage of that support and turn the war on terror into the kind of nationally unifying cause that the Cold War had been.

But early Alt-Rightists immediately sensed an opportunity. Just days after the attack, Steve Sailer on *VDARE* perceived that an era had come to an end: "The clever hopes of the low dishonest decade that began in the complacency following the glorious but painless triumphs of the Gulf War and the fall of the Soviet Union expired on Tuesday, September 11, 2001," he wrote.[12]

Precursors of the Alt-Right argued that the 9/11 attacks were the predictable result of an interventionist foreign policy[13] and the "Brave New Borderless World"[14] it had supposedly tried to create. Their proposed response to 9/11 was a more isolationist foreign policy and less immigration. In effect, the early Alt-Right advocated a cautious and limited response to 9/11, while the George W. Bush administration and mainstream conservatives were far more ambitious and even aggressive. Mainstream conservatives thus tied their fate to the success of a bold stratagem while the developing Alt-Right merely needed to wait for the going to get tough. The tough going came soon and continued throughout the many shocks the American political system endured up to and past the 2016 presidential election. Thus the crises of the early twenty-first century shook up the conservative climate of opinion of that era just as the events of 1968 rocked the liberal intellectual climate of that time. In both cases the public became more receptive to new public ideas.

The Rise of the Internet

The rise of the internet as a new medium of mass political communication quite different from television, the medium that mainly played that role in the twentieth century, also offered an opportunity to the proto-Alt-Right.

Early literature on the impact of the internet on political life was mostly optimistic. Among the first scholars to reflect on this issue were Jerry Barman, founder of the Center for Democracy and Technology in 1994, and Daniel J. Weitzner, founding director of the MIT Internet Policy Research Initiative. The tenor of their evaluation in a 1997 article for *Social Research* on the democratizing impact of the internet was characteristic of the time:

> The experience of the Internet in America offers substantial reasons to
> be optimistic about the positive impact of new interactive digital media

on our culture and political life. . . . Traditional communications media, such as radio and television . . . have failed to enable full democratic participation because of architectural limitations. . . . The Internet presents us with an opportunity to support the highest goals of democracy. We ought to embrace the Internet and support its continued and growing use in political life.[15]

Later developments would cool this early enthusiasm. One of the first scholars to document the worrisome effects of the internet on democratic discourse was Jeffrey M. Ayers, who in 1999 published a particularly insightful article on the impact of the new medium on political contestation.[16] Ayers wrote not about conservatism and gatekeepers but about the protest movements and their activist leaders he had seen in action in demonstrations against global trade agreements. Nonetheless, his observations are relevant here:

Yet the Internet challenges the dynamics of diffusion in ways beyond those encouraged by the so-called CNN effect of television. . . . The process of Internet-carried contention may be less contained or constrained by activist-led movements but, rather, unleashed into a type of global electronic riot. . . . If so . . . this post-modern phenomenon of cyber-diffusion portends a reawakening of those favored objects of study of the collective behavior school, including riots, fads, and panics.[17]

The "CNN effect" refers to the influence of twenty-four-hour cable television coverage of international events on states' foreign policy. Cable television's broadcast of dramatic images and information was said to have a great impact on policymakers. In 1997, U.S. secretary of state James Baker said the main impact of the CNN effect was to "drive policymakers to have a policy position."[18] So although television addressed a mass audience, it had an impact through influencing policymakers and was mediated by professional journalists. That is, CNN and television generally put pressure on and influenced gatekeeping policy elites but did not fundamentally undermine their power.

However, Ayers found that relative to television, with its technologically enabled gatekeepers, and unlike predigital protest movements organized by activist leaders, the internet diffused more "unreliable and clearly unverifiable" material such that "impressions, fears, opinions, and conclusions all traded equally on the Web," which had the effect of "bringing the crowd back in" to political debate.[19] The internet thus undermined gatekeeping elites and their professional standards in a way television did not. With the coming of the internet, asked Ayers, "are we going to witness a revenge of the mob, with electronic panics replacing coordinated protests?"[20]

Once it was realized that the mobs brought back into political debate by the internet could be right wing as well as left wing, enthusiasm for the medium cooled still more. The origin of the far right's use of the internet is usually traced to the establishment of the white supremacist platform *Stormfront*, which began in 1990 as an online bulletin board for David Duke's Senate campaign, went public in 1994, and became the website Stormfront. com in 1995. Today, Stormfront.com is a major neo-Nazi digital platform.[21] By 2000 there were several hundred white nationalist sites operating on the web.[22] Most of these sites were openly racist or anti-Semitic, or were maintained by established hate groups such as the KKK or neo-Nazis. But some presented a "soft-core" or "buttoned-down" appearance in the hopes of reaching a larger audience. Jared Taylor's *American Renaissance*, which would develop into a major Alt-Right outlet, was of this type.

Several studies from the first decade of the twenty-first century noted the effective use of the internet by "White Power Movements" (WPMs) and other tributaries that eventually fed into the Alt-Right. For example, in 2004 the sociologists Robert Futrell and Pete Simi attributed the persistence of WPMs to their successful development of "free spaces," that is, "network intersections that link otherwise isolated activist networks through physical and virtual spaces," and noted the increasing importance to WPMs of the virtual free spaces of the internet. [23]

Futrell and Simi reported that "many WPM members see cyberspace as the most critical free space for overcoming obstacles that prevent greater communication among Aryan activists." The authors quoted several WMP members on how they perceived the internet as offering a method of ready communication previously denied to them. Following are some observations from WPM members as quoted by Futrell and Simi:

"The technological restrictions that have kept us from communicating with other Whites is [sic] rapidly coming to an end. . . . Broadcasting stations own or at least control the transmission of media between sender and receiver, but Internet radio uses the common infrastructure of the Internet for transmission which is not controlled by anyone."

"We think a lot about how to reach a wider audience with the [mainstream] media pushing all this anti-white propaganda. We can't let that media define us. We've got to find ways to get the message out and with the Internet we've had some success."

"Since we've been able to access the Internet and email Hammers [WPM members] in other countries it's changed everything. . . . I've been around a long time and it is really a lot different than before we had the Internet."

"You can really do a lot with the Internet. With our website we're trying to combine different aspects so that we don't just appeal to younger or older racists. We want it to be both educational and entertaining. . . . I love doing our show live online and talking with all these people about white power music, about the movement. . . . We just sit back, let them talk, and take it all in."[24]

The authors agreed with other scholars who had concluded that "cyberspace is a qualitatively new and effective channel for reaching existing members and potential recruits."

Purveyors of the schools of thought that fed into the Alt-Right increasingly took advantage of the opportunities the internet provided. *American Renaissance* began publishing as a traditional magazine in November 1990. By 2000 the publication had a web page, and in 2012 it ended distribution of hard copies and became a web magazine exclusively. In a letter to his subscribers, editor Jared Taylor explained his decision to go digital:

Dear Subscriber,

We will be shifting our efforts from the monthly publication into what we expect to be the very best race-realist website on the Internet. . . .

We have seen the costs of printing and mailing continue to rise while, at the same time, more and more people look to the Internet for information. The result has been a dramatic shift in our readership. We never had more than a few thousand subscribers to the monthly American Renaissance, while

our website, www.AmRen.com, gets 100,000 to 200,000 different readers
every month. . . .

When we began publishing in November 1990, it was very hard to get
unorthodox information about race. There were a few small publications
. . . and a few specialty book sellers. The only way to find out about them was
through luck, word of mouth, or diligent library research. . . . There was
only a meager network of racially conscious whites who rarely met each other.

The Internet has given rise to scores of racially conscious websites—many
of them excellent—and it has become easy to find like-minded people. . . .
A 12-year-old with a computer can find first-class race realism and white
advocacy. . . . There is an entire universe of heretical ideas and an increas-
ingly solid framework of institutions to support it. . . .

Now, of course, traditional publishers can no longer control what the
public reads. Small presses are proliferating, and loads of heresy slip past the
gatekeepers. Letters to the editor in daily papers used to be carefully vetted
and only an occasional dose of good sense got through. Now, many of the com-
ments to the electronic versions of newspapers read as if they were written by
AR subscribers.[25]

Taylor's letter is striking for several reasons. First, it documents how
the new medium of the internet allowed *American Renaissance* to break
out of the "meager network of racially conscious whites" and expand its
readership by several hundredfold. Second, the letter notes that by 2012,
"scores of racially conscious websites" had been established. Third, it
shows how the internet undermined the power of "gatekeepers" such as
editors at traditional publishing houses and periodicals. Finally, a qualitatively different technology and weakened traditional gatekeepers resulted
in "an entire universe of heretical ideas" reaching a mass audience.

In short, the internet, because it provided an alternative to more
capital-intensive communication technologies that strengthened the hand
of traditional gatekeepers, broke an important link in the ideational food
chain that all idea brokers, but especially conservatives, had become used
to. The link most damaged was that of the intellectuals. But all gatekeepers whose function had been to prevent "heresy"—and lies, nonsense, vulgarity, invective, and other unlovely material—from slipping through to a
mass audience were weakened.

Concerns that the internet would foster not a "renewal of citizen democracy" but "a revenge of the mob" have been reinforced by the rise of the Alt-Right. So much is suggested by the 2016 remarks of Andrew Anglin, editor of the *Daily Stormer*, one of the most popular and most radical of current Alt-Right sites:

> The Alt-Right is a "mass movement" in the truest possible sense of the term, a type of mass-movement that could only exist on the internet, where everyone's voice is as loud as they are able to make it. In the world of the internet, top-down hierarchy can only be based on the value, or perceived value, of someone's ideas. The Alt-Right is an online mob of disenfranchised and mostly anonymous, mostly young White men. This collective of dissidents argued with itself until it reached a consensus (consensus is yet to reach 100%, but it is damn close). We have now moved from arguments and debates and become a new political collective, a type of hive mind.
>
> *The mob is the movement.*[26]

If indeed the Alt-Right is a revenge of the mob brought on by a technologically enabled weakening of top-down hierarchy and an overabundance of grassroots participation, the implications for theories of democratic discourse are significant. One of the most well-known of such theories is that of Jürgen Habermas on communicative action. Very briefly, Habermas specifies the features of an "ideal speech situation" that optimizes the legitimacy of democratic deliberation as follows:

(3.1) Every subject with the competence to speak and act is allowed to take part in a discourse.

(3.2) a. Everyone is allowed to question any assertion whatever.

b. Everyone is allowed to introduce any assertion whatever into the discourse.

c. Everyone is allowed to express his or her attitudes, desires and needs.

(3.3) No speaker can be prevented, by internal or external coercion, from exercising his rights as laid down in 3.1 and 3.2.[27]

In 2011 John Branstetter summed up his review of empirical studies of web discourse as conducted on YouTube as follows: "Based on the current evidence, much of the political discourse on the internet is not consistent with Habermas' notion of ideal speech. . . . The idea that the internet is providing a qualitatively better form of political discourse is difficult to sustain." Overall, he found "the forms of communication that the internet promotes seem to be less rational, more vitriolic, and less oriented towards consensus-building than traditional media."[28]

More specifically, with regard to whether the internet meets Habermas's second requirement for an ideal speech situation ("Everyone is allowed to question any assertion whatever"), Branstetter found that complete lack of limits degrades the quality of argument:

> Rather than increasing society's capacity to reason collectively by allowing new arguments to emerge, the new formats and freedoms the web has afforded are simply being utilized to say things that the more institutionalized frameworks of television and the print media prevent because they may be "irrational." One could argue that more limitation placed on people's ability to question statements may actually facilitate the production of reason, rather than the other way around. What seems clear from the data is that when anyone is allowed to say anything, a great many choose to abandon rational argument. Institutional gatekeeping prevents this from happening.[29]

With regard to Habermas's third requirement ("Everyone is allowed to introduce any assertion whatever into the discourse"), Branstetter suggested the ideal speech situation left something to be desired:

> The web does provide a home for some of the more fringe elements . . . to be introduced into the discourse in ways that traditional media, regulated by editors, would not allow. . . . It is questionable whether these new positions actually contribute to discourse. . . . It is perhaps another case in which gatekeeping may not actually hamper the progress of communicative action. It may serve to simply filter out the content inconsistent with the development of collective reason. It is possible to argue that the popular expectation that the web is increasing the capacity to say anything about politics is being met. The assumption that this is *a priori* a good thing may be flawed.[30]

What is most striking about these findings is that they show while the internet indeed seems to meet the accepted criteria of an ideal speech situation, that situation may in fact not be so ideal. Branstetter praises Habermas's theory for striking an optimal balance between "liberalism and republicanism,"[31] but the evidence from the internet suggests the theory underestimates the importance of republicanism.

In the American tradition, republicanism can be thought of as practices to filter or modulate popular impulses. In *Federalist* No. 10, James Madison famously criticized "pure democracy" and praised republics for their ability to "refine and enlarge the public views, by passing them through the medium of a chosen body of citizens. . . . Under such a regulation, it may well happen that the public voice . . . will be more consonant to the public good than if pronounced by the people themselves."[32] Of course, one could raise serious concerns about the legitimacy of the gatekeepers of traditional media, who were not "chosen" in the way representatives in an electoral republic are. On the other hand, those gatekeepers, however imperfectly, did function as a republican filter to refine the public view, and their relative weakness on the internet corrodes democratic discourse.

Postexperts and Postintellectuals

With the shocks of the early twenty-first century making the public more receptive to new political ideas, and with the rise of the internet providing a new, cheap, and gatekeeper-free medium for disseminating them, a new breed of secondhand dealers in ideas received an opportunity. The political ideas that now found an audience on the internet were not new. Rather, there was a set of old ideas that had developed over decades but had been kept submerged by the old-style gatekeepers. It is useful to think of the proponents of various brands of extremism that had been banished from mainstream conservatism but somehow managed to survive as the experts that would stand atop the restructured ideational food chain that the Alt-Right finally pieced together. Here the word "expert" is being used purely as a term of art and is not meant to legitimate the substance of what such figures had to say. These thinkers were introduced in chapter 3 of this book. None of them had achieved the positions of professional distinction associated with true experts. But some of them were articulate, were well educated, held academic appointments, and had produced large amounts of work.

The New Left pinned its hopes for revolutionary change not on the compromised proletariat but on the lumpenproletariat; Paleoconservatives similarly looked not to the bourgeois but to the "lumpenbourgeoisie" or "postbourgeois" of the alienated Middle American Radicals. In the same vein we might say that in the first decade of the twenty-first century there had developed a set of what I would call far-right "lumpenexperts" or "post-experts." These postexperts included Samuel Francis, Kevin MacDonald, Paul Gottfried, and other proto-Alt-Right thinkers discussed in chapter 3.

To continue this analogy, just as traditional experts had their thoughts simplified and disseminated by traditional intellectuals, the postexperts received the same assistance from the "lumpenintelligensia" or "post-intellectuals" of the Alt-Right. The careers of some of these Alt-Right pioneers are considered below.

Hunter Wallace (Brad Griffin), Editor of Occidental Dissent

One of the most striking accounts of the development of an Alt-Right postintellectual just after the turn of the millennium comes from Brad Griffin, who usually writes under the pen name Hunter Wallace. He grew up in Barbour County, Alabama, where George Wallace was from, and would found the early Alt-Right website *Occidental Dissent* in 2006. In his essay, "My Alt-Right Biography," Griffin writes:

> In late 2001, I was posting on internet gaming forums when 9/11 happened and I came across Pat Buchanan's book *The Death of the West: How Dying Populations and Immigrant Invasions Imperil Our Culture and Civilization*. It was that book which cemented my worldview. I had become interested in immigration due to a new chicken plant which was attracting illegal aliens to my hometown. I was also interested in the debate about reparations for slavery at the time.[33]

All of the elements discussed above—the crises of the early twenty-first century, the work of the proto-Alt-Right experts (in this case, Pat Buchanan), the importance of the internet—come together in Wallace's story.

Regarding the crises of the twenty-first century's first decade, Wallace notes in the above excerpt the experience of 9/11. As noted in "My Alt-Right Biography," he saw the George W. Bush presidency as a string of disasters: "I hated everything about George W. Bush . . . I hated the Iraq War . . . and felt vindicated by the Crash of 2008." The entry of immigrants into Wallace's hometown stoked in him a fear of demographic change: "It began to dawn on me that by the mid-21st century Whites were going to become a minority nationwide and that the whole country was going to look like the Alabama Black Belt. I knew from first-hand experience what that was going to be like and that it was going to be an unmitigated disaster for my descendants."

It was in that political context that Wallace discovered the postexperts who had laid the foundations for the Alt-Right ideology. Besides Pat Buchanan, other proto-Alt-Right experts Wallace mentions by name in his biographical essay are Samuel Francis; the Mises Institute, a southern, "paleolibertarian" think tank devoted to Austrian economics; and William Pierce, author of *The Turner Diaries*, a white supremacist cult novel about racial war and ethnic cleansing in the United States. Wallace describes the sources of his early ideology as follows: "From the White Nationalists, the Alt-Right took its views on race and identity. From the paleoconservatives, the Alt-Right took its views on free-trade and culture. From the paleo-libertarians, the Alt-Right took its views on foreign policy."

As an undergraduate at Auburn University, Wallace tried on a range of antiliberal ideologies. "I was interested in White Nationalism, but I also went through a Nietzsche phase, an Ayn Rand phase, a Michel Foucault phase, an Aristotle phase, etc." But as his essay notes, Wallace's intellectual sustenance during the early twenty-first century was mostly served up by "all the people who had been purged over the years from 'respectable' *National Review/The Weekly Standard* conservatism and who had begun to congregate in the forum archipelago."

By the "forum archipelago" Wallace means the network of message boards that were first connected to digital game sites. The message boards then became independent in order to accommodate posters who were interested in other subjects, such as politics. After 9/11, Wallace discovered one of the first hubs of this network, *Stormfront*, and then *American Renaissance* and *VDARE*, and became an active poster on *Stormfront* for some years. After being repeatedly banned from one gaming site, Wallace set up a whole network of his own sites, The Phora, which he ran from 2001 to 2005 and describes as follows:

The Phora was . . . a purely anonymous messageboard where people who had been banned from other messageboards came together to discuss edgy ideas. It wasn't just a White Nationalist forum. I went out and recruited paleoconservatives, libertarians, communists, socialists, liberals, moderates, anarchists, nihilists, Neo-Nazis, trolls, gamers, etc. The idea was to throw all these people together in one forum and have them debate current events, economics, politics, history, philosophy, race relations, religion, science and any number of topics. As a model, it worked and for many years this generated all kinds of fascinating discussions on the internet where I learned a bunch of things. . . .

I suppose you could say that it was the fringe of White Nationalism . . . all kinds of small, niche forums that catered to an ever widening audience for White and European identity politics.[34]

How well did the postmodern Phora in fact work as a model of democratic discourse? What Wallace took away from his Phora experience was a root-and-branch rejection of rationalism, liberal democracy, and the United States. Wallace has claimed, "The Southern Nationalist message relies heavily on our most valuable asset: the unvarnished truth."[35] The following excerpts from an *Occidental Dissent* article by Wallace show what passed for truth in his eyes:

Confederate ideology has stood the test of time because it is closer to the truth than Yankee ideology:

(1) The African negro is less intelligent and less conscientious than the White race. 150 years after slavery, this observation is still true. It is still true after DWLs [Disingenuous White Liberals] did literally everything in their power [to] uplift the negro and force reality to conform, unsuccessfully it turns out, to the liberal dogma of racial equality.

(2) Freedom failed everywhere it was tried: it failed in Haiti, it failed in sub-Saharan Africa, it failed in Dixie, it failed in Detroit, it failed everywhere in Europe where African immigrants have settled. When the African negro is combined with freedom and equality, civilization suffers a predictable decline.

(3) As John C. Calhoun pointed out, liberty proved to be a curse rather than a blessing to the negro. Look at Haiti, Liberia, Sierra Leone, Detroit, Zimbabwe, and the Democratic Republic of Congo.

(4) Slavery was the only argument for the African negro. The average single black woman in the United States has a net worth of $5 dollars after nearly 150 years of free society. That means the average black woman has lost 99 percent of her value since the destruction of slavery. . . .

The question is not whether there will be a wealthy ruling class. That is always a given. The real question is whether the ruling class will have any sense of racial, ethnic, and cultural loyalty to the lower classes.

An aristocratic upper class, preferably a rural landed gentry that invests its wealth in localized leisure activities, which is drawn by the late [sic] of fate from the people of the community, is naturally superior to the type of vulgar ruling class thrown up by liberal capitalist democracy, which is always striving to multiply the gap between itself and the lower classes. . . .

150 years ago, the only useful enterprise known to mankind in which the African negro could be profitably employed was as manual labor in cash crop agriculture. It says a lot about modern liberalism that the only substitutes it has managed to find since that time are sports, entertainment, and narcotics trafficking.[36]

Fortified with this learning, Wallace pronounces, "With the benefit of hindsight, we can shoot down the Enlightenment assumptions of the USA's Declaration of Independence."[37] The Alt-Right forum archipelago in which he received his political education was, it seems, a less than ideal learning situation.

Richard Spencer, Editor of Radix Journal

According to a frequently cited article in *Breitbart*, "An Establishment Conservative's Guide to the Alt-Right":

The media empire of the modern-day alternative right coalesced around Richard Spencer during his editorship of Taki's Magazine. In 2012, Spencer founded AlternativeRight.com, which would become a center of alt-right thought.

Alongside other nodes like Steve Sailer's blog, VDARE and American Renaissance, AlternativeRight.com became a gathering point for an eclectic mix of renegades who objected to the established political consensus in some form or another.[38]

Spencer claims he was "one of the founders of the Alt-Right as we know it. I coined the term[s] 'Alternative Right' and 'Alt-Right.'"[39] He received a bachelor's degree from the University of Virginia and a master's degree from the University of Chicago, where he took a class on Nietzsche and wrote his thesis on Theodor Adorno. At Chicago, Spencer became aware of Jared Taylor's work, which was the main cause of Spencer's embrace of racialism.[40] In 2005 Spencer enrolled in a doctoral program in European intellectual history at Duke University but left without obtaining a degree. While at Duke, Spencer met and worked with a fellow conservative activist, Stephen Miller, who went on to write Trump's inaugural address and work in the White House. (Miller now repudiates Spencer's views.)[41] After leaving Duke, Spencer was an editor first at the *American Conservative*, a paleoconservative magazine, and later at *Taki's Magazine*, owned by long-time conservative activist and wealthy playboy Taki Theodoracopulos. Under Spencer's editorship, *Taki's Magazine* developed into what might be called an "Alt-Lite" platform, one that, like the better-known *Breitbart News*, featured harsh rhetoric and sensationalist journalism on race, immigration, and other polarizing issues.

Spencer left *Taki's Magazine* in December 2009 to start his own web magazine, *AlternativeRight.com*. Three years later Spencer left *AlternativeRight.com* and started a new web magazine, *Radix Journal*, where he posted a letter explaining what he thought he had accomplished at his old site. He noted:

> Since March of 2010, the alt-right blogosphere has grown into something like a collective brain. Our website did not create this movement, of course. But it was inspired by it and sought to contribute to it.
>
> It's also worth noting the degree to which AltRight functioned successfully as a "Big Tent."
>
> Looking back over his career in the Beltway, Sam Francis noted that the non-mainstream Right (such as it was . . .) amounted to a collection of colorful personalities and their devoted followings—each of which distrusted, if not positively *loathed*, one another. (Little has changed.)
>
> AltRight, on the other hand, along with friendly sites and bloggers, offered a model of a non-aligned Right that could actually get along.
>
> I often got chided for my putative attempt to align traditional Catholics, atheistic Darwinists, Nietzscheans, National Anarchists, White Nationalists *et al*. But this critique never touched me, and not because I imagined AltRight as an effort in team-building . . . it was instead in-

tended as a conversation within an extended family—what social, cultural, and political discourse could be like in a society when egalitarianism is expunged and European identity is taken as a given.[42]

AlternativeRight.com was thus another digital Phora like the one Wallace had created, one that provided a safe space for a reactionary rainbow coalition of fringe movements that had endured a long exile from the political mainstream.

What sort of political discourse came out of this ideal speech situation for marginal antidemocratic ideologues? Spencer's letter describes in more detail the resulting social thought in which "egalitarianism is expunged":

> I wanted to see if I could help create an alternative to "conservatism" as we knew it. AltRight was never to be "to the right" of, say, *National Review* on an imaginary sliding scale. It was to emerge from a different universe—to have a different starting point and vision of society. . . . It's probably not an exaggeration to say that Alex's "Equality As Evil" represents a culmination of the kind of intellectual world I sought to foster. . . .
>
> To think that we all must agree on dogma is to adopt the very American notion . . . that to be a citizen, you must "believe" in some cocktail of dumbed-down Enlightenment precepts, consumer capitalism and welfare socialism, love of all mankind, free speech (expect for bad, anti-American speech), democratic representation, *und so weiter*. . . .
>
> But politics isn't ultimately about "believing" in anything; politics is, to be frank, the (often brutal) use of state power to achieve the aims of the governing class. What's most interesting about the world is *not* politics, really, but the human flourishing that occurs *outside* it, or rather *in the shadow* of state sovereignty.[43]

The "Alex" referred to above is Alex Kurtagic, a Spanish-born cultural critic frequently published in Alt-Right web magazines whose nearly hysterical attacks on political egalitarianism can indeed without exaggeration be termed the culmination of the intellectual world fostered by Spencer and the early Alt-Right. The following quotation gives a flavor of Kurtagic's thought:

The morality of equality is an evil and destructive morality. What is equal is replaceable, and what is replaceable has no value. Equality makes everyone a slave. Value comes from two sources, superiority and scarcity. What is superior is higher in quality than what is average. And what is scarce, what is rare or unique, has higher value than what can be found everywhere. The ultimate consequence of an egalitarian morality is the destruction of human value.[44]

The point to note here is not the extreme radicalism or moral nihilism of this passage but the weakness of its argument. Quite obviously, what is equal is not necessarily replaceable. A hundred pounds of feathers and a hundred pounds of gold are equal in weight but not replaceable in any respect except perhaps as ballast, for which they are never used. What is replaceable of course can have value; insurance providers calculate the "replacement value" of insured items all the time. Scarcity, in the sense of rareness or uniqueness, has, in itself, no bearing on value. A rare or unique bit of junk no one wants is as worthless as one of a type that is ubiquitous. An item is valuable only if it is scarce relative to the demand for it. It is entirely possible to be scarce in this relevant sense and therefore valuable and yet quite common, as are iPhones, BMWs, and diamond engagement rings. Superiority in some particular regard, however significant, has no bearing on political equality: Einstein, the person on the street, and the village idiot all have one vote. Equality cannot possibly make anyone a slave. A slave derives his status because he is unequal before the law, and if he is made equal in that sense then he is no longer a slave. But if factual equality—rather than equality before the law—is being spoken of, how can equality of height, strength, intelligence, and so forth make people slaves? And if it did, who would be a slave to whom?

Again, the point here is not that that the political discourse facilitated by *AlternativeRight.com* culminated in an intellectual world that was politically incorrect, antidemocratic, and nihilistic, although it certainly did. The point is that the political discourse of Spencer's Alt-Right world was intellectually bankrupt and incapable of holding up under any reasonable scrutiny. Poverty of thought, beyond offensiveness of speech, is the true sin enabled by the early Alt-Right.

Greg Johnson, Editor of Counter-Currents Publishing

Greg Johnson is editor in chief of *Counter-Currents Publishing*, which has been described by the multimedia platform *Mashable* as "one of the pillars of Alt-Right publishing."[45] Before his career as an Alt-Right post-intellectual, Johnson had what he describes as a "brief and inglorious" academic career.[46] In 2001 he received a Ph.D. in philosophy from Catholic University of America. His dissertation, titled "A Commentary on Kant's 'Dreams of a Spirit-Seer,'" was on that philosopher's account of the eighteenth-century Swedish mystic Emanuel Swedenborg.[47] In 2002 Johnson took up a teaching position at the Swedenborgian House of Studies, a seminary program at the Pacific School of Religion, because he had no other offers.[48] Despite not being a Christian, Johnson "did a pretty good imitation" of a Swedenborgian minister until 2005, when the school bought out the remainder of his contract.[49] Johnson also tells us he has been "a libertarian, then a conservative, then a White Nationalist, and now I am a member of the Racially-Conscious Left."[50] Interestingly, Johnson is perfectly aware this evolution involves leaving liberal democracy far behind, for he explains:

> Most White Nationalists in North America develop out of the conservative movement or milieu. . . . (Of course, both American conservatism and libertarianism are ultimately species of liberalism.)
>
> The reason that White Nationalists develop *out of* conservatism is that conservatism itself is *not* an adequate framework for the preservation of the white race. It is not intellectually adequate, because it is beholden to race-blind universalism and egalitarianism.[51]

Johnson's reactionary career began early. "When I was around 16," he writes, "I decided I was a right-winger because I did not believe in human equality. (Then I was pretty much a libertarian.) . . . That really is the essential issue, to my mind."[52] By 2000 Johnson's libertarianism had metamorphosed into white nationalism, and he "began thinking of creating a metapolitical journal that would lay the foundations for White Nationalism in North America," an idea he brought to fruition with the establishment of *Counter-Currents Publishing* in 2010.[53] But Johnson regarded the *Occidental Quarterly*,[54] which began publishing in 2001 and whose found-

ers included Samuel Francis, Kevin MacDonald, and Jared Taylor, as ful-
filling that need and became editor of the quarterly in the fall of 2007.[55]

As editor of the *Occidental Quarterly*, Johnson edited and published
MacDonald's *Cultural Insurrections: Essays on Western Civilization, Jewish
Influence, and Anti-Semitism* and used his position to facilitate others transi-
tioning from libertarianism to white nationalism.[56] According to Johnson:

> Now, another current of thought that is sort of flowing into the Alterna-
> tive Right that's very important is the breakdown of the libertarian move-
> ment. . . . In 2008 when the Ron Paul movement was getting started, I
> started noticing how overwhelmingly white Ron Paul supporters were and
> it was an implicitly white thing. They weren't aware of the fact that this
> was a very white form of politics. It made sense more to white people than
> to any other group.
>
> I was betting at the time that a lot of these people would start break-
> ing away from this and moving in the direction of white identity politics.
> When I was the editor of *The Occidental Quarterly* near the end of that
> time, I actually set in motion an essay contest on libertarianism and white
> racial nationalism. The purpose of that was to get our best minds to think
> about this idea and create an analysis and work towards creating talking
> points that we could use to ease the way of a lot of people towards our
> position.[57]

In the spring of 2010 Johnson founded *Counter-Currents Publishing*
with the purpose "to create an intellectual platform for White Nationalist metapolitics." A sister print journal was abandoned as inefficient in an
online age.[58] One white nationalist wag was quite right when he quipped
that *Counter-Currents* could as well be called the "*Racialist Reader's
Digest.*"[59] But Johnson had the internet rather than dentists' offices as a
distribution system.

The talking points that came out of Johnson's digital colloquium for
the Alt-Right's best minds had two distinctive characteristics: antidemocratic radicalism and implausibility. Johnson's rhetoric is relatively mild,
and he often condemns violence, but otherwise the extremism of his
thought is hard to overstate. Many examples could be provided, but for
present purposes two will suffice:

Lenin, Trotsky, and Mao were admired and analyzed in New Left circles because of their political writings. . . . Continuing the analogy: Mussolini and Hitler wrote, said, and created many things of permanent value to the New Right. Thus we will learn what we can from them and their movements.[60]

And elsewhere Johnson writes:

The original historical sense of the Jewish question . . . is . . . how Jews, being a distinct nation, can be given legal equality and citizenship within other nations. Our answer is: they shouldn't. They belong in their own nation-state. . . . Jews are not just *different* from whites, but powerful and malevolent enemies who bear significant responsibility for causing white decline and opposing white renewal.[61]

These sentiments are not only wild-eyed extremism, they are preposterous to boot. The catastrophic failure of Mussolini's and Hitler's movements, even from the perspective of their own bellicose nationalism, is obvious. Anyone who thinks that "many things of permanent value" were achieved by these two mass-murdering incompetents casts grave doubt on his or her own competency, to say the least.

As for Johnson's account of the "Jewish question," its absurdity, which is obscured by its gross anti-Semitism, deserves note here. According to Johnson, "The Jewish question is a simple, straightforward application of the basic principle of ethnonationalism. . . . Thus if England is to be English, Sweden to be Swedish, Ireland to be Irish, alien populations need to be repatriated to their own homelands, Jews included."

If this is so, why should not Americans of English, Swedish, and Irish ethnicity be repatriated to their own homelands too? Perhaps it will be said that Anglo-Americans are not an alien population. Native Americans will likely disagree. However that may be, what claim, by Johnson's standards, do Swedish Americans and Irish Americans, whose ancestors arrived in America no earlier than those of Jewish Americans, have to U.S. residency? If ideas such as these are the best Johnson's metapolitical forum can produce, the intellectual foundations of white nationalism are weak indeed.

Wallace, Spencer, Johnson and early Alt-Right postintellectuals generally were characterized by their marginal professional credentials, ideological reinventions, extremist orientation, and intellectual syncretism. The ideal speech situation of the internet turned out to be less than ideal.

Conclusion

The American production system of public ideas in operation from the late 1970s to the turn of the millennium turned out to have more virtues than it was sometimes given credit for. There was no formal censorship, for government prevented no one from disseminating their ideas. Of course, no one was guaranteed access to the resources necessary for dissemination, and gatekeepers could deny access to the particular resources they controlled. Writers and speakers blocked from any given forum were free to find another forum or start their own. Many did so, and a wide range of media, organizations, and networks developed to provide outlets for ideas across the breadth of the conventional political spectrum. But not every ideological orientation could muster the resources necessary to develop effective outlets and these fringe movements did not get a hearing.

This ideational production system, far from suppressing, in fact facilitated healthy democratic discourse. Without anyone's speech rights being violated, and without anyone being denied a fair chance to find a forum and an audience, antidemocratic and irresponsible discourse was marginalized even while a wide range of lively debate was maintained. The perfect political storm of the early twenty-first century upset this world, which was certainly not the best possible but was quite serviceable. We must now deal with the new intellectual world that took its place.

Part III
Alt-Right Ideology

5
Primer on Ideologies

As was discussed in chapter 2, the Alt-Right sees itself not as a constituency with political goals but as an intellectual movement that shapes how people think about politics. The Alt-Right models itself after another intellectual tendency it despises but seeks to emulate, neoconservatism. Its object is for an "elite" to articulate in detail a set of ideas grounded in a political philosophy and then disseminated through policy networks to political entrepreneurs and the mass media. The philosophy at the top of this ideational trickle-down process must be challenged, lest by osmosis it continue to leak into American political culture. To stop that process, Alt-Right ideology must be confronted, which means it must be exactly understood. But first a few things have to be said about the nature of ideology.

First, "ideology" as used here refers to a more or less consistent set of ideas about politics that is expressed most fully in the work of an elite of professional thought leaders such as scholars, journalists, and intellectuals. The term "elite" is used to denote a relatively small group of people who influence the thinking and behavior of a larger group. There are, of course, variations among these leaders that must be noted. But when a high degree of similarity of thinking persists among one set of thought leaders that distinguishes it from other sets, one may speak of a distinct ideology. In the case of the leaders associated with the Alt-Right websites identified earlier, there is considerable similarity of thinking, and so we can speak of a distinctive Alt-Right ideology (though here too there are important variations).

The extent to which an ideology expressed by an elite is embraced by mass audiences of party members, voters, activists, and others is an open question. It is not necessarily the case—indeed, it is unlikely—that the whole mass of followers of a political movement knows and accepts completely the ideology articulated by an elite. The ideological elite of the Alt-Right is relatively small, perhaps no more than a few thousand people. But the ideological elites of analogous political movements, such as the New Left or neoconservatism, were also small. The weight of influence of an ideological elite is not necessarily commensurate with the proportion of rank-and-file true believers. Such an elite, if it is organized and media-savvy, can have a disproportionate amount of influence—for good or ill. Such was the case of the most extreme New Leftists and Maoist-Leninist-Guevarist radicals of the 1960s, and such is the case of today's Alt-Right.

One major purpose of Part III is simply to document Alt-Right ideology as it is expressed at the digital outlets this book focuses on. Once the record is clear, the questions Part III seeks to answer are the following:

1. Does Alt-Right ideology represent a radical break with the philosophy of liberal democracy that, throughout the postwar years, has been assumed, with few exceptions, by the entire spectrum of American politics, from right to left? Or is the Alt-Right merely a populist variation on well-known, garden-variety conservative Republicanism?

2. What is the nature of Alt-Right rhetoric? When Alt-Rightists speak, are they merely politically incorrect, blunt, and perhaps usefully transgressive? Or is their vocabulary unnecessarily vulgar and hurtful? Do they impugn the motives rather than address the arguments of their adversaries? Do they elevate mere policy disagreements into matters of treason? In short, does the Alt-Right adhere to an ethics of controversy that facilitates rather than undermines democratic discourse?

3. What is the quality of Alt-Right thought? Are its practitioners developing controversial but cogent arguments? Are they calling at-

tention to unpleasant but relevant evidence? Or does their reasoning provoke opposition because it is weak? Is their evidence challenged because it is wrong?

With regard to the first question, the issue of the radicalism of Alt-Right ideology, if the Alt-Right is merely a variation on conventional conservatism, one may object or agree but need not prepare for the coming of a new political regime. But if the Alt-Right represents an effort to shatter the assumptions of American politics and create a new, post-liberal-democratic order, that is something else again. Proposals for strikingly radical change warrant especially careful examination, even skepticism. Thus the question of how radical the Alt-Right is bears on the question of how we should think about the Alt-Right, and determining how to think about something is one of the main objects of any inquiry.

Whether the Alt-Right represents a radical break with the status quo requires establishing what the status quo is. That is, the baseline, the broad underlying principles of the conventional American political spectrum, has to be determined. Only then can we answer whether the Alt-Right really is a radical departure from them. Now, perhaps the best-known and most accepted statements of those principles are in America's foundational documents—the Declaration of Independence, the Constitution, the *Federalist Papers*, the rhetoric of Lincoln and other great leaders, and similar sources. Since the following chapters often compare Alt-Right ideology with the statements of principles in those documents, what is meant by principles has to be explained.

By "principle" I mean an idea that is central to a system of thought, an idea that is essential to the logic, truth, and plausibility of that system and that, if refuted or denied, causes that system to collapse. Thinkers may, of course, informally and in their personal lives, make comments or think thoughts that clash with their political principles, which proves only that the thinkers are inconsistent, not that their principles are necessarily wrong. Such inconsistent thinkers may be hypocrites, but since hypocrisy is the compliment that vice pays to virtue, they may still genuinely adhere to those principles, which, of course, may still be valid.

Moreover, not every important idea or belief that a given thinker holds necessarily represents a principle of a system of thought he or she has built. Euclid's geometry begins with a statement of certain axioms or principles. Now it is very possible that Euclid believed that only men could understand geometry. But even in that case, it would be wrong to say a principle of Euclidean geometry is that only men can understand it and that Euclidean geometry is somehow "male." Euclid's personal opinion about women's aptitude for geometry would be entirely separate from the *principles* of that geometry. In this hypothetical case, when it turns out that women can indeed understand geometry, what would be undermined is not the principles of Euclidean geometry but Euclid's unrelated opinion about women.

This distinction between principles of thought and personal opinion is crucial because it undermines a whole genus of argumentation often deployed against American political philosophy. Jefferson, it is pointed out, thought blacks were less intelligent than whites, and supported plans to repatriate black people to Africa. The argument therefore concludes that Jefferson's assertion in the Declaration of Independence that "all men are created equal" can't possibly be meant to extend to blacks. The problem with this argument is that Jefferson's disparaging opinions about blacks are not incorporated into the argument of the Declaration any more than Euclid's hypothetical disparagement of women is incorporated into his geometry.

The point is that, just because Jefferson or any of the founders held certain opinions about blacks, women, or anything else, it does not follow that those opinions are built into their political principles. No doubt many of the founders and other American statesmen held assumptions about blacks, women, and other groups that would today be called prejudiced. But then, the American founders had strong assumptions about many things. They assumed eighteenth-century technology, an agricultural economy, premodern standards of health and longevity, Newtonian physics, and Aristotelian logic. Sometimes those assumptions drove their political judgments and policy choices. For example, Jefferson strongly believed that America had to retain its agricultural economy and, despite constitutional reservations, went forward with the Louisiana Purchase because he assumed such an economy would require new land. But this does not prove that American political principles assume an agricultural economy. Similarly, Alt-Right thinkers are unconvincing when they argue that since Congress in 1790 passed a naturalization act that limited citizenship to "free white persons," white racialism is assumed by the Constitution.[1] That Congress acts on certain assumptions in no way proves those assumptions are built into the Constitution or American political principles generally. Many such extraneous assumptions of the founders were sooner or later undermined, which had no bearing on the validity of the essential principles of their political philosophy. That past American statesmen assumed, tangentially, the country would be run by white men in no way proves that American political philosophy is "white" or "male," and less still that the only way to be faithful to those principles today would be to disempower blacks and women.

Nor is it correct, as is sometimes argued, that if a particular assumption does not appear in American foundational documents, this very absence proves not that the assumption is irrelevant but rather that it is so obviously central the founders didn't bother to mention it. For example, when I pointed out to Peter Brimelow, editor of *VDARE*, that the founders nowhere in the Declaration, or the Constitution, or the *Federalist Papers*, or anywhere say that America must be a white nation, he responded, "I think it's because they took it for granted. And this is not a right-wing position, you know. People on the left say the same thing. They say, 'America was racist from its founding.' "[2] But, in itself, the absence of a claim hardly proves its presence. There are, of course, such things as unstated assumptions, but such assumptions have to be proved with reference not to obiter dicta or external comments but to the logic and meaning of the argument that supposedly incorporates them.

Moreover, when a thinker in his political actions fails to follow up effectively on his political principles, that failure does not necessarily invalidate those principles. Suppose it is agreed that Jefferson did indeed believe the races were politically equal but then made questionable decisions about how to apply that principle: He did not push nearly hard enough to abolish slavery, and he favored the resettlement of blacks in Africa. This shows only that Jefferson exercised poor political judgment, or perhaps that he concluded, rightly or wrongly, that political circumstances did not allow for the full application of the principle of racial equality. But such judgments, whatever we think of them, do not prove Jefferson rejected the principle of equality or that it is inconsistent with the logic of Jefferson's overall political philosophy.

Does all the attention paid here to foundational statements of American political philosophy imply that America is a "propositional nation"? That idea holds that being American is primarily a matter of adhering to the basic propositions of the foundational documents. The most famous recent statement of the idea that the United States is such a nation was made by Barack Obama, who said: "Being an American is not a matter of blood or birth. It's a matter of faith. It's a matter of fidelity to the shared values that we all hold so dear. That's what makes us unique. That's what makes us strong. Anybody can help us write the next great chapter in our history."[3]

Contributors to Alt-Right outlets passionately reject the idea that being an American mainly involves acceptance of the nation's foundational political propositions; they insist that blood and birth are indeed relevant. Thus in *VDARE* John Derbyshire argues as follows:

> It's rather easy to mock this concept of a proposition nation. Suppose I were to trek up into the highlands of Ethiopia, get myself invited into the hut of some illiterate Amhara goatherd, and explain our founding documents to him; and suppose he were to respond with enthusiastic agreement. Did he thereby instantly become an American?
>
> Conversely, here is a U.S. citizen every one of whose forebears arrived here before the Revolution, and whose male forebears fought with distinction in our country's wars. He strongly disagrees with the principles of the Founders, and would have preferred we become a Christian theocracy. Should he be stripped of his citizenship?[4]

Of course, Derbyshire is right in the hypothetical cases he poses here, and the answer to the rhetorical questions he poses must be no. But the propositional-nation idea can be refined and made plausible. The first step is to acknowledge that legal citizenship is a central aspect of being American (or any other nationality). American citizens who embrace theocracy, communism, fascism, or any other antidemocratic ideology of course retain their citizenship. And foreign nationals—whether they be illiterate Ethiopian goatherds or English graduates of Oxbridge—do not become U.S. citizens merely by agreeing with the founders' political principles. Thus citizenship is a vital aspect of national identity.

However, as a general matter, identifying as a particular nationality is thought to involve more than just legal citizenship; it involves as well culture, residence, family ties, a sense of belonging, and more. Adherence to a set of political principles can be such a characteristic, and so can language, religion, and ethnicity. Exactly what characteristics, besides citizenship, define a nationality varies from nation to nation. For some countries, ethnicity is an important part of national identity. One can be not just legally but also ethnically German, French, or Japanese. But in the multiethnic Soviet Union there was no such thing as being ethnically Soviet; the sine qua non of Soviet national identity was acceptance of Marxism-Leninism.

In the relative importance of ethnicity, on the one hand, and a belief in certain propositions on the other, American nationality more resembles that of the Soviet Union than that of Germany, France, or Japan in the sense that it is based more on shared political affinity than on ethnic identification. There is no such thing as being ethnically American. This is true even if for much of the world the prototypical American is WASP. Were it otherwise, the very substantial numbers of U.S. citizens who are of other races, ethnicities, and religions would be . . . what, exactly?

The obvious reality that ethnicity is less important in American national identity than it is for other countries is acknowledged—and elicits a telling conclusion—in an interesting article from *The Right Stuff*, one of the most extreme Alt-Right outlets:

> When German or Swedish nationalism is spoken of, we know exactly to whom that refers, that is, ethnic Germans and ethnic Swedes, respectively. Who is American has never been so neatly or officially defined. Ultimately we need to be able to say clearly who the "we" is in our American nationalist movement, and the best way to do that is with a name. I propose White Europeans on the North American continent begin calling ourselves "Amerikaners."
>
> Why not stick with "American"? Because "Amerikaner" connotes ethnicity and rootedness and distances ourselves from the disastrous ideals of America and all that it entails.[5]

The article usefully admits that American national identity, unlike, say, German or Swedish nationality, is not rooted in ethnicity, which is a big problem from the point of view of the Alt-Right. Solution: jettison the term "American" altogether precisely because it does *not* connote ethnicity but *does* imply "the disastrous ideals of America," that is, those foundational propositions so much disliked by the Alt-Right. We have here, then, an Alt-Rightist admission that being American—as opposed to being "Amerikaner"—is more about propositions and less about ethnicity than are other forms of national identity. Of course, this is not to say that ethnicity counts for nothing in American politics. But to break fundamentally with the foundational propositions of U.S. politics represents a more radical break with American national identity than would a similar break with the propositions of a nation whose identity is more tied up with ethnicity than with ideas.

The main features of Alt-Right ideology are a rejection of the American variation on liberal democracy, racialism, and anti-Americanism. The various Alt-Right thinkers and outlets differ in how they understand and emphasize these positions. The next chapter provides an overview of Alt-Right ideology as it is expressed by several sources and notes their important disagreements.

6
The Alt-Right on the Foundational Principles of American Politics

One purpose of this chapter is to determine whether Alt-Right thought represents a radical break with American political principles. The issue is important, but not because radical breaks are necessarily bad while fidelity is necessarily good, or vice versa. The real question is what is being broken with or adhered to. American political principles are a variation on the philosophy of liberal democracy. A fundamental break with liberal democracy is a matter of deep concern not because fundamental breaks are bad but because liberal democracy has served the country and the world well and the alternatives to it are very unappealing. Another concern is *how* one breaks with or adheres to the principles of liberal democracy, or any political philosophy. Breaking with liberal democracy can contribute usefully to political discourse if the overall quality of thought behind the critique is strong; unintelligent advocacy is not helpful. How, then, by these standards, does the Alt-Right critique of American foundational political principles measure up?

Before we take up that question a potential misunderstanding must be addressed. This chapter presents a good deal of material to show that the Alt-Right's racialist and inegalitarian account of American foundational

123

principles is grossly incorrect. The point, however, is not that American political principles, and still less American political practice, are entirely free of racism and provided, from day one, a perfectly satisfactory vision of the liberal democratic ideal. As theoreticians of democracy and equality, the American founders and their followers often fell short. Regarding American political practice, slavery, segregation, and the continuing struggle for racial justice are only the most obvious examples of how the nation has never fully lived up to the promise of its stated principles. In deciding whether the principles of the American founders were or are racist, each person must take an honest look at the full record. The main argument of this chapter is that the Alt-Right interpretation of our foundational principles is neither honest nor comprehensive. Anyone who wants to argue that America was indeed founded on racist principles will have to provide much better evidence and reasoning than the Alt-Right does. That some legitimate scholars have judged the founders guilty of racism hardly vindicates the Alt-Right's shoddy reasoning, which this chapter documents.

The Alt-Right on the Declaration of Independence

Before we look at what the Alt-Right has to say about the Declaration of Independence, some brief remarks on the document's overall structure are useful. Stephen Toulmin's famous model fits the Declaration's argument well.[1] The argument's *claim* is "therefore . . . these United Colonies are, and of Right ought to be, Free and Independent States." This claim is supported with *evidence* in the form of a list of grievances against the king of England. The list is long, with thirty-nine grievances given (if each of the nine examples of "pretended legislation" is counted as a separate grievance). But why should a list of grievances, however long, prove the colonies are free and independent? Supporters of the divine right of kings would argue that revolution is never justified under any circumstances. What is needed is a *warrant*—an assumption shared by the speaker and the audience—that explains why the evidence supports the claim. The Declaration's warrant comes in the following passage of its second paragraph:

> Prudence, indeed, will dictate that Governments long established should not be changed for light and transient causes; and accordingly all experi-

ence hath shewn, that mankind are more disposed to suffer, while evils are sufferable, than to right themselves by abolishing the forms to which they are accustomed. But when a long train of abuses and usurpations, pursuing invariably the same Object evinces a design to reduce them under absolute Despotism, it is their right, it is their duty, to throw off such Government, and to provide new Guards for their future security.

If the Declaration's readers accept that "a long train of abuses and usurpations, pursuing invariably . . . absolute Despotism" justifies revolution, and if they acknowledge that the long list of grievances is accurately so characterized, then the claim of independence is established.

But will the Declaration's readers accept the warrant of its argument? Jefferson is canny enough to deploy a warrant his largely Anglo-American audience will have trouble rejecting. For the Declaration's warrant is a close paraphrase—nearly a plagiarism, by today's standards—of the authoritative political philosopher of its time, John Locke. Here is the relevant passage from Locke's *Second Treatise on Government*:

> *Revolutions happen not* upon every little mismanagement in publick affairs. *Great mistakes* in the ruling part, many wrongs and inconvenient Laws, and all the *slips* of humane frailty will be *born by the people*, without mutiny or murmur. But if a long train of Abuses, Prevarications, and Artifices, all tending the same way, makes the design visible to the People, and they cannot but feel, what they lie under, and see, whither they are going; 'tis not to be wondered, that they should then rouze themselves, and endeavor to put the rule into such hands, which may secure to them the ends for which Government was at first erected.[2]

By Jefferson's day it was widely accepted that Locke's argument had established the legitimacy of the Glorious Revolution of 1688, which no political faction wanted to deny. By obviously lifting his words from Locke, Jefferson forestalls even Loyalists and Tories from rejecting the right to revolution. Indeed, the entire second paragraph of the Declaration is a distillation of the *Second Treatise* calculated to elicit near universal agreement from contemporary readers.

The openly Lockean roots of the Declaration are important because they provide an answer to several objections often raised on the far right against America's founding document. Jefferson's words are hardly arbitrary "gauzy bunk," "ceremonial language," or "we-only-said-that-to-get-her-into-bed" drivel, as contributors to Alt-Right sites have claimed.[3] The second paragraph's language has to be exactly what it is, recognizably borrowed from the *Second Treatise*, in order to command agreement from anyone unwilling to disparage the foundational Glorious Revolution, and so to serve as a warrant.

Further, the obvious Lockeanism of the Declaration illuminates what the document means by "self-evident," and rebuts far-right scorn of that phrase. Alt-Right progenitor Samuel Francis disdainfully comments that if Jefferson's propositions were self-evident, "there would never have been any dispute about them, let alone wars and revolutions fought over them. No one fights wars about the really self-evident axioms of Euclidean geometry."[4] But the Declaration does not assert "these truths *are* self-evident"; it asserts, "*We hold* these truths to be self-evident."[5] The claim is only that "we," the document's author and audience, already accept and demand no further proof of its Lockean principles, which therefore can serve as its warrant. The truths of the Declaration are presented as self-evident in a rhetorical, not philosophical, sense and its argument implies no strong claims about their epistemological status. Indeed, the final language of "self-evident," which was suggested by Benjamin Franklin during the editing process, represents a backing away from the theological and philosophical overtones of Jefferson's original formulation, "sacred and undeniable."[6] Therefore the Declaration's argument does not, as Francis and other critics have claimed,[7] rest on the validity of Locke's tabula rasa theory, or any theory, of human understanding or nature. Nor does the document logically assume the state-of-nature account of the origins of government, as Calhoun and other antidemocratic thinkers have argued, even though its exposition is consistent with that theory.

Another important point about the language of the Declaration concerns the word "men" in its most iconic phrase. It seems Jefferson used that word to refer to people of both sexes. The 1756 edition of Samuel Johnson's dictionary gives the first definition of the word "man" as "human being" and the second as "not a woman."[8] Nothing in the text of the Declaration suggests only males were being referred to. In this book the phrase "all men" is meant to include women too. To avoid confusion I use the phrase "all people" whenever that seems appropriate.

The ground of the Declaration's truths is simply the political experience of its audience, as Locke and others helped them interpret it.[9] Historical events and their social consequences convinced the Anglo-American world of the late seventeenth and eighteenth centuries—from political thinkers like Locke and Jefferson to the people on the street they influenced— that the broad outlines of what is now called liberal democracy served well enough to merit acceptance. Whatever weaknesses there may be in Enlightenment philosophy do not necessarily undermine that conviction, which has since been reinforced by the Civil War, the twentieth-century contests with totalitarianism, and the ongoing struggles for human rights. A truly radical rejection of the principles of the Declaration—as interpreted and modified in light of experience and reflection—is nothing less than a repudiation of the entire ground and structure of modern liberal democracy. The question now raised is whether Alt-Right thought really represents such nihilism.

"All Men Are Created Equal"

The best way to appreciate the radicalism of the Alt-Right is to note that it is based on an explicit and fundamental rejection of the principle that all men are created equal. A few quotations will show that this is indeed the position of Alt-Right thinkers.

Here is Richard Spencer, who describes himself as "one of the founders of the Alt-Right as we know it"[10] and edits *Radix Journal*:

> Alexander Stephens, Vice-President of the Confederate States of America . . . stressed that the Confederacy was based on the conclusion that Thomas Jefferson was wrong; the "cornerstone" of the new state was the "physical, philosophical, and moral truth" of human inequality.
>
> Ours, too, should be a declaration of difference and distance—"We hold these truths to be self-evident; that all men are created *un*equal." In the wake of the old world, this will be our proposition.[11]

Interestingly, Spencer does not quote Stephens's specification of what the cornerstone truth of the Confederacy was: "Its corner-stone rests upon the great truth, that the negro is not equal to the white man; that slavery—subordination to the superior race—is his natural and normal condition."[12] (That the most radical spokesmen of the Alt-Right also assert the inferiority of blacks is taken up in more detail in chapter 7.)

Jared Taylor considers himself and his website, *American Renaissance*, part of the Alt-Right. He too excoriates Jefferson's famous dictum:

> Jefferson didn't believe all men were created equal . . . and to handcuff Jefferson to those five words is profoundly stupid. The Declaration of Independence explains to George III why the colonists wanted out. It starts with rhetorical throat-clearing in which the signers say they are *the King's* equals and have the right to leave. When the founders got around to writing the rules for actually running their new country—either in the Articles or the Constitution—they didn't put in any gauzy bunk about equality.[13]

Greg Johnson, editor of *Cross-Currents Publishing*, also rejects Jeffersonian egalitarianism. He writes:

> The true Right, in both its Old and New versions, is founded on the rejection of human *equality* as a fact and as a norm. The true right embraces the idea that mankind is and ought to be unequal, i.e., differentiated. Men are different from women. Adults are different from children. The wise are different from the foolish, the smart from the stupid, the strong from the weak, the beautiful from the ugly. We are differentiated by race, history, language, religion, nation, tribe, and culture. These differences matter, and because they matter, all of life is governed by real hierarchies of fact and value, not by the chimera of equality.
>
> The true right rejects egalitarianism root and branch.[14]

Hunter Wallace (the pen name of Brad Griffin), founder and editor of *Occidental Dissent*, answers the question, what is the Alt-Right?, as follows: "We don't belong to the liberal family . . . nothing is less self-evident to us than the notion that all men are created equal."[15]

Perhaps Alt-Right author Gregory Hood, writing in *American Renaissance*, achieved the ne plus ultra of vituperation against the Declaration's cornerstone when he wrote: "No phrase in history has done more harm than 'all men are created equal.'"[16] Then again, Hood's extraordinary claim was anticipated by the Alt-Right's forefather, Samuel Francis, who maintained that Jefferson's phrase "has to be considered one of the most arcane—and one of the most dangerous—sentences ever written, one of the major blunders of American history."[17]

Such excoriation of the Declaration's iconic phrase coming from the American right wing is highly unusual. In his recent history of the American far right, the political scientist George Hawley notes:

> Even the most vocal and extreme figures associated with the American conservative movement will express reverence for the ideals expressed in the Declaration of Independence and in their rhetoric they often empha-size that their preferred policies will ultimately lead to a more equitable society. They may argue that their interest is in equality of opportunity rather than equality of results, but in either case, they are careful not to reject equality as an ideal.[18]

Here Hawley is writing not about mainstream conservatives but about right-wing critics of American conservatism, as the title of his book has it. In other words, as recently as just a few years ago even the very far right embraced Jeffersonian political egalitarianism. (Obvious exceptions are violent and quasi-criminal operations such as the KKK and neo-Nazis.) Even the John Birch Society expressed pride in "the environment for life, liberty and the pursuit of happiness enjoyed by the average American Negro" and in "the governmental principles of our once great republic, and the gradual progress we had been making . . . towards a still better framework for human life on the part of individuals of all races, colors and creeds."[19] So the Alt-Right of today is much more radical in its criticism of Jeffersonian egalitarianism than previous right-wing extremists were.

When conservatives did speak about equality they offered, as Hawley notes, not a rejection but a clarification of the concept. In the past, when conservatives interpreted the idea that all men are created equal, their point was that people are obviously unequal in certain traits: some are strong and some are weak, some are tall and some are short, some are intelligent and some are not. Hayek took that position when he wrote in *The Constitution of Liberty:*

> To rest the case for equal treatment of national or racial minorities on the assertion that they do not differ from other men is implicitly to admit that

factual inequality would justify unequal treatment; and proof that some differences do, in fact exist would not be long in forthcoming. It is the essence of the demand for equality before the law that people would be treated alike in spite of the fact that they are different.[20]

It was not just conservatives who interpreted Jefferson's dictum to apply to political rather than factual equality. The social democratic philosopher Karl Popper, for example, argued that "'equality before the law' is *not a fact but a political demand based upon a moral decision*; and it is quite independent of the theory—which is probably false—that 'all men are equal.'"[21]

The point is, earlier expositors of the proposition "all men are created equal" were clarifying that the equality in question was not one of traits or characteristics but of rights and political status.

The Alt-Right disagrees with Hayek and Popper. Its thinkers either (1) explicitly reject not only the "factual equality" *but even the political equality* of all people, or (2) introduce so many qualifications and modifications of Jeffersonian political egalitarianism as to render it a dead letter, or (3) deny that Jeffersonian egalitarianism should extend to nonwhites.

EXPLICIT REJECTION OF POLITICAL EQUALITY   Richard Spencer offers an explicit rejection of political equality. Here is an excerpt from an interview I conducted with Spencer:

> TM: So you reject the idea that all men are created equal?
>
> RS: I reject that statement totally. I reject it in all its forms and context. . . . I reject it in the hardest way possible.
>
> TM: Let me just try to be quite clear on that. . . . We're talking . . . not about . . . intelligence, any factual, biological equality. We're talking about political equality in the sense of everybody has the same package of inalienable rights. Now what do you make of that reading of the Declaration?
>
> RS: I reject that utterly. I think that's just silly. Thomas Jefferson might as well be talking about everyone has the right to a unicorn.
>
> TM: Hayek says, "It is the essence of the demand for equality before the law that people would be treated alike, in spite of the fact that they are different." Now, interpreting "all men are created equal" in that sense, can you accept the idea of all men are created equal?

RS: Well I think that's much more attractive . . . but I would actually still reject that. First off, I really can't get over my defense that human beings do not have rights. . . . There is no deep right that any human being is born with or possessed with. You acquire a right by becoming a member of a community. So basically, Jefferson gets it backwards. . . . You owe it to your own children, to your neighbor, to your race, to your nation to treat people differently, to not treat them equally. . . . Like a Hispanic immigrant is just never going to be a member of my family and my people and my civilization. . . . This is not like a license to treat people with utter, abject immorality. Of course not, but . . . I don't owe this Hispanic immigrant anything. He's not part of my group. And in fact, I have a duty to treat him differently.[22]

In an interview with me, Mike Enoch, editor of *The Right Stuff*, expressed an equally radical inegalitarianism:

ME: We have equal rights, basically is what he [Jefferson] is saying. . . . I think that I don't agree with that because rights are socially constructed; rights are created by the state. The state is a group of people that create the norms of society and back those up, you know, with the threat of violence. . . . And that's what creates rights, and it grants those rights to, you know, to the people that it grants them to. . . . I do not believe that the state has a duty to provide equal rights.[23]

These statements are entirely dispositive on the matter of whether the most radical Alt-Rightists fundamentally reject Jeffersonian political equality; they do. But other Alt-Right thinkers are—or present themselves as—somewhat less radical.

JEFFERSONIAN EQUALITY OF RIGHTS MODIFIED AND QUALIFIED INTO NOTH-ING   Jared Taylor and frequent *VDARE* contributor James Kirkpatrick are examples of Alt-Right thinkers who modify and qualify Jeffersonian egalitarianism into a dead letter. Here is an excerpt from my interview with Taylor:

TM: Tell me in what sense you think the phrase "all men are created equal" is "nonsense" and "gauzy bunk," etc.

JT: Because there is no two men on Earth who are created equal. We all differ in countless, countless ways. Even identical twins are not created equal in terms of the measurable traits of all human beings. . . . We are equal in the sense that all men do have the right to life, liberty and the pursuit of happiness. We are equal in that regard. . . . [In] that sense, that very limited sense, Jefferson could have left off the entire five words "All men are created equal" . . . and the meaning of the document could have been the same but this aspect; this notion of the rampant equality would have been absent from American mythology.

TM: It's obvious, and I think it was obvious at the time, that if anybody thought Jefferson was saying, "Oh, I mean all men are equally tall, equally smart, equally strong," everybody would have laughed at him. So clearly what's being talked about here are certain inalienable rights, among which are life, liberty, and pursuit of happiness. You don't have a problem with that, do you?

JT: No, but . . . I think in the context of that document, those words have a meaning, the meaning of those words is equal to zero. In other words, I think his intent could have been gotten across simply by saying, all men have an equal right to life, liberty and the pursuit of happiness.

TM: However . . . the phrase as I'm interpreting it and as, for instance, Lincoln interpreted it . . . equality doesn't mean color, size, intellect, moral development, social capacity. It's all about inalienable rights. In that sense . . . you don't have any problem with that phrase?

JT: No, no I don't. Furthermore, I do underline this idea that because he did use this, in my words, meaningless five words. They have been blown up to . . . have this hold on the American imagination that has been extremely dangerous.

TM: You're concerned that the phrase "all men are created equal" might be taken [to mean] . . . Jefferson is saying we're all equally strong, equally smart. And you're saying he would've been better off to leave that out, as long as he was clear all men, understood as men of all races of course, are equal in terms of political rights. Is that correct?

JT: Well, not necessarily.

TM: Explain. Ah! Now we put our finger on it, Mr. Taylor.

JT: He's saying those three things.

TM: Yes . . . "endowed by the creator with certain inalienable rights, among which are life, liberty and the pursuit of happiness." So my understanding is the full complement of political rights is held equally by all people of all races. You don't have any problem with that, do you?

JT: Maybe he's saying that, maybe he's not.

TM: Well, what are you saying?

JT: The fact is I don't think it's useful to quibble over what Jefferson meant, and I don't think we necessarily have to tie ourselves [to] whatever interpretation we give of the Declaration of Independence.

TM: Whatever Jefferson said, you have no problem with the assertion that all men, in other words, people of all races, have certain equal political rights and are political equals to one another. That's your position, right?

JT: No, it's not my position either. There are differences between citizens and noncitizens. There are differences between the mentally competent and mentally incompetent. There are differences between people who are behind bars because they've committed a crime and people who are free. . . . To the extent that you're trying to find in the people that are classified as the Alt-Right, some willingness to deny certain rights to people of certain races, you're not going to find it in me.

TM: Okay, that's clarifying. All right, thank you. So let me ask you this, then. So we're agreed people of all races have the same political rights?

JT: Hold on. So long as they are citizens of the United States, because noncitizens don't have lots of the rights that [citizens do].

TM: To have the right to vote you need to be a citizen. However, if you're a noncitizen, you still have the right to life, liberty and the pursuit of happiness. The government cannot just show up and blow you away on the ground that, hey, noncitizens don't have any rights. Correct?

JT: Well, on the other hand, they have no right to pursue happiness in the United States if their visa expires.

TM: There's no question that governments have the right to institute immigration laws. I would simply say this, you hold the right to pursue happiness, but if you're here illegally you can be asked to leave, and you go pursue your happiness somewhere else.

JT: Absolutely.

What, then, is Taylor's bottom line on Jeffersonian egalitarianism interpreted as equality of rights? In this interview Taylor said "we are equal in the sense that all men do have the right to life, liberty and the pursuit of happiness" and that he would not "deny certain rights to people of certain races." Excellent. But when asked specifically, four separate times, Taylor would *not* say his position was "people of all races have certain equal political rights and are political equals to one another." In fact, he asserted, "No, it's not my position either." That is, once it is stipulated that "all men" refers to people of all races, Taylor's support for equality of rights becomes impossible to pin down.

And what to make of Taylor's claim that the pivotal phrase of the Declaration—"all men are created equal"—is just "meaningless five words" that could be struck altogether without changing the meaning of the document? In fact, eliminating those words would be inconsistent with Jefferson's argument, strikingly change the meaning of the Declaration, and undermine the equality of rights Taylor says he supports.

To understand why this is so, I recall Spencer's explicit rejection of even the qualified understanding of Jeffersonian egalitarianism as simply a matter of rights rather than factual equality. Spencer said, "There is no deep right that any human being is born with or possessed with. You acquire a right by becoming a member of a community. So basically, Jefferson gets it backwards."

That is, for Jefferson, people are born with rights; they do not receive them from the community. Jefferson has to take this position because he is making a case for revolution. Rights are primary and communities are to be judged against them. If the community regularly violates your rights, the problem is not with your rights but with the community, against which you may rebel if absolutely necessary. For rights to serve as such a standard of judgment, men have to be born with them—*created* equal.[24] If the community decides what rights you hold it can moot your call for revolution by simply revoking or denying the rights you claim to have. In calling for revolution, Jefferson cannot take that position. And if the community is the final arbiter of what your rights are, what is to stop the community from simply defining your rights however it pleases, and then declaring, without possibility of appeal, that despite appearances, all is well and you are equal?

Thus the denial of equal creation leads to a denial of equal rights and is a prolegomenon to a defense of slavery. This line of argument was developed by the apologist for slavery John C. Calhoun. Calhoun denounced "the prevalent opinion that all men are born free and equal; —than which nothing can be more unfounded and false." He held that men, "instead of being born free and equal, are born subject, not only to parental authority, but to the laws and institutions of the country where born and under whose protection they draw their first breath." One's political status is then to be determined by the laws and institutions of the country, which can and should apportion rights unequally, based on perceived merit. According to Calhoun:

> It is a great and dangerous error to suppose that all people are equally entitled to liberty. It is a reward to be earned, not a blessing to be gratuitously lavished on all alike; —a reward reserved for the intelligent, the patriotic, the virtuous and deserving; —and not a boon to be bestowed on a people too ignorant, degraded and vicious, to be capable either of appreciating or of enjoying it.[25]

Political equality thus becomes not an inalienable right one is born with but a reward to be doled out by the community or country to the virtuous, but not to "a people" too vicious to make use of it. Of course, to Calhoun, the ignorant, degraded, and vicious people in question turn out to be blacks, who deserve only slavery.

It is precisely to forestall interpretations like those of Calhoun and Spencer and to prevent equality of rights from becoming a dead letter that Jefferson's five iconic words are indispensable to the meaning of the Declaration. Taylor completely undermines his claim to accept the equal rights of all men when he disparages Jefferson's phrase as "meaningless."

James Kirkpatrick, a regular contributor to *VDARE*, in correspondence with me similarly modified Jefferson's words so as to undermine political egalitarianism:

> TM: So to make my question more precise, do you believe "all men are created equal" in the sense of having equal political rights?
> JK: No. And neither did Jefferson, obviously. There's a nuanced way in [which] this expression is true, in the sense that no *citizen* should be deprived of life, liberty or *property* without *due process*. This is obviously what Jefferson meant. . . . But things get taken to their logical conclusion. When you reduce your political philosophy to a slogan, "all men are created equal," eventually people start believing it. . . . It's all very

well to invent abstract universal rights in an all-white Christian society in which only property owning males vote. Today, it's hard to take some of these premises seriously. But I also have no illusions about some return to monarchy or whatever else.[26]

Kirkpatrick begins by bluntly denying that all men have equal political rights but then admits the idea is true in "a nuanced way." But the nuances turn out to make all the difference.

Note that Kirkpatrick's modification of the Declaration specifies not "all men," but only citizens. He therefore makes the same Calhounist move that Taylor does: only citizens are equal, and since citizenship is a matter of law, one's political equality depends on whoever makes the law. Thus an enormous loophole is left open for lawmakers to decide that entire classes of people are not citizens at all and therefore are politically unequal. Of course, this is exactly the move the Supreme Court made in the infamous *Dred Scott* decision, which held that blacks were not citizens and that a compromise in Congress that restricted slavery in some parts of the country was not constitutional.

Also, in Kirkpatrick's formulation, the rights that are held "unalienable" in the Declaration become subject to "due process." Thus one can be deprived of one's rights as long as established procedures are followed. But what if established procedures systematically leave entire classes of people at a disadvantage?

Kirkpatrick does the most damage to the Declaration, however, when he replaces "pursuit of happiness" with "property." Much has been written about why Jefferson preferred his formulation to "life, liberty, and property," as the thought was often put in his time.[27] In any case, Jefferson's right to the pursuit of happiness embraces a broader range of human affairs than the right to property, if property is understood in the narrow sense of possessions. Further, specifying a right to property would have provided slaveholders with the argument that they had a right to their slaves, whom of course they considered property. In contrast, slaves or any subordinated people can vindicate their claim to equality by appealing to a right to the pursuit of happiness.

It is a historical matter of fact that the Confederate supporters of slavery altered the Declaration's key phrase exactly as Kirkpatrick does. After the election of Lincoln, seven states of the Lower South were the first to secede. Five of those states sent official commissioners to the slave states that remained in the Union to urge them to secede. To a man, these commissioners based their arguments on the defense of slavery and white supremacy rather than on states' rights or anything else.[28] Characteristic of these arguments were those of Mississippi's commissioner to Georgia and Alabama's to Kentucky. William L. Harris of Mississippi, in his address to the General Assembly of Georgia, gave Alt-Right fear-mongers of "white genocide" something to think about when he asserted his state "had rather see the last of her race, men, women, and children, immolated in one common funeral pyre than see them subjected to the degradation of civil, political and social equality with the negro race."[29]

Hardly less ferocious was Stephen F. Hale in his letter to Kentucky's governor, in which he argued that "the triumph of this new theory of government"—that is, "the equality of the races, white and black"—"destroys the property of the South, lays waste her fields and inaugurates all the horrors of a San Domingo servile insurrection, consigning her citizens to assassinations and her wives and daughters to pollution and violation to gratify the lust of half-civilized Africans."[30]

Harris and Hale based their arguments on Jefferson's trilogy of rights, suitably edited, of course, just as Kirkpatrick does. Harris claimed, "Our fathers secured to us . . . protection to life, liberty and *property*" and that "citizens of the South have been deprived of their property" because the North was not effectively enforcing the Fugitive Slave Act.[31] Hale similarly argued that "the primary object of all good governments is to protect the citizen in the enjoyment of life, liberty, and *property*," and argued, "Will the South give up the institution of slavery and consent that her citizens be stripped of their property? . . . It is impossible. Disunion is inevitable."[32]

Let us here ignore the neo-Confederate propensities of *VDARE* and assume that Kirkpatrick rejects these apologies for slavery. But it is a matter of record that the substitution of "property" for "pursuit of happiness" that he now makes opened the door to such arguments and today could be put to similar bad use. Kirkpatrick's rewording of the Declaration, far from being a matter of mere nuance, entirely vitiates the document's world-historical proclamation of political egalitarianism. This cavalier disdain for the foundational principles of American democracy is an excellent example of the Alt-Right's intellectual recklessness.

Another regular contributor to VDARE, Steven Sailer, would also undermine Jefferson's dictum. Here is Sailer in the process of denying the idea that America is a "proposition nation," one based on the acceptance of certain foundational ideas:

> Consider the most famous of all the Propositions: "All men are created equal."
>
> Well, guess what, I don't believe it—not in the sense of empirical equality of capabilities. But that interpretation has become increasingly dominant. . . .
>
> What I do believe in is the spiritual, moral, and legal equality of humans. . . . Jefferson and the signers of the Declaration probably meant something similarly sophisticated.
>
> Unfortunately, they didn't quite end up saying that.[33]

The Declaration is not exactly right, argues Sailer, because Jefferson "appears to have made a typo by leaving out the word 'in' in his most famous sentence," which should read, "'all men are created equal, *in* that they are endowed by their Creator with certain unalienable rights.'"[34] Because of this lack of a "bit of proof-reading,"[35] Sailer claims, "The relentless momentum in American public life is toward enshrining 'All men are created equal' as totalitarian dogma."[36]

Sailer's proposed edit of the Declaration is less damaging to the document's overall argument than Taylor's but nonetheless deserves comment because it raises important questions. Sailer's argument is that Jefferson and the signers meant to assert "the spiritual, moral, and legal equality of humans" but "didn't quite end up saying that" and instead implied an "empirical equality of capabilities," all because of a sheer typo or proofreading error that dropped a crucial word.

But there is no evidence of such a gross mistake. In none of the Declaration's early drafts did the word "in" appear at this point and then get accidentally left out later.[37] Further, the drafting committee that drew up the document included, besides Jefferson, two other masters of the English language—John Adams and Benjamin Franklin—who made important changes but never suggested Sailer's proposed insertion. In her definitive account, "Mr. Jefferson and His Editors," the historian Pauline Maier described the attention lavished on the drafting process as "an act of group editing that has to be one of the great marvels of history" and notes that "the delegates who labored over the draft Declaration had a splendid ear for language."[38]

Thus, Sailer is arguing that a meticulous editorial process involving the collective genius of America's greatest literary talents let pass, for want of a bit of proofreading, a gross typo that transformed the meaning of the Declaration from an assertion of "the spiritual, moral, and legal equality of humans" into a "totalitarian dogma." This implausible and entirely unsupported claim is another example of the true offenses of the Alt-Right: intellectual carelessness, poverty of thought, and rhetorical excess.

Why Taylor, Sailer, or any reasonable person should think the Declaration makes not the vitally relevant claim of equality of rights but the obviously absurd assertion of an "empirical equality of capabilities" or of all men being "equal in terms of the measurable traits of all human beings" is a mystery. In fact, as far as I have been able to determine, *no* informed thinker has *ever* maintained that all men are factually equal in these senses. There is no danger of the idea of radical, factual egalitarianism becoming "totalitarian dogma" because no serious person—and certainly not Jefferson—has ever said anything so preposterous. Why, then, does the Alt-Right fulminate against an interpretation of the Declaration no sensible reader has ever held? The most reasonable answer is that these Alt-Right figures simply do not accept the Declaration's political egalitarianism and, after occasional perfunctory and ambiguous statements of good will, knock the foundations out from under that principle. But whatever the answer, the Alt-Right's hyperbolic disparagements of America's foundational document are down on all fours with similar rhetoric of Calhoun and other defenders of slavery and serve only to discredit altogether rather than clarify Jeffersonian egalitarianism.

REFUSAL TO EXTEND EQUALITY OF RIGHTS TO NONWHITES   Another way to seemingly embrace Jeffersonian egalitarianism partly but still leave the door open to discrimination is to deny that the phrase "all men" was meant to extend to nonwhites. Jared Taylor makes this move in his monograph *What the Founders Really Thought about Race: The White Consciousness of U.S. Statesmen*, where he writes: "Today, the United States officially takes the position that all races are equal. . . . Many Americans cite 'the all men are created equal' phrase from the Declaration of Independence to support the claim that this view of race was not only inevitable but was anticipated by the Founders. . . . They are badly mistaken."³⁹

Right at the start of his essay, Taylor runs into the obvious objection to his claim that the founders rejected the political equality of the races: doesn't the plain meaning of "all men" refer to men of all races? Here is how Taylor deals with this obvious problem:

Despite what he [Jefferson] wrote in the Declaration, he did not think Blacks were equal to Whites, noting that "in general, their existence appears to participate more of sensation than reflection." He hoped slavery would be abolished some day, but "when freed, he [the Negro] is to be removed beyond the reach of mixture." Jefferson also expected whites eventually to displace all of the Indians of the New World. The United States, he wrote, was to be "the nest from which all America, North and South, is to be peopled," and the hemisphere was to be entirely European: ". . . nor can we contemplate with satisfaction either blot or mixture on that surface."

Jefferson opposed miscegenation for a number of reasons, but one was his preference for the physical traits of Whites. He wrote of their "flowing hair" and their "more elegant symmetry of form," but emphasized the importance of color itself: Are not the "fine mixtures of red and white, the expressions of every passion by greater or less suffusions of colour in the one [whites], preferable to that eternal monotony, which reigns in the countenances, that immovable veil of black, which covers all the emotions of the other race?"⁴⁰

The passages Taylor quotes show that Jefferson believed blacks were more emotional than whites and not as good-looking. Jefferson was, of course, wrong, and reading these comments is very disheartening to modern admirers of Jeffersonianism. But do they show that Jefferson held, as an essential principle of his political philosophy, that blacks were not the *political* equals of whites and that the principle "all men are created equal" did not apply to blacks?

To start answering this question, let us first note that the unpleasant passages Taylor cites come not from the Declaration but from Jefferson's other writings. They are not part of Jefferson's expressed political principles but are opinions expressed in other contexts and not necessarily incorporated into his political philosophy. Further, a very simple examination of the drafting of the Declaration of Independence shows that Jefferson clearly meant to extend the principle of political equality to all men, blacks as well as whites.

Jefferson's original rough draft of the Declaration—that is, the text before it was edited by Congress—contained a number of charges against the British king that were not included in the final draft that Congress approved. One of these passages accused the king of foisting slavery on the American colonies:

He has waged cruel war against human nature itself, violating it's most sacred rights of life & liberty in the persons of a distant people who never offended him, captivating & carrying them into slavery in another hemisphere, or to incur miserable death in their transportation thither. This piratical warfare, the opprobrium of *infidel* powers, is the warfare of the CHRISTIAN king of Great Britain. determined to keep open a market where MEN should be bought & sold, he has prostituted his negative for suppressing every legislative attempt to prohibit or to restrain this execrable commerce: and that this assemblage of horrors might want no fact of distinguished die, he is now exciting those very people to rise in arms among us, and to purchase that liberty of which he has deprived them, & murdering the people upon whom *he* also obtruded them; thus paying off former crimes committed against the *liberties* of one people, with crimes which he urges them to commit against the *lives* of another.[41]

The key feature of this passage has been pointed out by the distinguished political theorist and student of the Declaration, Danielle Allen.[42] In it Jefferson acknowledges the "sacred rights of life & liberty in the persons of a distant people"—that is, black Africans being carried into slavery—and specifically recognizes these persons as men, or rather "MEN." The striking capitalization is in the original. Thus we have a clear proof: if the foundational statement of American political principles famously asserts "all men are created equal," and then goes on to specify blacks are "MEN," it follows that this philosophy does in fact extend that equality to blacks.

It is true that Congress edited this passage out of the Declaration, but not because there was any objection to the idea that blacks were men.

South Carolina and Georgia had never opposed the slave trade, which they wanted continued, and so demanded that the whole discussion of slavery be struck.[43] Jefferson had to bow to their wishes. He never repudiated his claim that blacks were men and—despite his disparaging remarks about blacks' hair texture, complexion, intelligence, and so forth—never suggested that the unalienable rights of the Declaration did not extend to blacks.

Another favorite Alt-Right argument claims that since the 1790 Naturalization Act made only "free white persons" eligible for naturalization, therefore the phrase "all men" in the Declaration must really mean "all white men." Thus a *VDARE* article argues: "Of course, the Declaration of Independence does assert that 'all men are created equal,' but what exactly the Founders meant must be assessed in the light of the fact that many were slaveholders—and that the 1790 Naturalization Act restricted citizenship to 'free white persons.'"[44]

But this citation of the 1790 act, far from showing that "all men" in the Declaration really means "all white men," in fact shows exactly the opposite. The wording of the Naturalization Act shows the statesmen of the founding generation could and did specify race when they wanted to. If, therefore, they declined to specify race in the Declaration's iconic phrase, then "all men" means precisely what it says—not just white men but *all* men irrespective of race. Further, citing the wording of a policy provision subject to revision in order to trump the principles enunciated in a foundational statement of philosophy puts the cart before the horse. That legislation does not always live up to first principles does not necessarily speak against the principles. In that case it is the legislation that must give way. Or perhaps in the press of trying to balance a variety of principles, the legislators felt, rightly or wrongly, some could not be fully realized at a particular historical moment. Of course, in due time, it was the policy that was revised to align with the Declaration, not the other way around, which suggests it was the principle of political egalitarianism that was found to be sound.

Another argument deployed by Alt-Right thinkers to deny the phrase "all men" was meant to extend to people of all races involves pointing out what the Declaration says about Indians. The relevant passage comes up in the list of grievances charged against the king: "He has excited domestic insurrections amongst us, and has endeavoured to bring on the inhabitants of our frontiers, the merciless Indian Savages whose known rule of warfare, is an undistinguished destruction of all ages, sexes and conditions."

Alt-Rightists claim the disparaging reference to "merciless Indian Savages" implies the unalienable rights of the Declaration were not meant to extend to Indians and nonwhites generally. Thus James Kirkpatrick of *VDARE* has said, "After all, Jefferson did not consider slaves part of the polity nor the 'merciless Indian savages' he condemns in the document. Nor did women have equal political rights in the sense of having a right to vote."[45]

And according to another *VDARE* contributor, "Our Founding Fathers often spoke in universal language but really only practiced their beliefs within the context of European descendants. Thomas Jefferson claimed 'all men are created equal' and then called Indians 'savages' in the very same document."[46]

There are two errors here. First, Jefferson's unfortunate characterization of Indians nowhere says they are not men, nor does it deny that they enjoy the same unalienable rights as everyone else. People of all temperaments, levels of "civilization," and behavior enjoy the same set of primordial rights under the philosophy of Jeffersonian democracy. Yes, this means even killers and criminals, however merciless or savage they may be. Of course, such rights, while unalienable, are not absolute. Since all persons enjoy them, one person's rights are limited by those of everyone else. If I mercilessly murder someone, I certainly may be punished for violating *his* rights. Such punishment in itself does not violate *my* rights, which never involved a license to murder. It is a mistake to think that when a convicted criminal is punished his rights are therefore taken away. So the Declaration's disparaging description of Indians does not imply that they or nonwhites in general do not enjoy exactly the same rights all men do.

Second, it may be that the founders only *practiced* their beliefs within the context of European descendants, but the question is about their *principles*. As we have seen, the plain language of the Declaration and the history of its drafting show the unalienable rights it describes were meant to extend, in principle, to people of all races. That granted, the founders faced the tangled question of how to realize those rights in practice. As a practical matter, and however unfortunately, an immediate end to slavery and the granting of voting rights to women were politically impossible in the founders' day. Further, the political agenda of the founding generation was already crammed with world-historical challenges, including independence and the restoration of republicanism. Therefore, some of the founders, including Jefferson, felt the best that could be accomplished regarding slavery was a repatriation of enslaved persons to Africa. That was, of course, an utterly wrongheaded, unrealistic, and immoral judgment. But the founders' bad judgment on that issue doesn't prove they did not believe, or that the Declaration does not mean, that in principle, equal rights ought to be extended to all people. Over time, the impossibility of repatriation became obvious, antislavery sentiment spread widely, and an end to slavery became a live political option and finally a reality, as did women's suffrage. In other words, it took a long time for the principles of the Declaration to be fully understood and then realized. Such is the nature of the struggle to achieve liberty. That obvious reality doesn't undermine the validity, then and now, of the principles of the Declaration.

In short, the political equality of all people, regardless of race, is a central principle of the American founding philosophy as expressed in the Declaration. Even if, in the founding era, that principle was not fully articulated in all its detail, or realized in political practice as much as would have been desirable, the principle remains valid. That should be obvious, at least to Americans of today.

VDARE'S CAUTIOUS SUPPORTERS OF "ALL MEN ARE CREATED EQUAL"   Some contributors to Alt-Right sites do accept Jeffersonian egalitarianism so long as it is made very clear that the equality in question is strictly one of rights, but remain doubtful that such equality can be realized in a multiracial country like the United States. Writers of this persuasion can be found at *VDARE* but seldom at other Alt-Right sites. *VDARE*, though some of its contributors consider themselves Alt-Rightists, is thought of by its founder and editor, Peter Brimelow, to be a forum site that publishes anyone who has something to say about what he considers to be the "post '65 immigration disaster."[47] Thus *VDARE* carries the relatively mainstream syndicated commentators Patrick J. Buchanan and Michelle Malkin, including columns in which they express support for Jeffersonian equality of rights.[48] And other writers more closely associated with the site show greater sympathy with Jefferson's words than do other writers considered in this chapter.

Brimelow himself in an interview acknowledged that all men are equal in the sense that they have the same bundle of political rights and said that "obviously people aren't created equal but what the founding fathers meant is that there's a moral equality."[49] John Derbyshire is a frequent contributor to *VDARE* who prefers the term "dissident right" to Alt-Right.[50] He agrees with Brimelow's assessment of Jeffersonian egalitarianism but is skeptical about whether it can be realized in a multiracial society:

> Well, as an idea it's obviously absurd. We're not all created equal. Some are tall, some are short, some are fast, some are slow, some are smart, some are stupid. It's obvious that we're not all created equal; you can't take it too literally. In the context of this sort of ceremonial language that the Declaration is using, I think the best translation of it would be that it's just an 18th century gentleman's way of saying that we're going to start a new social order, and there won't be any blood aristocracy. There won't be any aristocracy of blood in our new social order. That's what I think he was saying. . . .
>
> On the other hand, if you're going to say that different racial groups, different races, people with different kinds of ancestry, people from different local varieties of the human species—which they are—have general statistical differences between [them] . . . but we're going to treat them equally. . . . That's a somewhat different proposition and it's clearly in practice much more difficult to me. . . . I would put that in the basket labeled worthwhile ideals. Whether it can be obtained in practice, is much more difficult. . . . It's a grand idea. I would love to live in a society like that. Whether a society like that can actually exist, is an incredible problem. And the evidence to date is maybe it can't.[51]

Here Derbyshire makes some of the same criticisms of Jeffersonian egalitarianism that we have already found wanting and implausibly argues that the phrase's main point was merely to reject blood aristocracy, an issue that is not mentioned in the document at all. But at least Derbyshire acknowledges political equality among a diverse population as a worthwhile, though perhaps impractical, ideal, and states he would love to live in such a society. At this point in the interview I couldn't resist asking the following question:

TM: "It's a nice proposition, but can it work in practice?" Gee, I can think
of a country . . . [where it] comes pretty close to working in practice,
can't you?

JD: Well, let me think. Well, India doesn't do too badly; they've got a lot
of groups there.

TM: That wasn't what I had in mind. . . . What do you think I'm thinking?

JD: Um, I don't know?

TM: How about the United States of America?

JD: What?

TM: How about the United States of America?

JD: No, it doesn't work well here at all.

After this exchange we discussed how successful the United States has
been in achieving the Jeffersonian ideal of equal rights for people of all
races. Derbyshire pointed out that black social progress after the end of
legal segregation has not been as great as had been hoped. He also cited
affirmative action as an example of unequal treatment of different races.
I argued that the issue is whether political equality of the races has been
at least more nearly approximated. Less success has been achieved with
equality of social outcomes than could be wished, but this disappointing
outcome hardly proves that political equality is nearly unachievable in a
multiracial democracy. Nor does the relatively small impact of affirmative
action, whatever one thinks of it, substantially change the picture. In the
end, Derbyshire was willing to grant that "we have in fact obtained the
desideratum of absolute equality under the law." But if the desideratum
is equality before the law, then our acknowledged inequalities in height,
speed, intelligence, and so forth are clearly not germane; in which case,
why brand Jefferson's foundational idea "obviously absurd"?

Brimelow and Derbyshire at least show themselves to be finally more
comfortable with political equality than other Alt-Right thinkers. Perhaps
we should be grateful for small favors. Overall, *VDARE* contributors, with
their many objections, stipulations and quibbles that are often not to the
point, end up undermining and discrediting Jeffersonian egalitarianism
almost as much as the more radical Alt-Rightists.

"The Consent of the Governed": Electoral Democracy

The Alt-Right's rejection of Jeffersonian democracy is thoroughgoing. Once egalitarianism of rights is denied, the next step is a denial that the protector of those rights, government, derives its just powers from "the consent of the governed." The Declaration does not specify how that consent is to be obtained, but in the modern world the main way of so doing is electoral democracy: periodic, contested elections with a universal or nearly universal adult franchise to determine the leadership of the government. It is therefore unsurprising that the Alt-Right is consistent in its radicalism and rejects electoral democracy. Richard Spencer put the matter this way:

> RS: I'm not in favor of electoral democracy. I don't believe . . . tallying up votes is the best way to make a decision. I don't believe in that.
>
> TM: What's a better way to make a decision than electoral democracy?
>
> RS: Wise people who care, who have a long-term view and care about the future of their people.
>
> TM: And where do they come from? And how do you recognize them?
>
> RS: That's the trick. That's the trick. . . . I am not going to lie to you and . . . [say] that we can just poll every human being with a pulse and that is going to lead us to the right or sound answer.[52]

At the most, then, only "wise people who care" should be allowed to participate in politics, according to Spencer, and certainly not "every human being with a pulse," which would be to practice, as a writer for the *Occidental Observer* put it, "one idiot, one vote."[53] Writers for *The Right Stuff* agree:

> The solution to all of these problems is to destroy the concept of voting as a right. By limiting suffrage, we increase the value of votes and voters. By limiting suffrage to those who represent virtues beneficial to society, we promote those virtues bilaterally and at the same time. Expecting people who have done nothing to improve their lot in life to vote in any way other than destructively or in a manner consistent with their free willing [freewheeling] life style is tantamount to societal suicide.[54]

And again:

> If we must be a democratic society, the franchise should be limited. Universal democracy is a bad system. It gives power to the worst and shackles the fittest. It is a degenerative institution in which the weak and unproductive collaborate against the strong and sustainable.[55]

But then, there still remains the trick of identifying the wise who will be allowed to vote. Another writer for *The Right Stuff* has a simple answer; limit suffrage to the rich:

> This approach of test passing to qualify should be used in selecting the voting population. A base example of how the test could be done is that the person must earn over $100,000 gross in that year. The reasoning is that someone who achieves high-percentile market value has demonstrated a longer time horizon coupled with understanding—well enough—the intricacies needed for making policy decisions.[56]

But will income really turn out to be a good test of wisdom, virtue, fitness, and strength? Isn't whatever test that is established likely to be abused? Won't there be a great struggle over what the test should be, with the potential losers driven to civil war? Bring it on, says yet another writer for *The Right Stuff*:

> Drastic measures are required. We're too far gone now. A small elite always rules over the herd, and this elite has the power to mold public opinion. We must become the elite, by any means necessary. Martial law is probably required, and that means the imposition of a fascist leader's arbitrary will. . . . Our democratic constitutions are tantamount to a suicide pact for the Western world. The general public is overwhelmingly in support of Democracy, and it will be the death of us.[57]

Thus the Alt-Right critique of Jeffersonian democracy leads to acceptance of "imposition of a fascist leader's arbitrary will," which provides an answer to the question of just how radical this new movement is.

The Alt-Right on the *Federalist Papers*

The Alt-Right treats the *Federalist Papers* no better than it does the Declaration of Independence. The movement's account of the *Federalist Papers* generally singles out for attention John Jay's *Federalist* No. 2. Over the years *American Renaissance* and other Alt-Right outlets have cited this essay often, always as evidence for the founders' alleged white consciousness and preference for racial homogeneity. For example, in 1997 Jared Taylor wrote:

> For most of its history the United States was self-consciously homogeneous. In 1787, in the second of *The Federalist Papers*, John Jay gave thanks that "Providence has been pleased to give this one connected country to one united people, a people descended from the same ancestors, speaking the same language, professing the same religion, attached to the same principles of government, very similar in their manners and customs. . . ."
>
> This is not exactly a celebration of diversity. . . . It was only in the 1950s and 60s that the country turned its back on nearly 200 years of traditional thinking about race and began its long march down the road to nowhere.[58]

A year later, *American Renaissance* would publish an article by Sam Francis that would give Jay's words an explicitly racialist interpretation: "The racial unity of the nation is clear in Jay's phrase about 'the same ancestors.'"[59] Fifteen years later Taylor would again cite *Federalist* No. 2 to this effect in his monograph, *What the Founders Really Thought about Race.*[60] *VDARE* contributors Peter Brimelow, Steve Sailer, and Tom Tancredo have also cited Jay's essay as evidence that "the Founders . . . were highly conscious of America's specific ethnic and cultural heritage, i.e. national identity . . . [which was] the reason, Jay said in *The Federalist Papers*, why the experiment of federal government could be made to work at all."[61]

But *Federalist* No. 2 is a weak reed on which to rest that claim that white racial consciousness is central to the argument of the *Federalist Papers*. For the importance of Jay's contribution to that volume is doubtful. Jay wrote only five of the papers, compared with twenty-nine written by Madison and fifty-one by Hamilton. In a standard textbook on the history of political philosophy, Martin Diamond's chapter on the *Federalist Papers* remarks that "Jay's small contribution may be disregarded here."[62]

Further, the major themes of the volume—Union, republican principles, federalism, separation of powers—are dealt with by both Hamilton and Madison in several papers; Jay's invocation of "one united people" is not taken up elsewhere. Unlike Madison's *Federalist* No. 10 and *Federalist* No. 51 and Hamilton's papers on the presidency and the judiciary, *Federalist* No. 2 is not given much weight by interpreters outside the Alt-Right.

Further, *Federalist* No. 2 says nothing about what the Alt-Right claims is its main topic—race. Francis is just wrong when he claims that "Jay's phrase about 'the same ancestors' " implies the "racial unity of the nation." Strictly speaking, ancestors need not be of the same race as the present generation if there has been intermarriage. More important, if the key point is race, why not mention race explicitly rather than—at most—obliquely?

But for obvious reasons Jay could not possibly invoke race as a source of national unity. For if racial unity is a foundation of national identity, would not that imply that black slaves are a distinct nation? Jay certainly does not want to suggest any such thing, which would imply the legitimacy of an independent black republic or, alternatively, the necessity of slavery forever to prevent that outcome. The first option would have horrified the South and undermined the cause of national unity that Jay was supporting. The second option would have undermined support for the Constitution in the Federalists' New York audience, among whom opponents of slavery were an important constituency. So *Federalist* No. 2 cannot and does not bring up the matter of race, which would have been hard to deal with without taking an explicit stand on the thorny issue of slavery. This obvious awkwardness in Jay's argument is likely the reason Madison and Hamilton do not pursue the theme of "one united people" in their papers on national unity.

Again, Jay does not explicitly mention race in *Federalist* No. 2, but as one of the founders of the New York State Society for Promoting the Manumission of Slaves, Jay did have occasion to address the issue directly. In a 1785 letter to Benjamin Rush, Jay wrote: "I wish to see all unjust and all unnecessary discriminations everywhere abolished, and that the time may soon come when all our inhabitants of every colour and denomination shall be free and equal partakers of our political liberty."[63]

That is, when Jay does explicitly take up race, his commitment to political egalitarianism is absolutely clear. His wish that "all our inhabitants of every colour . . . shall be free and equal partakers of our political liberty" flatly contradicts a putative "racial unity of the nation" for it acknowledges that Americans are of various races. Not once in their many appeals to *Federalist* No. 2 do Alt-Rightists acknowledge Jay's well-documented repudiation of white consciousness.

It is important to note that a reasonable interpretation of *Federalist* No. 2 as a nationalist document is entirely possible. Sanford Levinson usefully points out that Jay is responding to the anti-Federalist argument that the states are too diverse to be governed under a strong central government. Jay's point, Levinson convincingly claims, is that the heterogeneity of the states has been overstated. Levinson sees in Jay's argument an underlying assumption that democratic government requires "a common heritage and a vision of a collective future and that genuine multiculturalism is dangerous," which assumption Levinson rejects but also thinks deserves serious consideration.[64] Thus stated, the nationalist assumption has been and continues to be a matter of legitimate debate. But it is also entirely different from the frank racialism of the Alt-Right, which insists America must be white-dominated in order to be decent and suppresses or distorts arguments by the founders that inconveniently suggest otherwise. Whatever may be said about moderate nationalist concerns, the radicalism, crudity, and distortions of the Alt-Right discourage rational consideration of them.

Race comes up explicitly twice in the *Federalist Papers*: once in *Federalist* No. 42, during a discussion of the slave trade, and again in the treatment of the three-fifths clause in *Federalist* No. 54. The Alt-Right ignores both passages.

In *Federalist* No. 42, Madison wishes the Constitution did not postpone Congress's ability to ban the slave trade until 1808 and hopes that soon after that date this "barbarism of modern policy" will be "totally abolished," much to the happiness of the "unfortunate African."[65] But it is *Federalist* No. 54 that fundamentally undermines the Alt-Right's claims about the white consciousness of the founders.

Federalist No. 54 gives a more detailed and highly illuminating account of what Madison thought about race. This paper makes a backhanded defense of the three-fifths clause, that is, the provision that each slave ought to count as three-fifths of a person in determining the states' populations for purposes of taxation and representation. This widely discussed provi-

sion is an obviously brutal solution to the sad question of how to take
account of slaves. Of interest here, however, is the case for racial egalitarianism that Madison makes in his qualified defense of that clause.

All of the *Federalist Papers* were written for a New York—that is, a
northern—audience. Madison's main rhetorical strategy in No. 54 is to
create a character—"one of our Southern brethren"—who makes the
defense of the three-fifths clause. In so doing, Madison avoids the em-
barrassment of arguing for the problematic provision in his own voice.
Further, Madison thus makes national unity, the fact that the South wants
the clause whatever its substantive merits, the main point of his argument.
The Southerner's case for the three-fifths clause is striking. He admits
that the clause considers the slaves as being "in the mixed character of
persons and of property." But why are slaves to be considered partly property? Madison's answer, given in the voice of the Southerner, is that slaves
are to be considered partly property only because the law, not nature, has
so made them:

> It is only under the pretext that the laws have transformed the Negroes
> into subjects of property, that a place is disputed them in the computation
> of numbers; and it is admitted, that if the laws were to restore the rights
> which have been taken away, the Negroes could no longer be refused an
> equal share of representation with the other inhabitants.[66]

Hence, change the laws, end slavery, and blacks deserve "an equal
share of representation with the other inhabitants"; that is, blacks are then
the political equals of whites. Later, in *Federalist* No. 54, Madison says it is
"unnatural" to consider "this unfortunate race" in the "light of property."
In other words, blacks were in Madison's time unequal, because they were
enslaved, by law only, not by nature. The law thus violated blacks' rights.
Change the laws, restore the rights, and blacks are the natural equal of
whites. That is to say, Madison's argument clearly implies the political
equality of the races and condemns slavery as a violation of the rights of
blacks.

Although *Federalist* No. 54 puts a certain distance between these sentiments and its author by employing the character of "an advocate for the
Southern interests," Madison endorses the Southerner's reasoning, saying
that "although it may appear to be a little strained in some points, yet on

the whole, I must confess that it fully reconciles me to the scale of representation which the convention have established." So although Madison approaches the whole delicate matter of slavery a bit gingerly, he makes the fundamental point without ruffling any more feathers than he has to: blacks and whites are political equals and the laws should treat them as such.

The third contributor to the *Federalist Papers*, Hamilton, does not discuss race in that work. But Hamilton's commitment to racial equality is documented. Hamilton's letter to Jay, written during the American Revolution and calling for the enlistment of black soldiers and eventual general emancipation, is famous:

> I have not the least doubt, that the negroes will make very excellent soldiers, with proper management. . . . I frequently hear it objected to the scheme of embodying negroes that they are too stupid to make soldiers. This is so far from appearing to me a valid objection that I think their want of cultivation (for their natural faculties are probably as good as ours) joined to that habit of subordination which they acquire from a life of servitude, will make them sooner bec[o]me soldiers than our White inhabitants. . . .
>
> The contempt we have been taught to entertain for the blacks, makes us fancy many things that are founded neither in reason nor experience. . . . An essential part of the plan is to give them their freedom with their muskets. This will secure their fidelity, animate their courage, and I believe will have a good influence upon those who remain, by opening a door to their emancipation. . . . The dictates of humanity and true policy equally interest me in favour of this unfortunate class of men.[67]

Three founders, three contributors to the *Federalist Papers*, three explicit and easily available commitments to racial egalitarianism: all three are ignored by the Alt-Right, which dwells repeatedly on one off-point observation and on that weak basis insists on the white consciousness of the entire American founding. This is mere misrepresentation, intellectual malpractice, and further evidence of the weakness of Alt-Right reasoning.

The Alt-Right on the Constitution

The Alt-Right attacks the Constitution as bombastically as it does the Declaration. A 2016 article in *Radix Journal* titled "Paper Worship" proposes how to engage "cuckservatives," that is, benighted mainstream rightists who continue to respect the Constitution:

> I am talking about the Constitution. . . . This primitive article of antiquity will not solve the problems we face in the 21st century. . . . We must do everything possible to discourage our people from elevating the zombie Constitution to the level of an unalterable sacred scripture. . . . Nothing they love will exist if we do not rid ourselves of such a pernicious and constricting piece of paper.
>
> My proposal: Any cuckservative witnessed making mindless hosannas to "defending the Constitution" will immediately be tarred and feathered with the label of Paper Worshipper. . . .
>
> Leave no space safe for Paper Cucks. No quarter for Parchment Fetishists. No mercy for Vellum Supremacists. Their pantywaisted reign of procedural suicide ends now.[68]

Hunter Wallace decries "the Constitution Cargo Cult" thus:

> As for the charge of Constitution skepticism on the Alt-Right, I would say we would have to plead guilty as charged. There are many reasons why the Alt-Right is dismissive of the US Constitution. . . . I dislike the Constitution because I believe the Union should have never been created in the first place. Instead, the United States would have been better off evolving as several regionally based nation-states. . . .
>
> Considering the present state of the Western world, there isn't much that is positive that I can say about the liberal order which is enshrined in the Constitution. Indeed, it is a cause of many of our problems and blocks any solution to them.[69]

VDARE has run a series of articles by one Joe Fallon attacking the Constitution in extravagant terms, such as the following:

The Constitutional Convention of 1787 was not a lawful assembly that produced an extraordinary political document, but an illegal cabal that staged a coup d'etat. . . .

The justification for this treason was the conviction shared by many politicians—including George Washington, Alexander Hamilton, and James Madison—that the first republic was too weak to be effective. . . .

By its actions, the Constitutional Convention proved itself to be a conclave of conspirators who betrayed their sacred oaths to the constitution of the first republic and usurped power. The subsequent adoption of the U.S. Constitution, and the establishment of the second republic, was achieved by extraconstitutional means. It was a bloodless coup d'etat. It was, in fact, a very civil coup d'etat. But it was a coup d'etat, nonetheless.[70]

An apparent exception to this contempt for America's Magna Carta is an anonymous article titled "An Alt-Right Defense of the U.S. Constitution," published by an Alt-Right organization with a board of directors that includes Richard Spencer and Mike Enoch. The defense offered turns out to be an exception that proves the rule and, in a way, is highly revealing:

An unfortunately common disparagement of Alt-Right activists is that the United States Constitution has failed our people and that "cuckservatives" are hopelessly moronic for worshipping the "failed document."

I disagree, for it is not the Constitution which has let down "ourselves and our Posterity," but rather, our politicians and the (((special interests))) they support. . . .

Despite what liberals would have us believe, the Constitution is not a color-blind suicide pact; the United States government acts in accordance with the Constitution when it protects its citizens from foreign elements.[71]

Several points here deserve note. First, the phrase "(((special interests)))" is a reference to the Jews. The practice of putting triple parentheses around the names of Jewish people or organizations is a well-documented Alt-Right meme, one that apparently began at *The Right Stuff* under Enoch and that the movement does not deny.[72] So the "defense" of the Constitution offered here turns out to be that the Constitution was fine until it was corrupted by the Jews and the politicians who curry favor with them.

Second, the author *defends* the Constitution because, supposedly, it is *not* "color-blind." In other words, we are being told that the Constitution is not racially neutral, as the document's defenders used to argue, but rather is pro-white, an expression of white consciousness, *which is the best thing about the Constitution.*

This extraordinary claim raises many issues that cannot be pursued at length here. It has been known at least since the publication in 1836 of Madison's notes on the debates of the Constitutional Convention that the Constitution included several features favorable to slave-holding interests in order to secure southern support and national unity. Since then, debate has continued over whether these compromises were necessary, whether they represented the best that could have been achieved, and whether they have been expunged by later developments. Defenders of the Constitution argue that, under the circumstances, the document represented a workable departure point for its time and has been improved since then. Other observers are very critical, and some even argue that the Constitution was pro-slavery and continues to disadvantage minorities.

But fringe groups and die-hard segregationists aside, since the defeat of the Confederacy no serious constitutional observer has *defended* the Constitution as being pro-white. Yet now the Alt-Right openly embraces white consciousness as a constitutional principle. The debate in the movement is between those who think the Constitution's framers did a fine job of incorporating racialism into the document, only to have their good work undone by the Jews, and those who think Washington, Hamilton, Madison, and the rest were race traitors and coupists and the Constitution betrayed "ourselves and our Posterity" from the start. The sheer radicalism of this school of thought is apparent. Also notable is the weakness of its argument. The Alt-Right account of the Constitution rests almost entirely on a labored interpretation of the phrase "to ourselves and our Posterity" from the Preamble and exemplifies many of the movement's intellectual failings.

The Preamble to the Constitution reads in full:

We the People of the United States, in Order to form a more perfect Union, establish Justice, insure domestic Tranquility, provide for the common defense, promote the general Welfare, and secure the Blessings of Liberty to ourselves and our Posterity, do ordain and establish this Constitution for the United States of America.[73]

Alt-Rightists claim that the apparently anodyne reference to "ourselves and our Posterity" represents a commitment to white consciousness as a constitutional principle. *Counter-Currents Publishing* offers several expressions of this claim. According to the site's editor, Greg Johnson, "The Preamble makes it clear that the Constitution was created and ratified by white men to provide good government for themselves and their posterity, not all of mankind."[74] Another article on the site, "White American Identity Politics," describes the Preamble as an "explicit dedication to the interests of the White founding stock" and concludes that this "explicit mandate of the Constitution demands the protection of liberty for the posterity of the White race."[75] Another contributor, Gregory Hood, writes:

> There exists no simpler, shorter, or more poetic expression of nationalism than five words from the Constitution of the United States—"For Ourselves and Our Posterity." For all the flaws of the Founding, no White Nationalist can dispute the beauty of that phrase, nor its relevance to our cause. . . .
>
> The Founding Fathers may have talked a lot about equality—but they assumed that America would be a white country of primarily Northern European stock. . . .
>
> Our nation and our people are one and the same—and it belongs to Ourselves and Our Posterity, alone.[76]

Contributors to *VDARE* rely on the Preamble's brief phrase to rebut the notion they detest, that the United States is a "propositional nation." That idea is false, former anti-immigration congressman Tom Tancredo writes, because

> the founders explicitly said, in the Preamble to the U.S. Constitution, that their purpose was "to secure the blessing of liberty to ourselves and our posterity"—their posterity, not the people of the world but the posterity of a specific, essentially British, community that—in the case of New England, for example—had grown rapidly through natural increase with essentially no immigration for nearly 200 years.[77]

VDARE contributor Steve Sailer also rebuts "the Propositionists" by appealing to "the Preamble to the Constitution, which puts forward a carefully considered explanation of what the United States exists *for*, one that is hard to reconcile with the current assumption that it exists primarily to take in immigrants." Sailer then quotes with approval an online poster who writes: "America is not a propositional nation, America is a prepositional nation: "*to* ourselves and our posterity." Here then is Sailer's point: the Preamble uses the words "for" and "to," which are prepositions and not propositions at all. Therefore the Propositionists, if there are any, who believe the United States "exists primarily to take in immigrants" are confuted by the clear words—two of them—of the Constitution itself.[78]

None of the Alt-Right's arguments about the Preamble are any better than Sailer's. First, the Preamble says nothing clear or explicit about the Constitution or Union being white, or British, or northern European. None of these terms or any racial, ethnic, or gender characterizations come up in the Preamble or anywhere else in the Constitution. Hood acknowledges that "whatever certain racial laws existed within the country, it was never *explicitly* stated that the United States was to be a country for a particular people,"[79] but in so doing he refutes himself, for how can the Preamble be an expression of white nationalism if it makes no mention of race?

The convention's Committee on Style was responsible for the Preamble, which was written from scratch by the committee's dominant member, Gouverneur Morris.[80] Throughout his career Morris was a passionate opponent of slavery and an advocate of political equality for blacks. During the American Revolution, Morris participated in drafting a constitution for New York State which he proposed should encourage future legislatures to abolish slavery "so that in future ages, every human being who breathes the air of this state, shall enjoy the privileges of a freeman. . . . The rights of human nature and the principles of our holy religion loudly call upon us to dispense the blessings of freedom to all mankind."[81] At the Constitutional Convention Morris, who spoke more often than any other member, famously fulminated against slavery, which he called "the curse of heaven on the states where it prevailed" and a "defiance of the most sacred laws of humanity . . . in a government instituted for the protection of the rights of mankind."[82]

Alt-Rightists would have us believe that after having delivered this philippic against slavery and defense of human freedom, Morris then served up in the Preamble a beautifully poetic expression of white nationalism.

If that overnight conversion happened, no one at the convention or in the ratification debates noticed. Nothing in the sketchy legislative history of the Preamble suggests race was considered at all.[83] In *Federalist* No. 84 Hamilton, also a member of the Committee of Style, makes mention of the phrase "to ourselves and our Posterity" and argues that the Preamble "is a better recognition of popular rights" than a Bill of Rights would be, but says nothing about race.

Alt-Rightists sometimes respond to this total absence of textual support for their position by reading a racialist element into the word "posterity." According to Peter Brimelow:

> The Founding Fathers were all white (and overwhelmingly Protestant). Their preamble to the U.S. Constitution said specifically that its purpose was "to form a more perfect union . . . [for] ourselves and our posterity"—by which they literally meant their physical descendants. . . . In other words, the U.S. was to be a nation-state, the political expression of a particular (white, British) people, as in Europe.[84]

By "posterity," Brimelow takes the founding fathers to have "literally meant their physical descendants."[85] However, neither Brimelow nor any other major Alt-Right figure has claimed to be a literal physical descendant of any of the founding fathers. Brimelow's account of posterity would disenfranchise the immense majority of present-day Americans of every race, ethnicity, and condition.

But what the Preamble literally says is that the Constitution of the United States was ordained and established by "We the People of the United States," not "We the Founding Fathers of the United States." So the posterity being referred to is that of the people of the United States, not that of the founding fathers only, and one hopes that despite what he wrote, Brimelow understands that. The question then is, whom does the Preamble mean by "the People of the United States"?

One *VDARE* contributor suggests that only the citizens of the United States were meant,[86] but the Preamble simply does not say "citizens," as it easily might have, but rather "people," so noncitizens were being included. Certainly one notable commentator has held that the Preamble and the Constitution overall considered "the negro race as a separate class of persons, and . . . *they were not regarded as a portion of the people or citizens of the Government then formed.*"[87] This was the opinion of Chief Justice Taney in *Dred Scott*, a decision so flagrantly ill decided that it provoked the universal opposition of the Free States, precipitated the Civil War, and resulted in the Fourteenth Amendment, which expunged its logic from legal reasoning. Alt-Right constitutional interpretation amounts to nothing less than a call to revive *Dred Scott* and embrace its dis-Unionist consequences.

Commentators since *Dred Scott* have given the Preamble's phrase a broad interpretation. Justice Harlan argued that "all under the sovereign jurisdiction and authority of the United States" were being referred to.[88] Justice Story suggests the Preamble is "for the sake of all mankind."[89] So a quite universalistic construction of the Preamble is appropriate, and there is certainly no reason to think that only whites were meant. Frederick Douglass was entirely correct in saying of the Preamble, "Its language is 'we the people;' . . . not we the high, not we the low, but we the people; . . . we the human inhabitants; and, if Negroes are people, they are included in the benefits for which the Constitution of America was ordained and established."[90]

Who, then, are the posterity of the people of the United States, broadly understood? Samuel Johnson's dictionary of 1755 defines posterity first as "succeeding generations" and second as "descendants," but says nothing about "literal physical" descendants.[91] Eighteenth-century legal dictionaries available online do not define posterity, but the term comes up in the discussions of inheritance. Modern dictionaries define the term as "the people who will exist in the future" (*Cambridge English Dictionary*) and "all future generations of people" or "the descendants of a person" (*English Oxford Living Dictionaries*). Posterity therefore does not necessarily mean the physical descendants of particular people, although it might. Equally plausible is the conclusion that "strictly biological descent will not do. The posterity of the 1787 'people of the United States' are 'the people of the United States' after 1787.'"[92] The record of the debate over the Preamble is too thin to support a construction so strong that it disenfranchises the majority of today's Americans. Nothing about the Preamble's text or history suggests the Constitution was ordained and established for the benefit of whites only.

Of course, if it could be absolutely demonstrated that the founders intended the Constitution to be racially exclusive, then it should simply be said that the founders were wrong, we now intend to give the document a politically egalitarian interpretation, and we will root out all provisions inconsistent with that determination. Fortunately, Americans do not have to make such a radical break with their past. All key developments in American history since the founders' day indicate that only a race-neutral constitution can be consistent with liberal democratic principles and serve as a workable governing document for present-day America.[93]

In short, the Alt-Right account of the Constitution is racialist and anti-democratic. But that is just the tip of the iceberg. Perhaps one might argue that a certain amount of iconoclasm, even wrongheaded iconoclasm, is useful. Or perhaps not. But Alt-Right constitutionalism is also bombastic, inaccurate, poorly reasoned, dishonest, and moot. Here again, it is the intellectual deficiencies of Alt-Right thought that are the true hell of the situation.

The Alt-Right on Lincoln

Of course, Lincoln, who emancipated the slaves and put down the southern secessionists, is despised by the Alt-Right. *VDARE* and *Counter-Currents Publishing* have published many articles in which Lincoln is condemned as a "dictator who[se] . . . administration was characterized by paranoia, a lust for power, and rampant corruption,"[94] an "American Pol Pot, except worse,"[95] and similar outrageous hyperbole. The nadir of such calumny is reached by Hunter Wallace, editor of *Occidental Dissent*, in his article "Happy John Wilkes Booth Day!," where he writes, "I propose a toast: to the memory of the great John Wilkes Booth, slayer of tyrants, martyr for liberty, avenger of the South!"[96] (A notable exception to this malice is *VDARE*'s John Derbyshire, who writes, "I count myself pro-Lincoln."[97])

But for the purposes of this discussion, which is concerned with Lincoln as an expositor of foundational political principles, the main issue is his position on the Declaration's iconic phrase and how the Alt-Right presents and interprets his position. The account of Lincoln given by Jared Taylor in *What the Founders Really Thought about Race* goes to the heart of this issue. There we find the following passage, in which Taylor first presents what he thinks and then quotes Lincoln:

Americans believe it was "the Great Emancipator" who finally brought the egalitarian vision of Jefferson's generation to fruition. Again, they are mistaken. . . . During the Lincoln-Douglas debates he stated:

> "I am not nor ever have been in favor of making voters or jurors of negroes, nor of qualifying them to hold office, nor to intermarry with white people; and I will say in addition to this that there is a physical difference between the black and white races which I believe will for ever forbid the two races living together on terms of social or political equality."[98]

The bluntly racist *Daily Stormer* also presents this Lincoln quotation and concludes, "They tell you he was a hero. Was he really a hero? It doesn't seem so. Like everything else, we have been completely lied to. . . . Abe didn't even want to free the slaves, it was just a political move."[99]

Lincoln did indeed speak these words at the fourth Lincoln-Douglas debate of September 18, 1858. But he also spoke other, more consequential words that Taylor fails to cite. At the first debate, on August 21, Lincoln had already taken a firm position on whether Jefferson's egalitarian vision embraced blacks:

> I hold that, notwithstanding all this, there is no reason in the world why the negro is not entitled to all the natural rights enumerated in the Declaration of Independence,—the right to life, liberty, and the pursuit of happiness. I hold that he is as much entitled to these as the white man. I agree with Judge Douglas, he is not my equal in many respects,—certainly not in color, perhaps not in moral or intellectual endowments. But in the right to eat the bread, without leave of anybody else, which his own hand earns, he is my equal, and the equal of Judge Douglas, and the equal of every living man.[100]

Thus, before he made the disparaging remarks cited by Taylor, and among the first words out of his mouth at the debates' beginning, Lincoln asserted that considerations of color, physical differences, and intellectual endowments are *utterly irrelevant* to the essential question of whether people of all races are politically equal in the sense meant by the Declaration.

But why did Lincoln slight the abilities of blacks as he did? Certainly these remarks are at odds with the popular image of Lincoln, and it is better to acknowledge his limitations than to cover them up. But the historical context in which Lincoln operated also has to be acknowledged.

In 1858 blacks were denied citizenship in Illinois and so could not vote. Senator Douglas had supported the Kansas-Nebraska Act, which was a scheme to create a new slave state that involved repealing the limitations on slavery's expansion imposed by the Missouri Compromise. Douglas also supported the disastrous *Dred Scott* decision that further enabled the spread of slavery.

Lincoln, an ardent and lifelong opponent of slavery, decided not to let this proponent of neutrality toward that peculiar institution run for re-election unchallenged. In so doing, Lincoln broke with the abolitionists, who refused to participate in the electoral political process, which they saw as too compromised with the Slave Power. In contrast, Lincoln felt that no front in the struggle with slavery should be left uncontested, and therefore ran for office. Taylor notes that Lincoln was not an abolitionist,[101] but apparently does not understand this was so because Lincoln was pursuing an antislavery strategy complementary to abolitionism and not because Lincoln was any less against slavery than were the abolitionists.

But one who runs for office must take the voters as he finds them and identify some area of agreement with them as a point of departure. Lincoln took the electorate's devotion to Jefferson's words as that point of commonality, thus putting Douglas in the awkward position of having to criticize his party's founder. Partly because he knew he was speaking before a rough, all-white crowd that was extremely suspicious of blacks, but also because he realized the complete irrelevancy of factual equality to political equality, Lincoln accepted his audience's prejudices but insisted that the principles of the Declaration nonetheless extended to blacks, which was the crucial point.

Of course, had circumstances permitted, Lincoln would have done well to repudiate the race prejudice of his day. Further, today it is understood that full political equality requires that all adults be entitled to vote, hold office, serve as jurors, marry without government discrimination, and so on. But Lincoln perspicaciously saw that on granting that people of all races have political equality, the legitimacy of slavery becomes refuted; eventual emancipation is then put on the political agenda, and full political equality becomes purely a matter of when and how. That strategy had its limitations but was an enormous improvement over Douglas's position of coexisting with slavery forever and was well worth fighting for even if it involved making certain concessions to public prejudice.

What, then, can be said of Taylor's failure to note Lincoln's explicit acknowledgment that Jeffersonian political egalitarianism extends to blacks? The Great Emancipator would have been indulgent. His immediate response to Douglas's demagoguery was, "When a man hears himself somewhat misrepresented, it provokes him—at least, I find it so with myself; but when misrepresentation becomes very gross and palpable, it is more apt to amuse him."[102] Less saintly responses are possible. The bibliography to *What the Founders Really Thought about Race* cites volumes that provide the full text of the debates, so it is inexcusable that Lincoln's defense of blacks' rights under the Declaration is omitted from Taylor's monograph. Taylor's treatment of Lincoln's legacy is another illustration of a main thesis of this book: The Alt-Right's radicalism and prejudice are not its only offenses against healthy democratic discourse. The true hell of the situation is the movement's poverty of thought.

Conclusion

Alt-Right ideology involves a root-and-branch rejection of all the central propositions of American political philosophy and of liberal democracy in general. Rights, political equality, the rule of law, electoral democracy, and constitutionalism are all discarded, sometimes with certain caveats, often with disgust. The Alt-Right is not merely a more right-wing and politically incorrect version of conventional American conservatism; rather, it is a radical and intemperate break with the country's entire political tradition and order.

Further, the quality of Alt-Right thought is abysmal. The movement's thinkers show little familiarity with relevant facts, no effort at research, no ability to entertain criticism, and a willingness to distort or suppress inconvenient evidence. In particular, Jared Taylor's *What the Founders Really Thought about Race* stands out as strikingly disingenuous. Most Alt-Right thought is no better.

Certainly a rational exposition of American nationalism is possible and would be a contribution to our democratic discourse whatever one might finally decide about nationalism. But a rational exposition of American nationalism or anything else is not what the Alt-Right is offering. The shake-up in the production system of public ideas that occurred in the early twenty-first century gave the extremists who had been exiled from mainstream conservatism a chance to show the world what they had to say. It turns out they did not have much, yet they have found a broad audience.

7

Racialism

Definitions

The terms "racism," "race prejudice" and "racialism" must be defined from the beginning. A standard definition of racism is given by the online *Oxford English Dictionary* as "prejudice, discrimination, or antagonism directed against someone of a different race based on the belief that one's own race is superior."[1] Here racism is a kind of prejudice and so is equivalent to the term "race prejudice." But scholars and political actors sometimes mean more than race prejudice when they speak of racism, which they understand as "prejudice plus power."[2] Thus one textbook on social justice education defines racism as "White racial and cultural prejudice and discrimination supported by institutional power and authority, used to the advantage of Whites and the disadvantage of peoples of Color."[3]

The Alt-Right is usually and not inaccurately considered to be racist. Nonetheless, both of the above definitions of racism prove to have limitations when applied to analyzing the race thinking of the movement. If racism means simply race prejudice, then racism is a psychological phenomenon, a kind of belief, and may or may not be integrated with other beliefs and may not be conscious at all. But the race thinking of the Alt-

Right is consciously articulated and elaborately integrated into a whole constellation of beliefs about politics, culture, and much else. If racism is white racial prejudice backed up by white institutional power, then only whites can manifest racism. It is, of course, true that in past and contemporary American society whites have had the institutional power to act on their racial prejudice while blacks have not. Nonetheless many people, including many blacks, do not think of racism as necessarily a practice of whites only.[4] Further, defining racism as prejudice plus power usually leads to an analysis of institutional power understood as a set of economic, political, and social structures that empower some groups but not others. Analyzing power structure is certainly a classic approach of modern political science and could be usefully deployed against the Alt-Right, which is under the delusion that whites have been entirely disposed of power and now must endure oppression at the hands of what Hunter Wallace of *Occidental Dissent* calls "Black Run Amerika."[5]

But although this book is a work of political science, its main focus is not so much power structures as another classic concern of the discipline, ideology. As chapter 2 showed, the Alt-Right conceptualizes itself as mainly a metapolitical or ideological movement and is less concerned with achieving immediate policy and electoral victories than it is with influencing over a longer term how other political actors think about politics. Therefore I am primarily concerned with critiquing Alt-Right ideology. I focus on ideas because I posit—as American conservatives, following Richard Weaver, once widely did—that ideas have consequences.[6] Ideas are a distinct political resource that, along with other resources such as wealth, force, votes, and organization, can confer political power and are therefore an independent matter of concern. My goal here is to unpack Alt-Right ideology and disarm it by revealing its likely disastrous consequences. Therefore, although the person on the street is not mistaken in labeling the Alt-Right racist, for present purposes it is useful to write of the movement's *racialism*: a set of consciously articulated ideas about race that are integrated into an entire antidemocratic ideology.

Alt-Right racialism:

1. Bases political identity primarily on race and sees political advancement of one's own race as the main goal of politics. We can call this belief "race consciousness."

2. Holds that race can be objectively defined in terms of biological and genetic characteristics, that an individual's race can be determined based on those characteristics, that those characteristics significantly correlate with an individual's intelligence and temperament and with the average intelligence and temperament of the race to which he or she belongs, and that black race correlates with a lower intelligence and a more impulsive temperament than does white race. This set of beliefs usually earns the appellation "race realism."

3. Concludes that because of their genetic endowments, blacks are less capable than whites of decent behavior and building good societies, and that therefore blacks are morally inferior to whites and ought to be politically subordinated to them. That is, the Alt-Right is committed to white supremacy. The movement's ideologues loudly protest the label, but they offer no convincing defense against it.

These features of the Alt-Right's racialism are considered below.

Race Consciousness

In an interview with me, Greg Johnson, editor of *Counter-Currents Publishing*, explained how awareness of race distinguishes the Alt-Right from earlier right-wing tendencies:

> GJ: The right-wing ideologies that are acceptable—mainstream conservatism, libertarianism—don't work and the reason why they don't work is simple. They ignore demographics, they ignore race and therefore they are not capable of preserving the things that these people really want to preserve and promote because there's an . . . intrinsically European ethnic character to the ideologies and political systems that they want to defend, that they're not as universal and portable and salable and transmissible as they used to think. . . . There's an ineluctably ethnic, racial dimension to politics and they realize that the mainstream right is basically moralistically committed to ignoring that. . . .
>
> The mainstream right is destined always to lose . . . the things that are most important, namely . . . a country that values private property and free enterprise and gun rights and religious freedom . . . because

once the people who created that system are being replaced with people who are radically different in both their genetics and culture and history, those things will inevitably disappear. They realize they have to fight. It's not just a cultural war, it's not just an ideological war, it's also a struggle over race and demographics, and that's the difference between the Alt-Right and the old right.[7]

Jared Taylor also explained race consciousness in an interview with me:

JT: Ultimately . . . what I care most about is the survival of my people as a distinct people. . . . White people.
TM: That's . . . race consciousness as a political principle. . . . Whatever race it is you're in, you should grab on to that and make the advancement and the assertion of that race an axiom of your political ideology.
JT: I believe the founders thoroughly believed that.
TM: You believe that. Is that correct?
JT: Yes, that racial consciousness is an essential part of group identity and it should be an inevitable part of national identity as well.
TM: And it should be an inevitable part of our political ideology, kind of on a level that . . . other more traditional concepts are on?
JT: I'm not quite sure. Yes, I would put it right at the center of any kind of understanding of the political order of a healthy nation is the recognition that racial homogeneity is essential to cultural survival and to national integrity.[8]

Richard Spencer also insisted on the centrality of race for political identity:

RS: I would also say that most everyone if not everyone of the Alt-Right would agree with the statement that . . . race is the foundation for identity. . . . It is a genetic reality. Race . . . matters and [has] deep consequences for society. It's not just like, say, hair color or eye color or like athletic talent. It's much more important in its ramifications. . . .
TM: It seems to me one of the features of Alt-Right thought is that it raises racial consciousness and specifically white racial consciousness, to a political principle . . . that's on a level with the rule of law and democracy

and anything else you want to talk about. Is that where you're going?

RS: Correct.

TM: So talk to me about race consciousness and what it means to you and what the implications of it are.

RS: Race isn't just some issue. It isn't just some little thing that we might want to pursue here and there. It's this core idea that really informs everything. You know this is how I understand identitarianism . . . you have to ask and answer that question "who are you?" before you answer other political questions. So before you start talking about what foreign policy should we have? What's our economic policy? How are we going to regulate the sidewalks this year? Even a question that mundane, literally.

TM: But you . . . give a racial answer to that question. . . . You say, "Who am I?": I am not a soul before God, I'm not a utility-maximizing individual, I'm not someone who is trying to seek the good. You answer, "Oh, I'm white." And what I don't understand is, why make that move?

RS: Because nothing else makes sense without race. Race is a grounding for everything.[9]

Since race is a grounding for everything, it a grounding even for morality. Thus one contributor to *The Right Stuff* asserts: "Moral value (at least from a social standpoint) is based around someone's solidarity on family and ethnic lines," with the following consequences for political ethics:

> We all understand now that tolerance is not a virtue if the thing being tolerated is evil (bad for our people and against the natural order). . . . Wishful thinkers long for freedom. . . . This is a compromise. Instead, we should long for total victory, where the only freedom is freedom to do good (meaning, what is good for our people).[10]

In this formulation, since racial group interest is the decisive consideration in morality, tolerance of, and compromise with, other races is evil, and the goal of politics can only be "total victory" for "our people."

I have interviewed other prominent Alt-Rightists who do not hesitate to draw this conclusion. Here is Mike Enoch, editor of *The Right Stuff*, responding to the question of whether there is in Alt-Right ideology any "natural stopping point" to the drive for total political victory of the white race:

> ME: The government to me and to us, the Alt-Right, I think for the most part, it's representative of a people. So the rights of people that aren't part of that people don't matter. It's not the concern. . . . I want the government to be a white government for white people in a white nation. I don't care about the rights of blacks.
>
> TM: Aren't you basically giving yourself a blank check for the state to treat its black citizens or members any way they want to? . . . The white government can say, "This is not a government for black people. You black people, we're going to segregate you [or] we decided instead of segregating you we're going to send you [to] the gas chambers, we're going to send you back to Africa." . . . There is no natural stopping point that I can see in your position.
>
> ME: You're saying we have to answer morally for advocating for ourselves and our rights, when no other group is asked that question. There is no other race that is asked, "Where does it end?". . . I'm saying, look, I don't care, what we are going to advocate is our rights, our people, and our sovereignty.

Enoch would forestall racial oppression by the easy expedient of achieving racial homogeneity. But in the case of a multiracial society such as the contemporary United States, he will not rule out such a possibility. Why, by this reasoning, a homogeneous white ethnostate should not oppress foreign nonwhite states is not clear.

Kevin MacDonald, founder and editor of *Occidental Review*, also embraces the idea of race consciousness as the grounding for politics and morality, but in an interview with me he came to a rather less horrific conclusion than writers for *The Right Stuff* do:

> KM: I'm an evolutionist. So from the evolutionist point of view, any ideology you have, whether it's a moral ideology, religious, whatever, ultimately it has to pass the test of satisfying the interests of the people who believe those things. And if it doesn't then it's not adaptive. From my point of view, it's really about advancing white interests and white identity, and obviously any system of government that does not advance

those things is not desirable. We have to get a system of government that works for us.

TM: I think we've got ourselves into a problem here because we've got a society which for better or worse is multiracial. So if whites say politics is about advancing the interests of the white race and if blacks say no, politics is all about advancing the interests of the black race, and Asians say the same thing, and perhaps Jews do [too] . . . are all these interests compatible?

KM: No. Definitely not. . . . They're not compatible. They're conflicts of interest, that's life.

TM: So let me see if I understand this: Politics is all about advancing the interests of your race. The interests of your race are not compatible with the interests of other races. So politics is all about conflict between races in which one race strives to advance its interests at the expense of others?

KM: Yeah. I don't really disagree with that. . . .

TM: In a multiracial society that seems to suggest that politics is always going to be a struggle between the races.

KM: I don't think you're wrong. When they opened the gates to all these other groups, which you've seen in the last few years, gradually every election cycle we've seen the racialization of politics. . . . American politics has become a racial battleground. That's all we're saying.[11]

In our interview MacDonald, unlike contributors to *The Right Stuff,* specifically rejected the ideas of unequal rights for, or de jure segregation of, minorities in a multiracial society. But he sees such societies as headed for unresolvable racial conflict unless one group establishes dominance. MacDonald outlined to me what such a process could look like:

KM: One way would be to first of all end immigration and then start repatriating people who are, first of all, illegal, but [also] other groups. Encourage them, give them financial incentives to leave. . . . This could be done if we had the political will to do it. Think about it, look what [happened] after World War II in Europe. There was all this ethnic displacement. And you look at what happened with the partition of India. Gigantic population transfers in history. That could happen again.[12]

Reasonable people can differ on the merits of ending immigration and about what to do with illegal immigrants. But it is not comforting that

MacDonald cites the displaced persons' crisis of postwar Europe and the partition of India—tragedies in which many thousands of people died or suffered—as precedents for his preferred policy.

In short, an obvious problem with undiluted race consciousness as a political principle is that it acknowledges no internal breaks. By itself, advancement of racial interest rules no abomination beyond the pale. Of course, Alt-Rightists cannot argue that the pursuit of racial interest should be limited by respect for human rights since, as was noted earlier, they roundly reject such rights as gauzy bunk.

A morality independent of racial interest might set appropriate limits. Thus one writer at *Occidental Dissent* has suggested that "the limitations of traditional Western Christianity" as it was practiced in the antebellum South could "ensure that our ideas do not end in absolute horror and tyranny." But this is not helpful insofar as Christianity as it was understood in that setting endorsed slavery.[13] Further, and more fundamentally, for some prominent Alt-Rightists, morality is *not* independent of racial interest; good and evil are determined entirely by what does and does not advance the interests of one's race. This position leads straight to a racialized version of "might makes right." Thus the Alt-Right merely updates and collectivizes ancient Thrasymachian morality: justice is the advantage of the stronger race, with nothing barred. In our interview, Kevin MacDonald told me that he wishes blacks well and objects to large-scale immigration partly because it damages blacks' interests. But if political morality is entirely about advancing white interests, why care about black interests at all? One hopes that however absolute the devotion of Alt-Rightists to white racial consciousness, it is in fact tempered by a residual respect for human rights or another principle that sometimes gives them pause. Or perhaps the unpersuasive claim is that even without the limitations set by human rights, the white race will, once guaranteed a supermajority, out of prudential and cost-benefit considerations, not press its advantage against the powerless minority. But if those considerations change, and the majority race imagines itself presented with an opportunity for "total victory," what then?

If we conclude that white race consciousness as expressed by the Alt-Right is pernicious, we must address Enoch's concern that no other group is asked, "Where does it end?" That is, generally there is no objection to apparent expressions of race consciousness among blacks, for example. Is "Say it loud / I'm black and I'm proud" as objectionable as the "white consciousness" posters distributed by *American Renaissance* that feature images such as Thomas Jefferson exhorting viewers to "Embrace White Identity Today!"? According to Jared Taylor these posters merely "encourage whites to be proud of their heritage and to stand up for themselves, which is exactly what America promotes for every other racial group."[14] The claim is that white racial consciousness is no worse than any other form of race consciousness or, presumably, ethnic or gender consciousness. To respond, as some thinkers do, that all expressions of group consciousness—white identity, black identity, Latino identity, feminist identity—are anathema is logically consistent but unrealistic in America today. Thus an effective response to race consciousness as the Alt-Right understands it requires an account of how race, ethnic, gender, and other differences can find some form of expression without surrendering to the dismal conclusion that politics is no more than endless, unrestrained strife among irreconcilable identity groups.

Why not say instead that in a diverse society, the various races, ethnicities, and so on will be considered as different interest groups, with each one jockeying for position within a liberal democratic framework and accommodations being reached through ongoing pluralistic bargaining? This idea is hardly original; it was developed in detail by Nathan Glazer and Daniel P. Moynihan in their seminal account of ethnicity in America, *Beyond the Melting Pot*, first published in 1963. Those authors rejected the idea that national unity required melting down America's diverse population into a "homogenous end product" of generic Americans. Glazer and Moynihan instead argued that American society could live with ethnic diversity and indeed that "the ethnic pattern was American, more American than the assimilationist."[15] This could be accomplished, the authors posited, if America's many diverse groups were thought of as ethnic groups, and ethnic groups were thought of as a type of interest group. This approach involved conceptualizing blacks as not a racial group but rather an ethnic group. That is, Glazer and Moynihan legitimated *ethnic* identity but not *racial* identity. They argued black identity could be accepted if it were thought of as an ethnic identity rather than a racial identity. On the other hand, white identity, Glazer and Moynihan correctly stressed, was to be rejected as it was simply a cover for rejection of blacks.[16]

Unfortunately, Glazer and Moynihan made a bad slip that obscured their important insights. The insistence that blacks were not a racial group at all but an ethnic group provoked misunderstanding and legitimate anger. The implication seemed to be that the situation of blacks was really no different in kind from that of ethnic groups such as the Irish and Italians whose incorporation into American society was relatively painless. For good reason, blacks objected to the apparent suggestion that their lot was essentially the same as that of white ethnic groups.

Glazer and Moynihan's point can be salvaged, however, if it is recognized that any sense of group awareness—whether we are speaking of ethnic, racial, gender, or whatever type of group—can be accommodated within democratic politics if the group, however distinctive it may be, is thought of as an interest group. Doing so by no means requires arguing that blacks are "really" not a race at all but rather an ethnicity. Of course, blacks are a race, and as such they may function as an interest group as unproblematically as do women, manufacturers, gays, conservatives, Latinos, Catholics, etc. This is not to deny that interest-group pluralism has its problems, but that is a matter for another day.

Here we have an answer to the frequent complaint of the Alt-Right that white racial consciousness alone is held to be illegitimate but racial consciousness for blacks and everyone else is accepted. In fact, the form of group consciousness that American society can tolerate and sometimes even celebrate is *interest* group consciousness, not *identity* group consciousness. Interest group consciousness conceives of race, ethnicity, gender, class, religion, economic position, and other characteristics as potentially *contributing to* one's political orientation. It sees a particular group as one legitimate interest among others, all seeking to advance themselves within the context of a democratic polity, and it appreciates that other considerations besides group interest are legitimate guides to political action. Identity group consciousness sees race or some other trait as *overwhelmingly determinative* of political orientation. It regards other groups as threats to be overcome or at best neutralized in a no-holds-barred, zero-sum struggle for dominance, and it holds that group identity decisively trumps all other political and moral considerations.

Interest group awareness includes garden-variety forms of black, Latino, and feminist pride, although more problematic versions can be found. Even the Black Lives Matter movement, so often castigated by the Alt-Right as antiwhite, takes care to express its orientation in interest group rather than identity group terms. The movement's website asserts, "We are unapologetically Black. . . . To love and desire freedom and justice for ourselves is a necessary prerequisite for wanting the same for others" and so presents itself as one of a plurality of legitimate interests.[17]

Identity group awareness is exemplified by Alt-Right white consciousness and cannot be squared with liberal democratic politics. Historically, ideologies of white racial consciousness have never expressed themselves as bland interest-group politics but have always been radically corrosive forms of identity politics deployed in defense of slavery, disunion, segregation, and now the Alt-Right's political agenda.

Race Realism

Alt-Rightists often describe themselves as race realists, which they sometimes claim amounts to no more than the acknowledgment that "race is real" and important. Thus Mike Enoch states that one of the major "red pills" of the Alt-Right is "race realism, the reality of racial differences and the importance of racial differences."[18] *American Renaissance*, in explaining "what we believe," offers a similarly bland definition of race realism: "Race is an important aspect of individual and group identity. . . . Attempts to gloss over the significance of race or even to deny its reality only make problems worse. Progress requires the study of all aspects of race, whether historical, cultural, or biological. This approach is known as race realism."[19]

Critics of the Alt-Right then sometimes respond that race is an "illusion."[20] But thus framed, the debate is unilluminating. Obviously, race is real in some sense and important in human affairs. Santa Claus and the atom bomb are both real and important, but in very different ways: one is a toy-industry marketing device based on a folkloric character and the other is a geostrategic weapon that threatens human survival. The point at issue is *in what sense* is race real?

The Alt-Right makes two claims about the reality of race that supposedly are based on the latest scientific findings of genetics, biology, and other disciplines. The first is that race can be defined in terms of objective biological and genetic characteristics and that an individual's race can usually be determined based on those characteristics. Thus Jared Taylor writes, "Race is a biological fact."[21] Alex Kurtagic denies "the liberal/ Left's assertion that race has no biological basis, when the senses tell us otherwise and there is even race-specific medicine."[22] John Derbyshire tells us, "I'm a race realist. . . . I don't doubt that race is a real and important thing; more than that, it's fundamental to biology."[23] A contributor to Greg Johnson's *Counter-Currents Publishing* writes of "the biologically-distinct white race."[24] And Hunter Wallace of *Occidental Dissent* said in an interview that "there are the same evolved, inheritable differences between the races of mankind . . . there are genetic variations between men and women. . . . What we think of race today is clusters of people who are genetically related."[25]

The second supposedly scientific premise that the Alt-Right argues from is that an individual's genetic race is correlated with other genetic factors that partly influence his intelligence and temperament such that being black correlates with lower intelligence and greater impulsivity while being white or Asian correlates with higher intelligence and greater impulse control. Thus Jared Taylor writes, "Different races have different average IQs, and the evidence is overwhelming that these differences are, to a substantial degree, genetic."[26] And a contributor to *The Right Stuff* asserts "the root cause of why Blacks, relative to Whites, are criminal and poor . . . is genes related to traits like (but not limited to) intelligence and aggression."[27] Virtually all of the Alt-Right figures considered in this book claim that blacks on average are less intelligent and more aggressive than whites for largely genetic reasons.

But is it true that race is a biological fact and that the racial categories used by laypeople correspond to clusters of people who are genetically related? Or that genetic factors make blacks on average less intelligent and more impulsive than whites? What is relevant for the purposes of this book is the consensus of scientific opinion on these matters. Alt-Right racialists are trying to build an argument to refute political egalitarianism and delegitimate liberal democracy. The stakes are therefore tremendously high. In that highly consequential context, to come within a country lightyear of being politically actionable, the premises of the Alt-Right's argument would have to rest on an adamantine scientific consensus. Citing the same handful of thinkers over and over, as the movement does, will not suffice, even if all of them were eminent authorities, which they are not. The burden of proof Alt-Right outlets demand concerning the scientific consensus on another highly consequential issue, climate change, is extremely high. Steve Sailer, a long-time regular contributor to *VDARE*, has written: "I normally don't have much to say about climate change. I'm sort of an agnostic."[28] And an article from 2017 in *American Renaissance* advises us that "while much of our contemporary Western science is increasingly suspect—with political concerns such as anti-racism inhibiting inquiry in the social sciences—it is reasonable to be skeptic of the Left's primary scientific cause célèbre: climate change."[29] Thus on this vital issue the Alt-Right counsels us that a consensus shared by "97 percent or more of actively publishing climate scientists" deserves no more than agnosticism and skepticism.[30] Is there, then, on so-called race realism, the virtually unanimous scientific agreement the Alt-Right elsewhere demands?

The Oxford Handbook of Philosophy and Race provides authoritative summations of expert opinion on a wide range of issues including the science of race. The editor of that volume summarizes the conclusion of human geneticists, evolutionary biologists, epidemiologists, and population scientists, and other specialists as follows:

> The consensus about human physical reality is that the idea of human races is neither supported by reliable data concerning human differences, nor does it add any meaningful information to such data. And so the answer to the . . . question, *Does race have a foundation in human biology?* is No.[31]

The chapter in the handbook titled "Biological Anthropology, Population Genetics, and Race" also acknowledges that consensus:

> In the past, considerable attention has been given to the question of whether human races exist in a biological sense. Our current understanding of human genetic variation is at odds with traditional views of race. The past use of race as a unit of evolutionary change has been rejected. . . . The real question is whether anything is gained by applying the biological race concept to the analysis of human biological variation and evolution. . . . The fine detail of our species' evolutionary history and its impact on patterns of genetic variation are lost when trying to categorize and classify into races.[32]

As for the genetic explanation of black-white intelligence differentials, the most comprehensive overview of the relevant scientific knowledge remains *Intelligence: Knowns and Unknowns*, the 1996 report of a task force established by the Board of Scientific Affairs of the American Psychological Association. The task force was established in the wake of the controversy occasioned by the 1994 publication of *The Bell Curve*, the hotly contested analysis of intelligence and class in American society by Charles Murray and the late Richard J. Herrnstein. The task force was charged with producing an "authoritative report on these issues—one that all sides could use as a basis for discussion," and the final report received the unanimous support of that body.[33]

The APA report notes that African American IQ scores for a long time had averaged about fifteen points below the scores of whites. As for the cause of the differential, the report notes that "environmental factors can produce differences of at least this magnitude," and then sums up:

> The cause of that differential is not known . . . it is apparently not due to any simple form of bias in the content or administration of the tests themselves. . . . Several culturally-based explanations of the Black/White IQ differential have been proposed; some are plausible, but so far none has been conclusively supported. There is even less empirical support for a genetic interpretation. In short, no adequate explanation of the differential between the IQ means of Blacks and Whites is presently available.[34]

Intelligence: Knowns and Unknowns says little about political issues except with respect to the central point: "The commitment to evaluate people on their own individual merit is central to a democratic society."[35]

In short, it is entirely false to say "the evidence is overwhelming" for the Alt-Right's supposedly scientific claims about race. In fact, the great majority of professional scientists in relevant fields find the evidence decidedly underwhelming at most. That generalization, like all others, needs some qualification. There is serious discussion among real experts on how to interpret specific findings about genetics and race and intelligence. Let such debate continue. But the scientific consensus is negative on the biological nature of race and skeptical on genetic explanations of racial IQ differentials. The scientific consensus on these matters may be wrong, but it is very firm and based on vastly more real evidence than the Alt-Right can muster. And no professional scientists are willing to join the movement in its leap of nihilism from speculation to political inegalitarianism.

Robert Nozick's sprawling tome *Philosophical Explanations* contains an observation about racism that strikingly applies to the Alt-Right's race realism:

> A racist is not simply someone who believes there are or may be racial differences along dimensions of value—whether or not there are is an empirical question. A racist, I am inclined to say, is someone who wants there to be racial differences along dimensions of value and who wants these differences to go in a certain direction. . . . To avoid falling into wanting there to be such racial differences . . . we might avoid reaching a conclusion or (especially) a stand on the issue.[36]

So-called race realism perfectly exemplifies Nozick's definition of racism. Alt-Rightists go well beyond reluctantly concluding, on strictly empirical grounds, that average differences between the races in important traits likely have a biological component. Alt-Right thinkers evince a passionate desire, a will to believe, that such a component not only exists but is overwhelming and fatal to political equality. They ignore the fact that the vast majority of qualified researchers believe no such thing and they cite repeatedly the handful of marginal figures committed to racial inegalitarianism. Far from avoiding hasty conclusions, in their outlets they sedulously reinforce their racialist worldview with a steady stream of filtered information and disinformation. Far from race realism, the Alt-Right espouses race irrealism in a discourse bubble designed to spare its denizens from serious consideration of the pressing challenges faced by diverse democratic polities.

But the most important point to make about possible racial differences in genetics or traits or any "dimension of value" is that such differences, even if definitively established (which, as has been shown, they are not) are utterly irrelevant to the case for the political equality of all people. The moral and political demand that all people are politically equal is based on centuries of experience demonstrating that on balance, the social consequences of political egalitarianism are much better than those of political inequality. If it should turn out that the current firm scientific consensus against the biological nature of race and the genetic roots of racial differences requires modification in light of further research, fine. David Reich of Harvard University has suggested that this consensus has hardened into an orthodoxy that may be challenged by scientific progress. But he also writes: "An abiding challenge for our civilization is to treat each human being as an individual and to empower all people, regardless of what hand they are dealt from the deck of life."[37] That is the truly essential point.

White Supremacy

Some Alt-Rightists jump straight from their poorly supported race realism to the claim that blacks are simply inferior to whites. Thus one contributor to *Counter-Currents Publishing* writes it "is obvious to race realists . . . mestizos and negroes aren't very bright, and they tend to be incompetent at whatever they try to do. . . . The reality is that black lives don't really matter that much. It is the white race that is the indispensable race."[38] And in *The Right Stuff* a writer who goes by the name of Charles the Hammer denies that "even if people aren't equal in capacity, they're still morally equal":

> Once someone can get past the lie that all people have equal capacity for achievement and that putting loads of different ethnic groups in one spot is a good thing, the next big hurdle [to accepting Alt-Right ideology] is coming to grips with the fact that some people are just shitty people. . . . I've more or less come to grips with the fact that a mixed society with anything above 3rd world standards is not possible. Blacks, Latinos, etc. simply are not capable, as groups, of participation in high-trust, highly civilized societies that Europeans have created. No amount of "education" or dem[ocratic] programs can change this.[39]

These writers, as Leninists used to say, simply "blurt out" their real opinion: the races aren't equal in capacities, therefore neither are they morally equal, therefore some people—nonwhite people—"are just shitty people," "don't really matter that much," and are inferior human beings.

But most Alt-Rightists respond that to posit a genetic explanation of average differences between racial groups in significant psychological traits is not, in and of itself, racist. Their argument is something like this: acceptance of the reality of average differences in physical strength between the sexes, and the acknowledgment that those differences are in part based in genetics, is not misogyny, the belief that women are in some overall sense inferior to men. The claim of these more sophisticated Alt-Right apologists is that women are, on average, physically less strong than men, not that men are *better than* women and ought to enjoy a superior *political* status over women. Similarly, Alt-Rightists say their claim is merely that whites are on average more intelligent than blacks, not that whites are superior in some overall sense and not that blacks should be politically inferior to whites.

This line of defense is developed by Spencer and a co-author in an article published in *Radix Journal*, which deserves to be quoted at some length:

> The reluctance to discuss—or even to admit to—the existence of racial differences is commonly motivated by fear of possible invidious distinctions between "superior" and "inferior" races.
>
> But claims of superiority beg many questions. First, racial differences must relate to some particular trait. West Africans may, indeed, be a "superior" race *when it comes to sprinting.* In reference to other traits, other races may be more gifted. No race is best in everything, and it is meaningless to speak of any race being superior *per se.* Moreover, there is no unequivocal reason to hold that longer legs or lighter skin are more desirable than their opposites. It all depends on context. Ultimately, there is no unequivocal reason to think that the recognition of racial differences in particular traits implies any overall "superiority."
>
> Second, the existence of racial differences does not logically imply that one race should rule over others or benefit at their expense. No one has ever claimed that the superiority of West Africans at sprinting entitles them to preferential treatment over Whites and Asians. The same goes for all other races and all other traits. This may sound like an elementary point, but much opposition to the open discussion of racial differences is based upon a tacit assumption that recognizing such differences would *ipso facto* justify the mistreatment of one or more races. But this is simply a fallacy.[40]

In an interview with me, Jared Taylor similarly defended himself against the charge of believing that blacks are inferior to whites. Here are relevant portions of that interview:

JT: I think it is an unfair and loaded term to say that white people are better or black people are better. I think that's an unfair and . . . an emotionally charged way of describing something that should be couched in more precise terms.[41]

Here Taylor does not deny that white people are better; he says only that speaking in such terms is "an unfair and . . . emotionally charged way of describing something that should be couched in more precise terms." Shortly this matter will be addressed here with suitable precision. But Taylor continued:

JT: Ultimately, it's very important that you should realize what I and I believe everyone in the Alt-Right wants for white people. We are perfectly happy to grant to every other group on earth, nobody is trying to deprive anybody else of their rights, nobody is trying to deprive anybody else of their culture. I wish all other groups well. I can like and admire many foreign societies. As you probably know I lived the first 16 years of my life in Japan. I want Japan to stay Japanese. If Japan ceased to be Japanese, which it would cease to be if it filled up with Brazilians, and Algerians and Tahitians and Haitians, that would be terrible, [a] terrible tragedy. All I'm saying is that we as whites have the right to pursue our destiny as white people, unencumbered by the embrace of people unlike ourselves. It's a matter of survival. It's a matter of pure reciprocity. And it is completely wrong and unfair to think us and only us as somehow bigoted and close-minded because we are earnest about the survival of our people and our culture. . . . Quote that verbatim and you can say anything else about me.[42]

In this summation of his position, while Taylor claims not to want to deny any group its rights, he fails to specifically acknowledge blacks as political equals.

The question, then, is this: Some Alt-Rightists perfunctorily acknowledge that a claimed difference in intelligence between blacks and whites "does not *logically imply* that one race should rule over others" (my emphasis). But the issue here is not one of logical implication. It is rather whether Alt-Rightists do *in fact* go on to argue that whites should politically dominate blacks because of alleged, genetically based differences. In the next section I show that Alt-Rightists do indeed go on to argue that these putative differences in intelligence and other traits make whites better at building decent societies than blacks; that white-dominated societies are necessarily better overall than nonwhite societies; and that for these reasons, whites *ought to be politically superior to or dominate over blacks.*

The Political and Moral Inequality of the Races: The Alt-Right's Record

Michael Levin developed his moral case for white political dominance in his 1997 book, *Why Race Matters*, which was discussed in detail in chapter 3. Levin's book is relevant here because of its influence on Alt-Right thinkers. Thus in 2005 the New Century Foundation, founded by Taylor, obtained the copyright to this book and republished it with a preface in which Taylor expressed admiration for the work. *Why Race Matters* is still available for purchase through the *American Renaissance* website, which describes it as a "masterpiece" and a "classic."

In *American Renaissance*, Taylor wrote a glowing review of *Why Race Matters* when it was first published. In his review, Taylor gets to the political bottom line of Levin's analysis: "Interestingly, Prof. Levin's exhaustive study of racial differences leads to policies strikingly similar to those of the pre–civil rights era American South. It may be no coincidence that the latest scientific findings support the traditions of whites who lived, for generations, in the most intimate contact with blacks."[43]

Thus Taylor's claim, based on Levin's work, is that the latest scientific findings on racial differences "lead to policies strikingly similar to those of the pre–civil rights era American South"—which were disenfranchisement, segregation, and Jim Crow. In other words, Taylor is doing here exactly what he says he will not do. He goes beyond claiming that the races *differ*, on average, with respect to some important trait, to asserting that because of such differences one race must be politically superior to the other, as whites were to blacks in the Old South. So Taylor's acknowledgment that "we are equal in the sense that all men do have the right to life, liberty and the pursuit of happiness" is meant so abstractly as to be compatible not only with segregation but with Levin's explicit "race conscious measures by the state in the exercise of its police power,"[44] which Taylor illuminatingly describes as the acknowledgment that different punishments may be appropriate for different races. For blacks it should perhaps be swifter and include corporal punishment, especially for men who treat a jail term as a badge of honor and a rite of passage. It might also be sensible to try some black juveniles as adults, since blacks mature more rapidly than whites. Finally, since blacks have frequently shown themselves unable to transcend racial loyalty, they might be excluded from juries in trials that could inflame racial passion.[45]

In other words, Taylor claims he does not think whites should be superior to blacks, but he does think that corporal punishment for black criminals and lighter punishment for similar white criminals may well be justified in light of what he imagines are the latest scientific findings on race. It suffices to say that if members of one race, when they are convicted of a crime, receive a light punishment, such as a fine or imprisonment, while similar members of another race receive a harsher punishment, such as fifty strokes with a cat-o'-nine-tails well laid on, the first race is politically superior to the second. Passages such as this—and there are many of them—dramatically undermine Taylor's impassioned insistence he is not a white supremacist.

In *American Renaissance* over the years Taylor has repeated support for white political domination over blacks. In 1991 he wrote an article titled "The Racial Revolution," in which he argued:

The best way to gauge the extent of the revolution is to compare the present to the past. The contrast is staggering. Practically every historical American figure was by today's standards an unregenerate white supremacist.

Until just a few years ago virtually all Americans believed that race was a profoundly important aspect of individual and national identity. They believed that people of different races differed in temperament and ability, and that whites built societies that were *superior* to those built by non-whites. They were repelled by miscegenation—which they called "amalgamation"—because it would dilute the unique characteristics of whites. They took it for granted that America must be peopled with Europeans, and that American civilization could not continue without whites. Many saw the presence of non-whites in the United States as a terrible burden.[46]

It must be understood that Taylor is here *lamenting* the "racial revolution" that has undermined "white supremacist" standards in modern America. He concludes his essay by remarking, "However, revolutions that violate the laws of human nature eventually founder. Someday ours will collapse, as biology reasserts itself over sociology, and white racial consciousness reawakens."[47]

So Taylor endorses the reawakening of "white racial consciousness" and its belief that "whites built societies that were superior to those built by non-whites," and its vision of "non-whites in the United States as a terrible burden." All this goes beyond merely claiming that black societies reflect black intellectual endowments as Taylor judges them. It is a value judgment in favor of white supremacy and against the "terrible burden" of nonwhites in the United States.

In a 2005 *American Renaissance* article on the disorders in New Orleans in the aftermath of Hurricane Katrina, Taylor concluded, "To be sure, the story of Hurricane Katrina does have a moral for anyone not deliberately blind. The races are different. Blacks and whites are different. When blacks are left entirely to their own devices, Western Civilization—any kind of civilization—disappears."[48]

The assertion that blacks and whites are different in important ways is debatable but not in itself necessarily objectionable. The same could be said of a claim that blacks on their own build civilizations *different from* Western civilization. Taylor has claimed that his race realism holds only that blacks build societies different from Western societies: "People of different races build different societies. Blacks—wherever they are found in large numbers—establish communities with certain characteristics, and whites and others do the same."[49]

But that is not what Taylor wrote in his article on post-Katrina New Orleans. He wrote that when blacks are left on their own, not merely Western civilization but "*any* kind of civilization—disappears" (emphasis added). The word "civilization" clearly expresses a value judgment in favor of that situation as opposed to a lack of civilization. So the moral of this article by Taylor is not just that the races differ but that blacks are inferior to whites in terms of the vital trait of capacity for civilization.

In 2013, *American Renaissance* published a review by Taylor, titled "The Long Retreat on Race," of a biography of James Jackson Kilpatrick Jr. Taylor accurately describes Kilpatrick as "a hugely popular conservative commentator of the latter part of the 20th century. . . . Before that, however, he was one of the country's best known segregationists." Sometime between the late 1950s and the early 1980s Kilpatrick went from being a staunch defender of Jim Crow to a more mainstream conservative who embraced *Brown* and rejected racism. The questions Taylor wants to answer in his analysis of Kilpatrick's development are, "How did he make the switch? Did he change his views? Sacrifice his principles?" To illustrate those principles, Taylor quotes without comment from an article that Kilpatrick sent to the *Saturday Evening Post* in 1963:

> The Negro race, as a race, is in fact an inferior race. . . . Within the frame of reference of a Negroid civilization, a mud hut may be a masterpiece. . . . But the mud hut ought not to be equated with Monticello. . . . Where is the Negro to be found? . . . He is lying limp in the middle of the sidewalk yelling he is equal. The hell he is equal.[50]

Here's what Taylor has to say of Kilpatrick's transformation from segregationist to *Brown* supporter: "What are those of us who prefer the early James Kilpatrick to make of his career? . . . If Kilpatrick really did change, then God rest his erring soul. If he trimmed all the way to the grave, he forsook his obligations to the truth and to his people."[51]

Taylor is writing here that he is one of those who "prefer the early James Kilpatrick," who wrote "the Negro race, as a race, is in fact an inferior race," to the later Kilpatrick, who rejected racism. And if Taylor really objects to the idea that blacks are an inferior race, why not say so when he quotes Kilpatrick's noxious words? What is all this but an endorsement of the idea that blacks are "in fact an inferior race"?

Taylor returned to the claim that nonwhites are inferior to whites in terms of their capacities for civilization and to build good societies in 2015 when he contributed to his website an "Open Letter to Cuckservatives." "Cuckservative" is a vulgar and derogatory term that Alt-Rightists, including Taylor, throw at traditional conservatives. The slur derives from "cuckold" and suggests that traditional conservatives are sexually inadequate. Taylor writes:

> You tell yourself that the things you love about America—and I love them, too—are rooted in certain principles. *That is your greatest mistake.* They

are rooted in certain people. That is why Germans, Swedes, Irishmen, and Hungarians could come and contribute to the America you love. Do you really believe that a future Afro-Hispanic-Caribbean-Asiatic America will be anything like the America your ancestors built? . . . Even when they violate your principles, white people build good societies. Even when they abide by your principles, non-whites usually don't.[52]

Here again Taylor is undermining his claim that race realism is merely the belief that the races are different. He says clearly that white people build, not merely different societies, but *"good* societies . . . nonwhites usually don't" (emphasis added). So Taylor is making a value judgment against nonwhites. Note that he claims this ability to build good societies is dependent specifically on *race* and not attributable to principles; so, he theorizes, whites have that ability and nonwhites usually don't. Under his theory it therefore follows that blacks cannot make up for this deficit even if they adopt good principles because race is determinative; what you believe or think counts for nothing. The upshot of what Taylor writes here is that whites are superior to blacks, for racial reasons, in the essential ability to build good societies.

What has happened here is that while very superficially giving the appearance of accepting Hayek's and Popper's distinction between factual equality and political equality and their insistence that alleged factual inequality must not trump political equality, the Alt-Right as represented by Taylor and others who take up arguments along these lines in fact rejects such qualified Jeffersonianism completely. It is not that the presumption in favor of political equality is so well grounded that factual differences should be politically irrelevant. Rather, the case for crucial factual differences between the races is held to be so absolutely overwhelming that the liberal democratic tradition of America, from the Declaration of Independence through the civil rights era, is to be tossed out and replaced with a neosegregationism more explicitly based on racial inegalitarianism than the prescientific variety enforced in the Old South.

Taylor's occasional professions of good will toward nonwhites must be acknowledged. And his repeated claims of genetically based racial difference, however dubious, do not in strictest logic imply racism. But the above review of his contributions to *American Renaissance* shows that he has repeatedly expressed the idea that blacks are morally inferior and should be politically inferior to whites. The same could be said of most contributors to Alt-Right platforms.

I gave much thought to whether the Alt-Right should be considered white supremacist. Peter Brimelow regards the term as a "stale smear" and for Jared Taylor it is "the most morally-loaded expression of contempt for a white person in the English language . . . the equivalent of calling blacks ni**ers."[53] If the term were an acknowledged expletive and had no specific meaning I would not use it. But while the online *Oxford English Dictionary* recognizes the racial insult Taylor references as "contemptuous" and "offensive," it says nothing similar about "white supremacist," which it defines as "an advocate or supporter of the doctrine that white people are superior to other peoples, and should therefore have greater power, authority, or status."[54] In that exact sense the Alt-Right is aptly termed white supremacist. Moreover, the coarseness and hyperbole of that movement's rhetoric, so amply documented in this book, although they should not be returned in kind, do not encourage an observer to mince words.

Why Political Egalitarianism Does Not Depend on Factual Equality of Abilities

The entire analysis of Alt-Right racialism presented here has argued, as thinkers in the liberal democratic tradition have since Locke, that people can be equal in terms of the rights they hold even if they are unequal in terms of important traits such as intelligence, temperament, strength, or virtues of whatever kind. But, one might ask, why shouldn't people who are superior in these factual traits be granted superior political status? And further, why shouldn't we discriminate against entire races on the basis of average traits if we imagine doing so will achieve desirable social outcomes?

Let us begin by looking at this issue on the level of individuals. Obviously, if a polity announces that superiority in terms of certain traits will translate into superiority in political status, it will trigger enormous conflict. Which traits will be relevant, how superiority in those terms will be established, who will make that determination, and what political advantages will be doled out, based on what determinations, will become the central issues of political life, and dispute over them will be intense. But eventually, perhaps after rivers of blood have been spilled, another obvious point will become clear. If it is really true that superior intelligence, say, is a tremendous natural advantage, makes one a better citizen, and brings with it social influence, why bother to make an *official* determination of who is more intelligent than whom? If the intelligent will naturally rise to the top and dominate society, why not simply let that happen and skip the expense, conflict, corrupting influence, and opportunity for mistakes involved with an official determination process? In other words, why not recognize that political equality is entirely compatible with factual inequality[55] and need not undermine whatever claims to power superior merit may have? The American founders understood this point. Jefferson rightly saw no contradiction in maintaining that all men are created equal and calling for an educational system in Virginia that would identify and cultivate a natural aristocracy of gifted students.

Again, the above case for political egalitarianism among individuals is obvious. Is the case for political egalitarianism among groups, whatever average differences there may be in important traits between those groups, any less obvious? If two individuals, one more intelligent than the other, both have the same rights, stand equal before the law, cast one vote, and so forth, why should things be any different for two groups of individuals, one on average more intelligent than the other? Here it is assumed for the sake of the argument that this average difference is real and has, all things being equal, a significant impact on important life outcomes for members of these groups. Why cannot it be said that these two groups, by hypothesis factually unequal, are nonetheless created equal in the sense meant by the Declaration, that is, are politically equal?

Again, as we have seen, some, but by no means all, Alt-Rightists occasionally claim to acknowledge the political equality of all groups. But we have also seen their claims are perfunctory, inconsistent, vague, and unconvincing. Alt-Rightists who disdain these evasions, such as Spencer, Enoch, Anglin, and their intellectual forefather, Mike Levin, raise a point that requires a response. The most radical Alt-Rightists are arguing—when they are engaging in real argument—that certain social benefits can be achieved if average group differences in important traits are taken into account. Here is an example of such an argument from a *VDARE* contributor:

Recognizing that blacks are more violent than whites . . . is not "racism." It is accepting reality.

Segregation may well be unjust in some cases. Yet if reasonable authorities conclude, having looked at the data on crime and inter-racial
violence, that blacks and whites live better apart, segregation may well
be necessary. That is not tantamount to hating blacks because of their
disabilities, or suggesting the law should deny them a living, or worse,
exterminate them, which would indeed be a terrible sin. Race-realism is
not "racism."[56]

This passage is extraordinary for several reasons. First of all, it shows
that race realism is not simply the claim that race has an important biological element; race realism becomes a justification for segregation, that
is, for the denial of political equality. Second, it justifies segregation based
on the average difference in crime rates between blacks and whites. On
average, under this *VDARE* contributor's reasoning, blacks commit more
crimes than whites, and therefore all blacks—the criminal and the innocent alike—must be denied the right to live, work, and associate—that
is, to pursue their happiness—as they please. Third, the imagined good
of this illiberalism is a vague social benefit: blacks and whites will "live
better" in some unspecified way under segregation. The likelihood that
blacks will feel they are not living better under this arrangement compared to whites is not considered. That is, the insight obtained after many
traumatic decades of segregation—that separate is inherently unequal—is
here discarded. Fourth, this return to Jim Crow is to be undertaken
merely because "reasonable authorities conclude" it should be so. But who
are these authorities? And how could they conclude, merely by looking
at some data, that the dearly bought achievements of desegregation shall
be entirely scrapped? Finally, we are asked to believe that none of this
amounts to racism: these reasonable authorities do not hate blacks; they
merely judge them unfit to live with because they are "more violent," on
average, than whites. And since no one wants to "exterminate them," no
great harm is done, according to *VDARE*'s writer.

Let us put aside, so far as is possible, the blatant unconstitutionality,
atavism, and outrageousness of this argument and use it as an opportunity
to ask why racial, ethnic, or any other kind of groups should not be denied
equal political status if it seems that some social benefit can be achieved
by so doing. The simple answer is that judging by group averages is unnecessary because institutions already exist for judging people as indi-

viduals. America's independent and professional criminal justice system, which certainly is in need of much improvement, has been built and is maintained at great cost. If, therefore, crime rates are high, let convicted criminals, of whatever race, be segregated from society by being placed in prisons. This is not a segregation of all blacks, including the innocent, in official ghettos. Why be especially concerned over interracial violence when the police exist to foil violence of every sort, whether inter- or intraracial, or whatever? (Of course, responses other than incarceration or policing are appropriate too, as long as they are nondiscriminatory and effective.)

Perhaps it will be claimed that judging people on the basis of race is legitimate only when there is no practical alternative, but the fact of the matter is there almost always are alternatives. Perhaps one can think up mental experiments in which minor advantages can be gained from various marginal practices (such as subject profiling) by taking race into account. But such benefits are entirely negated by the political cost of implementing these divisive tactics. Our finite resources will be infinitely better rewarded if we help our mainstream institutions, such as the courts, the market, and the democratic political system, make better judgments about individuals.

Moreover, judging people based on group averages rather than as individuals creates massive perverse incentives. If all members of some group—the violent and nonviolent, the innocent and guilty—are segregated or discriminated against, what incentive do the well-behaved group members have to keep up their good work? Unequal status turns such righteous people into chumps; they may as well embrace a life of crime since they get no credit for good behavior anyway. The group in question, which by hypothesis is on average more problematic than the rest of the population, now has an incentive to go over to the dark side 100 percent, which will benefit no one. Political inegalitarianism therefore harms not only those discriminated against but also those doing the discrimination, who end up with a worse problem on their hands than they have when all groups are considered equal.

To put the Alt-Right's racialism in perspective, consider how dramatic average group differences in important personal traits would have to be before anyone would seriously consider judging group members on the basis of those average differences rather than as individuals. The example of a prominent minority group is illuminating. Data clearly show this minority is dramatically more prone to violence and criminal behavior and more likely to be incarcerated and sexually predatory than the general population. Moreover, the case that all this misbehavior is rooted to some degree in genetic factors seems quite strong, with obvious biological differences setting members of this minority off from the rest of the population. The precise genetic differences distinguishing members of the minority and majority groups are a matter of settled science. Perhaps tellingly, professional sports are dominated by this minority. And yet this troublesome group enjoys full political equality with the rest of humanity. For example, it has never been suggested that the notorious habits of these folk have undermined their right to a presumption of innocence, or that in their criminal trials a lower standard of proof for them would be appropriate.

The minority group described here is men, who, according to the 2010 census, accounted for 49.2 percent of the U.S. population.[57] Despite its infamous record, the male sex enjoys full political equality with women, and yet life goes on and liberal democracy endures. If the rights to life, liberty, and the pursuit of happiness can be successfully extended to men, then a fortiori, political egalitarianism can function in a multiracial and multiethnic society. At least that seems to be a safe bet, one based on centuries of historical experience, and much safer than scrapping American foundational principles in favor of the Alt-Right's jumble of untried, antidemocratic nostrums.

Conclusion

This overview of Alt-Right racialism comes to the same conclusions that the review of the movement's illiberalism did in chapter 6. The Alt-Right's racialism is extremely radical and goes far beyond merely politically incorrect opinions about the nature of race, the abilities of minority groups, or the desirability of progressive welfare state programs. The movement is at odds not just with contemporary civil rights policy but with foundational principles of liberal democracy, especially political egalitarianism. Alt-Right rhetoric on the delicate matter of race is not merely outspoken, blunt, or insensitive. Despite some occasional and vague professions of good will, the movement's discourse on race is generally unnecessarily harsh, deliberately transgressive, coarse, and, quite often, hateful. More-over, Alt-Right racialism displays the same poverty of thought and lack of reasonableness that the rest of its ideology does. Here again, the revolution in the production of public ideas that occurred in the early twenty-first century, when it at last gave the Alt-Right a platform it previously lacked, did not produce a happy result.

8
Anti-Americanism

A racialist political perspective that demonizes Lincoln, then sugar-coats the Old South, will not find much to approve in the United States of the twenty-first century. All Alt-Right thinkers express at least a profound alienation from or even revulsion toward the United States. Many, though not all, Alt-Rightists come to what might fairly be defined as anti-Americanism, a radical critique and intemperate dislike, on balance, of present-day, actually existing America: its society, culture, government institutions, history, and multiracial, multiethnic population.

Intemperate Anti-Americanism

The Alt-Right's anti-Americanism takes various forms. Simple vituperation of contemporary America is quite common among Alt-Rightists. For example, Johnson's Cross-Currents Publishing has issued the book *Waking Up from the American Dream*, by Gregory Hood. Jared Taylor's endorsement of that book asserts, "In our movement, Gregory Hood is unquestionably the best writer of his generation," and Richard Spencer's says, "Gregory Hood is one of the most insightful and entertaining writers in the Alt-Right." Here is a passage from Hood's book:

Waking up from the American Dream means recognizing that American ideals have been tried, tested, and found wanting. . . . We are not "Americans," for how can one be [a] citizen of an abstraction? . . . We know this farce you call a country is a nightmare that just rolls on and on, and we want no part of it.[1]

Hunter Wallace, editor of *Occidental Dissent*, is also coarsely anti-American. He has written: "America has now evolved into its final form as a cultural and political dung heap of liberty and equality—just like every other republican experiment in the modern West."[2]

Other writers are more nuanced. In an interview with me Richard Spencer specifically identified himself as "anti-American," but adduced certain qualifications:

TM: I see you in particular and the Alt-Right in general on kind of a collision course with actually existing America.

RS: Yeah, I agree.

TM: Well, let me ask you this. So would it be accurate to describe your ideology as anti-American?

RS: Yes.

TM: Yes? What do you mean by anti-Americanism?

RS: I mean that we—the Alt Right—[are] a radical alternative to the political theology of the current year. Of 2016. . . . The Alt-Right is really an alternative to the theology of equality and universalism that is shot through American society. . . .

I think it is important to point out that the Alt-Right as I understand it and in terms of my hopes for it is a radical departure from the Americanism of the current day. And it's a radical departure, I think, [from] the enlightened liberalism of the age of the founders. So it really is something new. . . .

That being said, I'm also not like a[n] off-the-shelf anti-American in the sense that I hate everything about American history or that I hate American identity. I think there are actually some aspects, many aspects, of the American historical experience and the American identity that are quite admirable and heroic. . . . [The] notion of a strong man going out into a wilderness and taming it and surviving and confronting dangerous foreign races and living to tell the tale. . . .

But . . . in terms of what does America mean today? The Alt-Right in my eyes is a radical departure from that. It is an attempt for a new beginning.

Thus, for Spencer, there are aspects of the American historical experience that are admirable, but a radical break has to be made with the America of today, a stance that, he agrees, is accurately described as anti-Americanism.

America and "Anti-America"

Alt-Rightism often replaces patriotism with race consciousness, to the specific detriment of the United States. In his interview with me, Jared Taylor expressed a similar sentiment in the following exchange:

TM: Do you make a distinction between the real American nation, which is white, and then this thing that exists now, the United States of America, which is not really the historical nation at all but some kind of distortion of it?

JT: The American government is a huge enemy of the White majority.

TM: The American government? You're not talking about a particular president or party, you mean the government as a whole?

JT: The government and also the current ideology. The current ideology of equality, the notion that the races are completely equivalent—all of this serves to dispossess the White majority.

Often the Alt-Right's anti-Americanism involves sharply distinguishing between the sociopolitical entity known to the world as the "United States" and the "real" America. Then allegiance to the supposedly more real America is professed while the present United States is declared to be an alien entity or even the enemy. In an interview with me, Mike Enoch, editor of *The Right Stuff,* made this move of apparently pledging allegiance to America but then radically narrowing what he meant by America.

ME: I absolutely am not an anti-American. I'm a pro-American. I'm a patriot. [But] I've hated the United States government as long as I can remember.

TM: When I talk about America in terms of anti-Americanism, I mean the actually existing political entity known as the United States of America, with a specific set of rules and laws, a history, and a people. . . . I'm not talking about a particular administration. I'm not talking about a particular party. I'm not talking about a particular ideology.

If you ask some people, "Do you love your spouse?" And if the person says, "Yes, I love my spouse except I wish she hadn't put on that weight. And also I have this problem, and I have that problem, and if only my spouse were like this. . . . " Well, of course, nobody is perfect, and everybody could specify what they would like in an ideal partner. But if you push that line of argument far enough, one gets to the point where you have to say, "Hey, it looks you really don't love the actual spouse that you've got." So my question is—

ME: So you're saying, are we putting so many stipulations on what we want America to be that it's no longer the existing America? Therefore we're anti-American?

TM: That's the question, yes.

ME: I think that possibly [may] be a fair assessment, although I don't put it that way because I consider myself, I am pro-white American. And I think that fundamentally the American identity, when people think American they think white. They think of a white person. That's sort of the default thing that they think of. And so as long as that is the ethnic group that I identify with, that is the group that I support and whose rights I advocate for. So in that sense I'm pro-American. I am not pro the ideology of the United States government. I'm not pro even the apparatus of the United States government. So I think it's a tough question. I don't know.

TM: So let me understand this: when you say "pro-American," am I correct in understanding that you're pro-white American?

ME: Yes.

TM: In other words, blacks and Hispanics and Muslims are not part of the America that you're in favor of?

ME: Yeah, they've got their own identities.

TM: So they're not American at all?

ME: Certainly Muslims aren't, nor should they be, but blacks have a legitimate claim to an American identity. They're African Americans. . . . I don't think that it's fruitful for white and black Americans to continue to try to integrate. I think it causes too much conflict, and too many problems, and too much hatred. But certainly Muslims are absolutely excluded from American identity. They don't belong here.

TM: When I say I'm pro-American, and I do say that, I mean America in the sense I described it: actually existing. Now, however, the people at *VDARE* talk about the "historic American nation."

ME: The historical American people, yeah.

TM: And then they say, "I'm patriotic for the historic American nation." Well, again, this gets you to "I love my spouse, but." So if the historic American nation is what the nation used to be seventy-five years ago, and minus all of these features, then, you know, you may be pro the "historic American nation," but you're not pro-American in the sense that ordinary people think about America.

ME: Sure, why not? I mean, fine.

TM: Is that what you would say?

ME: I don't think it's a very important thing. I mean, sure, it's a semantic point, like I'm in favor of what I'm in favor of. Whatever. I just shrug at the whole question, like it's, you know.[3]

As came up in the above interview with Enoch, the strategy of splitting off a real America deserving of allegiance from the unworthy, actually existing country of today was pioneered by *VDARE*, which has long declared, "We are the voice of the Historic American Nation,"[4] in contrast to what it calls the "Anti-America."[5]

What exactly does *VDARE* mean by the "historic American nation"? It most emphatically does not mean the U.S. government. Peter Brimelow has specified that "the National Question isn't about the government of the United States—it's about the historic American nation, the real people that created America."[6]

So the "government of the United States" isn't part of the historic American nation. But who are "the real people that created America"? This question was put by one *VDARE* reader, who wrote: "I'd love to know what exactly Peter Brimelow means by expressions like 'Historic Nation of America' and 'generic Americans.' They sound like formulations which mean 'me and anybody else I like.'"[7]

On behalf of Brimelow, James Fulford, a regular *VDARE* contributor, explained:

As to who exactly that means, it might mean the "Old Stock" Americans, who were . . . already present in the US, meeting the boats that came in to Ellis Island in the 1890s, but we usually use it to mean "the Historic

American Nation as it had evolved up to 1960"—i.e. the "Old Stock" plus the Ellis Island contingent, who the Great Pause had encouraged to assimilate.

It would be easier to say who it doesn't mean—people like Filipino illegal immigrant Jose Antonio Vargas, the Arab taxi drivers who shut down JFK recently, people like that.[8]

So the historic American nation is the American population as it was about sixty years ago. People who can't trace their American roots further back than that are, along with the U.S. government, left out.

It might seem, then, that *VDARE*'s historic American nation at least includes African Americans, since they certainly have a heritage that traces back to before 1960. But perhaps not; Brimelow's usage of the term "historic American nation" often excludes blacks. In the following passage, for example, the terms "white" and "historic American nation" are used synonymously:

> In the US, the federal government is essentially abolishing the people and electing a new one. In 1965, the US was 90% white; it's now somewhere below 70% white—it's hard to determine exactly because the census is so poorly designed—and that's entirely because of public policy. The government is basically driving the Historic American Nation into a minority in the state it created. Whites will go into a minority in this country by 2040 or so.[9]

Elsewhere Brimelow is even more explicit in excluding blacks from the historic American nation. In an article with the illuminating title of "America, Anti-America, and the Role of VDARE.com," Brimelow commented on a newspaper headline that described the 2012 GOP presidential nominating convention as "an ocean of whiteness":

> Well, VDARE.com is here to point out a simple historical truth: in 1960, well within living memory, *these "whites" would have been have been called Americans*. At that time, the country was nine-tenths white. And essentially all the rest was black—not historically part of the political nation, but by 1960, being slowly and painfully assimilated.
>
> That "ocean of whiteness" IS America.

Looked at a picture of the Founding Fathers recently? . . .

"Whites" = Americans, of course.[10]

In short, the historic American nation is a nation of whites only. But what of blacks, post-1960 immigrants, the U.S. government, and everyone else? It turns out they belong to what Brimelow calls "Anti-America":

In contrast, the Democrats represent the nation of Anti-America.

That doesn't mean they are opposed to America . . . [ellipsis in the original] exactly. . . .

Anti-America is like antimatter. . . . To put it another way, Anti-America is America Through The Looking Glass. It's Bizarro World America. . . .

Simple arithmetic suggests that the Democratic Party will soon be able to assemble a majority out of Anti-America, and will need only a decreasingly small share of the *white (a.k.a. American)* vote.[11]

VDARE is not the only Alt-Right outlet to proffer loyalty only to an imaginary all-white America and to scorn the America that exists today. Greg Johnson heads in this direction when he writes:

There now exists a very real and very serious split between conservatives who remain firmly emotionally, spiritually and intellectually attached to the United States and those whose attachment has transferred from that nation state to the people who formed that nation state to protect and defend their natural rights and liberties: the European-American people of North America.[12]

Hunter Wallace deploys this move more openly in a 2011 article for *Occidental Dissent* titled "Why Do You Hate America?"

How can someone whose ancestors have lived in North America since before the American Revolution possibly come to hate the United States? . . .

This loaded question is exactly like asking a Russian why do you hate the Soviet Union or a Croat why do you hate Yugoslavia. The answer is because the Soviet Union wasn't Russia or because Yugoslavia wasn't Croatia. Similarly, what passes for America today isn't the "Real America."

A better question for a White Southerner to ask himself is why should you love Black Run Amerika? . . . Is this what you call America? If so, then it makes sense to hate America, as this is a false America, not the real thing.[13]

Thus, according to the Alt-Right, there is the historic American nation, the "Real America," which is white, and then there is the Anti-America or Black Run Amerika, which is the actually existing United States. According to the Alt-Right, only the real, white America is worthy of allegiance; the present-day United States deserves none. In short, the Alt-Right expresses revulsion for the actually existing United States of America of today.

Secession and Disunity

Some Alt-Right thinkers take their anti-Americanism to its logical conclusion: secession. For example, Michael Hart, author of *Restoring America*, which is published by VDARE.com Books, writes, "It is a major thesis of this book that ethnic hostilities within the present United States of America are so great that we can no longer function effectively as a single unified country. We must therefore split into two countries."[14]

VDARE is usually the least radical of the major Alt-Right platforms, but it treats secession as a live policy option, in contrast to more militant voices such as that of Samuel Francis, who in 1998 called the idea "an infantile disorder,"[15] and Richard Spencer, who realistically judges "Washington would send in tanks."[16] Yet Hart's book is not only published by VDARE.com Books but carries endorsements from *VDARE* editor Peter Brimelow and regular contributor John Derbyshire. Derbyshire's blurb claims the book is "pinned to reality at every point by historical precedent and scientific fact" and "Dr. Hart deals with every conceivable objection to his plan."[17] Brimelow writes that Hart's "proposal for a practical secession plan deserves careful attention from Americans."[18] Paul Gottfried, a frequent *VDARE* contributor, is an experienced writer and academic. Yet in a review of Hart's book titled "Secession Is Our Only Hope," Gottfried has only two objections: the federal government will not accept secession, and Hart, despite his advocacy of disunion, in fact accepts the "mainstream liberal historical interpretation of American history." Otherwise,

Gottfried writes, "Hart's ambitious scheme for secessionism has much to recommend it."[19] James Fulford, a *VDARE* editor and regular contributor, posted on the site an edited version of Gottfried's review and a link to the full version. Fulford also provides a useful documentation of his site's disunionist orientation in an article, "Nothing Succeeds Like Secession—A VDARE.com Secession Roundup," that links to thirteen other pro-secessionist *VDARE* articles.[20]

What is most striking about the enthusiasm of *VDARE* and other Alt-Rightists for secession is the poverty of thought behind it. *Restoring America* is most charitably described as an exercise in what internet trolls call LARPing, or "live action role playing." The entire book imagines a fantasy world completely divorced from political reality. Hart and his supporters fail to engage a host of obvious and insuperable objections.

First, secession is unconstitutional. The issue was decided in the 1869 Supreme Court case *Texas v. White*, where the court found "the Constitution, in all its provisions, looks to an indestructible Union composed of indestructible States."[21] More recently the late Supreme Court Justice Antonin Scalia, not known as a spokesman for an anti-America, observed: "If there was any constitutional issue resolved by the Civil War, it is that there is no right to secede. (Hence, in the Pledge of Allegiance, 'one Nation, indivisible.')"[22]

Alt-Right secessionists consider the unconstitutionality of their proposal to be a small, legalistic matter. Fulford argues that secession is "not really a justiciable question. . . . It's a political question." Certainly it is hard to imagine the Supreme Court ruling on a state's request to secede, but only because, as Scalia went on to note, the United States would not consent to be sued by a state on this claim. But secession is not merely a political issue; it is *the* political issue. The unconstitutionality of secession has been established with the spilling of rivers of blood. If this constitutional principle is defied without consequences, why should *any* provision of the Constitution be enforced? A successful secession would as a practical matter render the entire Constitution null and void and leave the country without any established governing procedures that could be counted on.

Second, wouldn't potential secessionists get cold feet once they started focusing on who would pay their Social Security benefits? Access to all federal entitlement programs would prompt similar questions. And how would the national debt, the armed forces, and other public obligations and resources be apportioned?

Third, Hart's proposal is to divide up the United States not by states but by counties, which is glaringly unworkable and positively frightening. A map provided in *Restoring America* shows an archipelago of tiny blue counties—the fragmented remains of the United States—strewn across the red expanse of the secessionist Federal American Republic. This dystopian image calls to mind the plea for national unity in *Federalist* No. 9. There Hamilton recoils from the vision of the United States "splitting ourselves into an infinity of little, jealous, clashing, tumultuous commonwealths, the wretched nurseries of unceasing discord and the miserable objects of universal pity or contempt. . . . Such an infatuated policy, such a desperate expedient . . . could never promote the greatness or happiness of the people of America."[23]

None of these obvious issues is addressed by Hart with anything more than perfunctory comments ("the two countries will have to agree on just how existing military equipment will be divided"), and some, such as constitutional and fiscal issues, receive not so much as a mention. Anyone who contemplates such a scheme undermines his or her claim to political and intellectual seriousness.

Other Alt-Rightists also support one form or another of disunion. Richard Spencer does not support secession but refrains purely for prudential reasons. Spencer is no supporter of national unity. He writes, "The ideal I advocate is the creation of a White Ethno-State on the North American continent."[24] Realizing this dream presumably would involve some kind of national breakup, insofar as the North American continent is now entirely occupied by three very non-ethnostates.

Jared Taylor supports secession with the object of creating separate, racially homogeneous nations. This is a logical conclusion of Taylor's claim that "human races are biological subspecies. . . . To imagine one subspecies of man living together on equal terms for long with another subspecies is but wishful thinking and leads only to disaster and oblivion for one or the other."[25] I discussed secession with Taylor, as follows:

TM: So here we are in a multiracial society. Is the situation that we now face, with multiracialism causing certain tension in democracy, not necessarily making it impossible but—

JT: Distorting it.

TM: Let's say distorting it. Is the better option to say, "Hey, multiracialism is not working so what we need is secession. We'd be better off with racially and ethnically homogenous, separate nations"?

JT: Yes, we would be much, much better off in a state of homogeneity. So the question is how to unscramble the omelet.[26]

Greg Johnson of *Cross-Currents Publishing* gives a clearer picture of just what such unscrambling would involve. Johnson has called for a kind of national separation through "a well-planned, orderly, and humane process of ethnic cleansing,"[27] which we discussed as follows:

GJ: I think the false assumption is that if all people have the rights to life, liberty and the pursuit of happiness that means that all people can live under the same system of laws in the same society, and I think that that's really the error. . . . I would say definitely black people have and always have had the right to life, liberty and the pursuit of happiness. However, that doesn't [mean] . . . that it's a really good idea to have a multiracial society where everybody's under the same system of laws. And what I really believe is that because people are different and unequal in a whole raft of ways, and that these differentiations are based on race and they're based on ethnicity, . . . when you try and put everybody in the same political order, you're going to have unnecessary and easily avoidable ethnic conflict. I'd like to eliminate that.

TM: Are we saying here that we're going to push the black people into some kind of a homeland or autonomous republic?

GJ: Basically, yeah. I would say that's [a] fair [assessment]. I think it would be more appropriate just to say, let's give you a homeland that you can live in. . . . African-Americans, here's a state in the South that is going to be the black homeland. . . .

TM: So we've got this homeland. What happens if somebody in the homeland says, I want to go back to New York City?

GJ: Nope.

TM: Not allowed, right?

GJ: Yeah, yeah.

TM: So we have a defensible border around this homeland, yes?

GJ: Yeah, yeah.

TM: Barbed wire? Dogs?

GJ: A wall. It depends on what needs to be done. A lot of movement of people and you would want some kind of border. Something like [what] you see between the West Bank, I suppose, in Israel, if need be. The Berlin Wall or something like that.

TM: Suppose somebody said, "Gee whiz, breaking up the United States, repatriation of ethnic populations, building a wall. Sounds risky, sounds like it might be a rough ride, and I'm not enthusiastic about secession. That was tried before; didn't go over so big. Maybe you've got some kind of a point here, but wouldn't it all be just easier if we somehow or another learned to get along with each other?" Why not try that?

GJ: We've been trying that for a long time and learned that that—

TM: For how long? Since 1968?

GJ: —entails telling certain lies and building certain inequities into the system. That has become intolerable.

TM: Is multiracial democracy possible?

GJ: I don't think so. I think that in a multiracial or multicultural society, you can't actually have a democracy where people are trying to create a government that serves the common good. Instead all the party politics are just disguised forms of ethnic, tribal factionalism.[28]

This proposal to repatriate blacks to a homeland surrounded by something like the Berlin Wall speaks for itself, but one historical parallel is worth making. What is the last American political party since the Civil War to endorse the "right of free withdrawal from the Union," that is, secession?

The party in question was none other than the Communist Party of the United States, whose candidate for president in 1932, William Z. Foster, outlined the plan for secession in his book, *Toward Soviet America*. Foster called for the creation of a black homeland in the American South in imitation of the Soviet Union's disastrous policy of creating pseudo-autonomous regions for ethnic minorities. Foster approvingly cites a passage from the *Program of the Communist International*, and then draws his party's conclusion:

"The recognition of the right of all nations, irrespective of race, to complete self-determination, that is, self-determination inclusive of the right to State separation."

> Accordingly, the right of self-determination will apply to Negroes in the American Soviet system. [29]

Stalin himself was the source of this horrific idea, which he insisted on even after visiting African American students "respectfully observed that the idea smacked of Jim Crowism on a grand scale."[30] In short, the Alt-Right's call for racial self-determination through state separation is merely a radical rightist variation on Stalinism.

Conclusion

A key conclusion is that the imaginary constructions to which the Alt-Right professes loyalty—the "historic American nation," the "Real America," a "white ethnostate on the North American continent," a "Federal American Republic"—have no more relation to the actually existing United States than did the "American Soviet system" dreamed of by the Stalinists. If we think of the old CPUSA as anti-American in the sense that it radically rejected American political philosophy and declared loyalty to a utopian ideal rather than to the United States, then the Alt-Right is at least as anti-American as the Communists ever were.

A second finding is the sheer irreality of Alt-Right thinking about America. In its advocacy of secession and other forms of disunion the movement has embraced what one of its own forefathers described as an "infantile disorder" and demonstrated a fundamental lack of seriousness. Here again, when the exiled extremists of the far right finally got a hearing, it turned out they had little worthwhile to say.

Finally, the irresponsibility of Alt-Right rhetoric is striking. Alt-Rightists excoriate the United States as a farce, a nightmare, and a dung heap, boldly advocate secession or disunion, and then blandly assure us that this desperate scheme will be achieved "peacefully, without violence,"[31] through a "humane process of ethnic cleansing." These perfunctory reassurances are entirely unconvincing. Here again, Hamilton's realistic evaluation of the upshot of disunion, expressed in *Federalist* No. 7, is wiser:

> It is sometimes asked, with an air of seeming triumph, what inducements could the states have, if disunited, to make war upon each other? It would be a full answer to this question to say—precisely the same inducements which have, at different times, deluged in blood all the nations in the world.[32]

Hamilton's critique of the anti-Federalist advocacy of disunion applies a fortiori against Alt-Right plans. At least the anti-Federalists did not propose to create a crazy quilt of homogeneous ethnostates and claim the result would be perpetual peace. In contrast, the Alt-Right proposes to create homelands for minorities precisely because it refuses to acknowledge nonwhites are the political equal of whites. We are then assured that once the unequal races and the benighted whites who tolerate them are walled off in their autonomous republics they will be treated with the utmost respect, and friendly relations will endure forever.

But what if the white ethnostates decide that turning over much of the continent to the undeserving is just a waste of resources and not required by their political morality anyway? The result would resemble a scene from *The Possessed* by Dostoevsky in which a deluded revolutionary theoretician presents his plan for utopia to a group of fellow radicals. Ten percent of humankind will become masters of the earth; the other 90 percent will become servants but thereby achieve the primeval innocence of Eden. And so peace will reign. But then a voice from the back of the room asks: Once the masterful 10 percent have been identified, why not simply blow up the less capable 90 percent instead of turning paradise over to them? The point is, despite the Alt-Right's protestations of good intent, their disunionist schemes leave the door wide open to war and genocide.

At least some Alt-Right thinkers appreciate that when anti-Americanism results in support for secession, their movement has lost touch with political reality. During our interview, Mike Enoch admitted as much when he said that detailed plans for secession amount to "LARPing, because we're talking about politics that aren't in any way realistic yet."[33] Out of such realism some Alt-Rightists rechannel their disgust with actually existing America in some more plausible direction. Giving up on schemes of disunion often results in a deep alienation from present-day America.

Samuel Francis gave expression to radical alienation early on. As noted, he believed proponents of literal secession suffered from "an infantile disorder," but in *Leviathan & Its Enemies* he presented certain secessionist impulses as positive. As we have seen, the portrait of contemporary America painted in Francis's magnum opus is so unlovely that repulsion toward, and withdrawal (or what Francis calls "secession") from, that regime is a natural response. In the following passage Francis describes this process of the psychological secession by the Middle American Radicals in whom he places his revolutionary hopes:

> The alienation and dispossession of the post-bourgeois proletariat . . . may precipitate a far-reaching conflict between this new force and the elite of the regime, resulting in the "secession" of the internal proletariat from the rule of the dominant minority. . . . It is this metamorphosis, rather than literal "secession" that would constitute the revolution of the post-bourgeois proletariat and its emergence as a new elite displacing the old dominant minority that "has become a prison-house and a City of Destruction."[34]

Such an internal or psychological secession rather than literal disunion is a more realistic matter of concern. The Alt-Right's indulgence in vituperative anti-Americanism and rhetorical excess in general shows obtuseness with respect to the costs of fanaticism and obliviousness to a classic conservative observation: ideas have consequences.

9

The Alt-Lite, *Breitbart*, Bannon, and Trump

Today (early 2018) the meteoric career of Stephen Bannon is all the talk of followers of American politics. From executive chairman of the largest far-right opinion outlet, *Breitbart News*, to the most-likely-to-succeed fellow traveler of the Alt-Right, to chief executive officer of the Trump presidential campaign, to White House chief strategist and holder of a full seat on the "principals committee" of the National Security Council,[1] and finally to persona non grata among nearly all his former associates, Bannon and his rise and fall have been widely chronicled. That story need not be recapitulated in detail here. In keeping with the goal of this book, this chapter examines the ideas espoused by *Breitbart News* and Bannon and their relation to Alt-Right ideology.

Andrew Breitbart founded the website *Breitbart News Network* in 2005; the site remained fairly small and had a strong connection to Israel. Bannon, a former naval officer and investment banker, became involved later and set about raising funds for its expansion around 2012, using his Wall Street connections. That expertise helped fund the site. When Breitbart died suddenly in 2012, Bannon became the *Breitbart* executive chairman and Ben Shapiro—a young conservative journalist—became editor at large.

Under Bannon, the site hammered big government, political correctness, all things Clinton, gun control, and undocumented immigrants, among other themes of the far right. Typical *Breitbart* headlines of this period included "Sarah Palin Defends Breitbart against the Wrath of the Whiners" and "Smiling Down Syndrome Kids Banished from French TV in Case They Offend Post-Abortion Women." In her attack on the Alt-Right during the 2016 presidential campaign, Hillary Clinton highlighted *Breitbart's* delight in outraging liberal sensibilities with headlines such as "Would You Rather Your Child Had Feminism or Cancer?" and "Hoist It High and Proud: The Confederate Flag Proclaims a Glorious Heritage." Thus perhaps the most direct parallel between *Breitbart* and the Alt-Right is an affinity for outlandish rhetoric.

Under Bannon, *Breitbart* became an early cheerleader for Trump. Shapiro, who would leave *Breitbart* in March 2016 over a disagreement with Bannon, characterized the new direction the site took as follows:

> Under Bannon's Leadership, Breitbart Openly Embraced the White Supremacist Alt-Right.
>
> Andrew Breitbart *despised* racism. . . . He insisted that racial stories be treated with special care to avoid even the whiff of racism. With Bannon embracing Trump, all that changed. Now Breitbart has become the alt-right go-to website, with [*Breitbart* contributor Milo] Yiannopoulos pushing white ethno-nationalism as a legitimate response to political correctness, and the comment section turning into a cesspool for white supremacist mememakers.[2]

Bannon himself seemed to admit to part of these charges when, in July 2016, while he was still *Breitbart* chairman, he said, "We're the platform of the alt-right."[3] After he was appointed White House adviser, Bannon appeared to change his description of *Breitbart*. He told the *Wall Street Journal* that, at *Breitbart*, the Alt-Right was among "10 or 12 or 15 lines of thought—we set it up that way" and the Alt-Right was "a tiny part of that." Even if this later characterization is correct, *Breitbart*—with a monthly average of 64 million visits between September 2016 and February 2018—is a major outlet of Alt-Right thought to a wide audience.

Alt-Right and Alt-Lite

But how exactly does Bannon define "Alt-Right?" What do other Alt-Right figures say about *Breitbart*? And what does a review of the contents of that outlet show about its ideology?

According to Bannon, at *Breitbart*, "Our definition of the alt-right is younger people who are anti-globalists, very nationalist, terribly anti-establishment."[4]

Alt-Right writers acknowledge their thinking is different from that disseminated at *Breitbart*, but see a connection with Bannon's former home. For example, Richard Spencer has said, "Breitbart has elective affinities with the Alt Right, and the Alt Right has clearly influenced Breitbart. In this way, Breitbart has acted as a 'gateway' to Alt Right ideas and writers. I don't think it has done this deliberately; again, it's a matter of elective affinities."[5]

Other Alt-Right writers say much the same thing Spencer does about their connection to *Breitbart*. Jared Taylor wrote to me:

I would say that of all the mainstream news sites that are *not* Alt Right, Breitbart is probably closest to the Alt Right. It is entirely possible that some of the people who write for Breitbart have been influenced by Alt Right thought, but when Steve Bannon himself says he is not a white nationalist I have every reason to believe him.[6]

And Greg Johnson wrote:

Bannon has a lot of reporters. Some popular ones (Milo, Katie McHugh) started flirting with Alt Right ideas or attracting Alt Right audiences. Bannon did not fire them, because unlike the gelded cucks at National Review and the rest of the conservative media, he does not let the Left choose his staff for him.

Bannon is a civic nationalist. We're racial nationalists. There are overlaps but disagreements on fundamental values. But Bannon is not stiffing us because his life is an experiment. He's living as if the future he is fighting for has already arrived: a world where the Left has no power. I think this is what makes him so appealing to Trump. Mainstream conservatives are graceful losers who have not retarded the Left one iota. Bannon wants to win and actually roll back the Left. That makes him a radical and revolutionary conservative.[7]

Hunter Wallace of *Occidental Dissent* used the term "Alt-Lite" to describe Bannon and *Breitbart*:

Steve Bannon isn't a member of the Alt-Right. . . . Like Donald Trump, Steve Bannon is more of a civic nationalist. . . . Steve Bannon is the most important figure in the Alt-Lite. . . . The Alt-Lite is a hybrid of mainstream conservatism and the Alt-Right . . . which has emerged since Conservatism, Inc. lost its legitimacy and ability to police the Right. We all see *Breitbart* as the premier Alt-Lite website which has popularized a diluted version of our beliefs. . . .

We like Steve Bannon.

We don't agree with Steve Bannon on everything, but he is far closer to us in spirit than to the "conservatives." He is a nationalist and a populist. He is an iconoclast who hates the conservative establishment. . . .

Steve Bannon isn't one of us, but he isn't an enemy either. He has gone out of his way to stick up for the Deplorables. If politics is about friend vs. enemy, then we definitely count Steve Bannon as a friend. He is on the side of the national populist revolution. His enemies are our enemies.[8]

Even though Mike Enoch of *The Right Stuff* feels that "*Breitbart* is sort of not quite Alt-Lite"[9] the term seems appropriate for Bannon's former outlet. As Wallace suggests, while *Breitbart* usually presents a watered-down version of Alt-Right thought, on one key ideological point Bannon, *Breitbart*, and the Alt-Right are in full agreement: politics is all about friends vs. enemies.

Bannon and the Alt-Right writers are agreed that there are clear differences between them, but also some overlap. But how important are the differences, and how big is the overlap?

A search of the online archives of *Breitbart* suggests that the site isn't much of a gateway to the more radical Alt-Right sites. None of the radical figures discussed here have written for *Breitbart*. Nor do links to the radical Alt-Right sites show up with much frequency in the readers' comment sections for *Breitbart* articles. When I checked those sections in December 2016 there were only about 140 links each to such sites as *American*

Renaissance, *VDARE*, and *The Right Stuff* and merely fifteen links to Spencer's *Radix Journal*. Interestingly, there were more than 10,000 links to the Alt-Right's bête noire, *National Review*.

The Surface of Alt-Lite Ideology

Alt-Right ideology is characterized by its rejection of the formulation that "all men are created equal," but *Breitbart* writers explicitly defend that idea. Lincoln and even Martin Luther King Jr. are praised for their fidelity to the Declaration. One article stated, "Just like Abraham Lincoln—the first Republican President—who gave his life to end slavery, Martin Luther King, Jr. had a radical vision for America, making real those words of the Declaration of Independence—that *"all men are created equal."*[10] It is impossible to imagine such sentiments being expressed at *Radix Journal*, *American Renaissance*, or *VDARE*. Some comfort can be taken from the knowledge that *Breitbart*'s writers have explicitly defended the idea that all men are created equal, though that seems the very least one could ask.

However, it is true that *Breitbart* has run attacks on American foundational propositions along the lines featured in more radical Alt-Right outlets. For example, the *Breitbart* article on the Confederate flag criticized by Clinton does more than simply flaunt the Stars and Bars the way a southern rock band might. It also claims that

> the Civil War was not fought over slavery, but in defense of states' rights. As for secession, the very existence of the United States derived from its secession from the British Crown. Why did the South, then, not have the right to secede in turn from a Union grown intolerable to it, with Abraham Lincoln assuming the role of George III? . . . Everything that America deplores in Washington today is what the Confederacy fought against.[11]

Breitbart senior editor Gerald Warner contributed this neo-Confederate polemic in 2015 during Bannon's watch.

Breitbart's treatment of Jewish issues is sometimes questionable but is far removed from the neo-Nazi anti-Semitism disseminated by the most radical Alt-Right outlets. A staple criticism of Bannon was that during his tenure, *Breitbart* indulged in anti-Semitism. Ben Shapiro—who, after opposing Trump and leaving *Breitbart*, received more than 7,400 anti-Semitic tweets[12]—characterized Bannon's relation to that bias as follows: "I have no evidence that Steve's an anti-Semite. I think Steve's a very, very power-hungry dude who's willing to use anybody and anything in order to get ahead, and that includes making common cause with the racist, anti-Semitic alt-right. . . . That . . . is appeasement of anti-Semitism.[13]

Bannon has repeatedly denied being an anti-Semite. The Alt-Right has "some racial and anti-Semitic overtones," Bannon said in the *WSJ* interview. He made clear he has zero tolerance for such views.[14] Bannon is quick to point out that *Breitbart* employs Jews, has a Jerusalem bureau, and reports on the ill effects of the Boycott, Divestment, Sanctions movement on college campuses. Nonetheless, most Jewish interest groups are deeply concerned.

The form of race consciousness that *Breitbart* indulges, while offensive, is still rather watered down when compared with the exacting standards of the Alt-Right. But what is the point of *Breitbart*'s constant baiting and insulting of immigrants, nonwhites, women, and other groups its writers perceive as progressive constituencies? (There are no such barbs directed against Alt-Right sites or figures, even though recently *Breitbart* editors claim not to adhere to far-right ideology.) *Breitbart* contributors argue that they have no alternative: they say contemporary political culture legitimates such tactics against the right, which has no choice but to respond in kind. Thus one *Breitbart* contributor denied that the platform engaged in the kind of "white identity politics" advocated by the Alt-Right relating to immigration issues, as follows: "Lately there has been a great deal of muttering about how the pushback against amnesty represents the rise of vile 'white identity politics.' . . . Personally, I despise identity politics of every stripe. . . . I want to tear down the system that makes such tactics necessary for social and political survival."[15]

Identity politics are "vile" but "necessary for social and political survival." Therefore, be vile, which *Breitbart* often is. Interestingly, the *Breitbart* article that recommended flaunting the Stars and Bars argued such inflammatory behavior was necessitated by leftist identity politics:

> Those who initiated identity politics are attempting to obliterate the Southern identity. There is only one response: defiance. Every tree, every rooftop, every picket fence, every telegraph pole in the South should be

festooned with the Confederate battle flag. Hoist it high and fly it with pride, it proclaims a glorious heritage. [16]

The Deep Structure of Alt-Lite Ideology

Some Alt-Right sites, especially *Radix Journal* and *Counter-Currents Publishing*, devote considerable attention to political philosophy and discuss at length thinkers such as Carl Schmitt, Martin Heidegger, and a range of European New Rightists. *Breitbart News*, as its name suggests, is largely a news and opinion outlet and devotes much less attention to philosophical concerns. Therefore the intellectual foundations of its editors' thought are not so obvious. Bannon's most extensive statement of his worldview can be found in the remarks he delivered via Skype to a conference hosted by the Human Dignity Institute and held inside the Vatican during the summer of 2014. In those remarks a broad sense of *Breitbart*'s ideology can be found, for Bannon explains that

> I believe the world, and particularly the Judeo-Christian West, is in a crisis. And it's really the organizing principle of how we built Breitbart News . . . to let people understand the depths of this crisis, and it is a crisis both of capitalism but really of the underpinnings of the Judeo-Christian West in our beliefs.[17]

Bannon criticizes the capitalism of today for having degenerated from the "enlightened capitalism"[18] of the West's heyday. Now, he says, capitalism "doesn't spread the tremendous value creation throughout broader distribution patterns that were seen really in the 20th century." This concern has a progressive overtone, although it is also consistent with the paleoconservative critique of free markets voiced by Samuel Francis and Pat Buchanan. The other prong of the crisis *Breitbart* seeks to communicate is, Bannon tells us, "an immense secularization of the West . . . [that] converges with something we have to face . . . we are in an outright war against jihadist Islamic fascism."

So far Bannon's diagnosis of the alleged crisis of the West, whatever one makes of it, seems relatively tame, and perhaps his mild characterization of *Breitbart* as "the voice of that center-right opposition" is fair.

But when an audience member expresses concern about Vladimir Putin and how Marine Le Pen and the rightist United Kingdom Independence Party are "strongly defending Russian positions in geopolitical terms," Bannon shows a different face.

> I think it's a little bit more complicated. When Vladimir Putin, when you really look at some of the underpinnings of some of his beliefs today, a lot of those come from what I call Eurasianism; he's got an adviser who harkens back to Julius Evola and different writers of the early 20th century who are really the supporters of what's called the traditionalist movement, which really eventually metastasized into Italian fascism. A lot of people that are traditionalists are attracted to that.
>
> One of the reasons is that they believe that at least Putin is standing up for traditional institutions, and he's trying to do it in a form of nationalism—and I think that people, particularly in certain countries, want to see the sovereignty for their country, they want to see nationalism for their country. They don't believe in this kind of pan-European Union or they don't believe in the centralized government in the United States. They'd rather see more of a states-based entity that the founders originally set up where freedoms were controlled at the local level. . . .
>
> However, we [of] the Judeo-Christian West really have to look at what he's [Putin's] talking about as far as traditionalism goes—particularly the sense of where it supports the underpinnings of nationalism—and I happen to think that the individual sovereignty of a country is a good thing and a strong thing. I think strong countries and strong nationalist movements in countries make strong neighbors, and that is really the building blocks that built Western Europe and the United States, and I think it's what can see us forward. . . .
>
> At the end of the day, I think that Putin and his cronies are really a kleptocracy, that [they] are really an imperialist power that want to expand. However, I really believe that in this current environment, where you're facing a potential new caliphate that is very aggressive that is really a situation—I'm not saying we can put it on a back burner—but I think we have to deal with first things first.

Bannon here references two thinkers, a Putin adviser associated with Eurasianism and Julius Evola, and Evola himself. The Putin adviser clearly is Alexander Dugin, former head of the Department of Sociology of International Relations of Moscow State University, whose work is well regarded in some Alt-Right circles but controversial in others. Dugin's Eurasianism has been described as "a syncretic combination—bordering on random compilation"[19] of many intellectual tendencies, salient among which are Heidegger's critique of modernity and Evola's "spiritual racism."

Evola was an Italian Dadaist painter, an occultist intellectual who supported Mussolini and after the war was an exponent of neofascism. Bannon and many other commentators describe Evola as a traditionalist, but the label is potentially misleading to anyone unfamiliar with Evola's thought. American readers are likely to think of a traditionalist as a Burkean conservative, someone who believes that political liberty is rooted in a particular organic tradition, such as "the rights of Englishmen." Such communitarian conservatism has nothing to do with Evola's radical strain of traditionalism, or rather "Traditionalism," for Evola frequently capitalizes the word "Tradition" and its cognates in his best-known work, *Revolt against the Modern World*, first published in 1934 and followed by later editions in 1951 and 1970.[20]

A Burkean defense of the particular liberties rooted in the Anglo-American political tradition was a prominent part of the mainstream conservative fusionism associated with the *National Review* and had Russell Kirk as its best-known exponent. Evola's Tradition is absolutely *not* a spontaneous outgrowth of the political practices and institutions of particular societies, nor does he see the task of "men of speculation" as being to discover and cherish the "latent wisdom" in national prejudices.[21] In Burkean traditionalism there are many political traditions, none of which is to be undermined by supposedly universal principles discovered through generalizing philosophy.

But according to Evola, there are not many traditions but only one real tradition. He writes of "the spiritual unity that is the life of the one common Tradition."[22] Here Evola is following earlier Traditionalists, who, as one scholar notes, focused on "the concept of Tradition, i.e., the teachings and doctrines of ancient civilizations and religions, emphasizing its perennial value over and against the 'modern world' and its offshoots: humanistic individualism, relativism, materialism, and scientism."[23] The antiquity Evola ascribes to this one common Tradition and to humankind's long loss of touch with it is far older than the roots of any modern national tradition. He writes that "in an antitraditional sense, the first forces of decadence began to be tangibly manifested between the eighth and sixth centuries B.C."[24] The central idea of this perennial Tradition is that "there is a physical order of things and metaphysical one . . . the superior realm of 'being' and the inferior realm of 'becoming.'"[25] Fidelity to this idea and its implications is the final imperative of politics and trumps every other loyalty. Thus in his final book, *Man among the Ruins*, Evola states:

> The Idea, only the Idea must be our true homeland. It is not being born in the same country, speaking the same language or belonging to the same racial stock that matters; rather, sharing the same Idea must be the factor that unites us and differentiates us from everybody else.[26]

Here Evola far outdistances those enthusiasts of American liberal democracy who believe the United States is essentially an idea rather than a nation and for whom the Alt-Right has such contempt. His Traditionalism has no respect whatsoever for the particular communities mainstream Burkean conservatives celebrate and subordinates everything to a single metaphysical Idea.

But what are the political implications of this great Idea of the one common Tradition? By Evola's account, even during the "Golden Age" ("an original civilization that was naturally and totally in conformity with what has been called 'the traditional spirit'"[27]) not everyone could maintain contact with the superior realm of being, and those who could do so through access to certain rites became the rulers over those who could not. The Idea of Tradition thus endorses rigid hierarchy, indeed a caste system of divine kings, a patriciate, and slaves. However, caste status is determined not ultimately by biological race but by proximity to the metaphysical, superior realm of being. Thus political status is theoretically based on spiritual status, but Evola then makes things worse with the extraordinarily unfortunate move of equating spiritual status with "race." He often fulminates against Nazi race doctrine and any form of racism based on biology but does not hesitate to assert there are superior and inferior races in spiritual terms. A chapter from *Revolt against the Modern World* titled "The Decline of Superior Races" indicates what this spiritual racism leads to:

The deterioration of the population affects only those stocks that should be considered bearers of the forces that preside over the demos and the world of the masses and that contribute to any authentic human greatness. When I criticized the racist worldview I mentioned that occult power when present, alive and at work constitutes the principle of a superior generation that reacts on the world of quantity by bestowing upon it a form and quality. In this regard, one can say that the superior Western races have been agonizing for many centuries and that the increasing growth in world population has the same meaning as the swarming of worms on a decomposing organism or as the spreading of cancerous cells.[28]

Thus Evola rejects racist worldviews based on biology and genetics, but only because he thinks the true ground of racism should be the occult power inherent in the superior Western races that places them in a favored relationship to the metaphysical realm of being. Non-Western races, whose members so alarmingly procreate, are likened to worms and cancers.

Actually, for Evola, not the Western races as a whole are superior but only those very few individuals among them that have somehow resisted the millennia-long slide away from being and by virtue of whom "Tradition is present despite all."[29] Such people "live on spiritual heights; they do not belong to this world." Any general effort by them to fix things "stands almost no chance at all" because the deterioration of this world is nearly total.[30] Therefore this tiny nucleus in whom the "'perennial fire'" of Tradition still burns might usefully direct their efforts not to improving the world but to hastening its decline. Evola suggests:

To some the path of acceleration may be the most suitable approach to a solution. . . . Thus it would be expedient to take on, together with a special inner attitude, the most destructive processes of the modern era in order to use them for liberation; this would be like turning a poison against oneself or like 'riding a tiger.'[31]

It turns out, then, that the traditionalism Bannon references in his Vatican remarks involves not preserving established institutions and customs but accelerating their destruction in service of the grand metaphysical idea of spiritual racism. Such a political vision is not exactly "the building blocks that built Western Europe and the United States," nor is it accurately characterized as "center right," whatever the former editor of *Breitbart News* thinks.

Traditionalism was a major influence on Aleksander Dugin, who has translated some of the works of Evola and other Traditionalists into Russian.[32] Perhaps the most concise statement of Dugin's thought is *The Fourth Political Theory*, available from the European New Right publishing house Arktos. Also of interest is Dugin's book *Martin Heidegger: The Philosophy of Another Beginning*, issued by Richard Spencer's Washington Summit Publishers with a preface by Paul Gottfried, who, along with Spencer, coined the term "Alt-Right."

Dugin is very clear that his Fourth Political Theory is a radical attack on liberal democracy. He writes: "Liberalism is the main enemy of the Fourth Political Theory, which is being constructed specifically to be in total opposition to it. . . . Liberalism must be defeated and destroyed."[33] However, Dugin explicitly borrows certain themes from liberalism, as he also does from Communism and fascism, which together are the first three political theories he is seeking to supplant. From liberalism Dugin takes the idea of freedom, which he goes so far as to say is his theory's "greatest value."[34] But Dugin then immediately explains that his idea of freedom has nothing to do with the freedom of the individual protected by rights that he sees as the center of liberal politics. True freedom for Dugin is that of human existence or being, that is, *Dasein*, which term Dugin takes from the preeminent German philosopher Heidegger, whose most important work was *Being and Time*. Dugin writes:

> The difference is that this freedom is conceived as human freedom, not freedom for the individual—as the freedom given by ethnocentrism and the freedom of *Dasein*, the freedom of any form of subjectivity except for that of an individual. . . . Placed in the narrow framework of individuality, the amount of freedom becomes microscopic, and, ultimately fictitious. . . . Liberalism . . . is . . . especially opposed to the realization of a great will . . . it protects not so much the rights of man, but, rather the rights of a small man.[35]

As opposed to liberal individuality and "the rights of a small man," Dugin endorses "the right of a great man (*homo maximus*)—a real man of

'Being and time' (Martin Heidegger)" to "establish order" through "the actual execution of tasks as well as the taming of the restless and exciting horizons of the will."[36]

As the above quotations show, Dugin is strongly influenced by Heidegger, who was a member of the Nazi party and whose thought is now widely acknowledged to have fascist, or at least illiberal, antidemocratic implications.[37] Dugin's project can be understood as making Heidegger's tyrannophilic propensities overt, rooting them in ethnocentrism, and applying them to post-Soviet Russian politics.

In Dugin's interpretation, *Dasein* does not exist in the abstract but always as one or another particular ethnos or nation. For him, the freedom of small men too weak individually to make much use of it is insignificant. Much more important is realizing the freedom of an ethnically defined nation, which has the collective resources to get something done. So the Fourth Political Theory is ethnocentric and nationalistic. The nation of concern to Dugin is Eurasia—basically the territory of the old Soviet Union plus the widest continental sphere of influence to which it aspired. But the resources of the ethnos or nation are of use only when they are directed by the great will of a great man who establishes order and so effectively executes tasks. In Dugin's estimation, Eurasia has just such a great man at hand in the person of Putin.

Like Evola, Dugin rejects biological racism, for his key analytic concept is ethnicity, not race, and he envisions a multipolar world divided up into co-equal, ethnically defined nations. But how to determine exactly which ethnicities will belong to what nations is likely to be a sticking point. Dugin takes seriously the idea that Alaska should be returned to Russia and has argued that in regard to Ukrainian nationalists, Putin should "kill them, kill them, kill them. There should not be any more conversations. As a professor, I consider it so."[38] It turns out that this multiplicity of illiberal nations, each embodying the distinct *Dasein* of a particular ethnos, will not be able to remain at peace, at least not with liberal states and especially not with the United States. In a 2015 exchange with an interviewer published in volume 2 of *The Fourth Political Theory*, Dugin gets to the heart of the matter:

[Interviewer] In one of your books on Heidegger [vol. 3] you raise the possibility that there are a multiplicity of Daseins. . . . To what extent do you want to see the actors and ideas you oppose (U.S. liberalism, especially) destroyed and to what extent do you want to let them be, so long as they let others be?

[Dugin] Liberalism is not an ideology that can let the other be. . . . Liberalism is part of exclusivist Modernity and Modernity is essentially totalitarian. . . . So we have no chances to create Eurasia, based on non-liberal and non-Modern tradition on the basis of [the] Fourth Political Theory, peacefully with the cold indifference of the liberal Americano-centric globalist West. The West will immediately intervene and it intervenes now. So war is imminent.[39]

The only hope for peace, by Dugin's account, is if the United States abandons its essentially totalitarian and interventionistic liberal democracy and embraces its own unique *Dasein* in the form of an ethnocentric, antiglobalist regime led by its own great man. According to Dugin, the American *Homo maximus* capable of destroying American liberalism is Donald Trump. Dugin was elated by Trump's election because "you must understand that we consider Trump the American Putin."[40] On Trump's victory, Dugin commented:

Anti-americanism is over. Not because it was wrong but exactly opposite: because American people started itself the revolution against precisely that aspect of USA we all hated. . . . We need a Nuremberg trial on Liberalism: the Last totalitarian political ideology of modernity.[41]

Thus in an international order compatible with Dugin's Eurasianism there may be peace, but only if American liberal democracy is defeated and destroyed and put on trial as the Nazis were after World War II.

Too much should not be made of Bannon's references to Evola and Dugin, which he did not repeat publicly after his Vatican remarks. *Breitbart* barely mentions either figure and, as noted above, does not flamboyantly reject liberal democratic principles the way they do. But to note how remarkable is Bannon's familiarity with these reactionary ideologues hardly constitutes "fake news," as one *Breitbart* article has claimed.[42] That *National Review* editors and Reagan administration officials used to sport Adam Smith neckties hardly proved they were laissez-faire purists but did offer insight into their intellectual milieu. The philosophical chasm between, on one side, the invisible hand and, on the other, spiritual racism and total opposition to liberal democracy is deep.

The Alt-Lite as the New Yippies

What, then, can finally be concluded about the ideology of *Breitbart* and the Alt-Lite? The best bright-line distinction between Alt-Right and Alt-Lite thought was offered by Richard Spencer:

> Trump and Bannon deserve credit for asking "is this good for us?" when considering issues of trade, immigration, and foreign policy. . . . However, as civic nationalists, their idea of "us" is the people who occupy the current multiracial landmass known as the United States. The Alt Right fundamentally differs from Trump's civic nationalism by considering "us" to be all people of European ancestry across the globe.[43]

This account recognizes the complete agreement of *Breitbart* and the Alt-Right on an essential point of antidemocratic, right-wing ideology: Politics is entirely a struggle between friend and enemy, us and them, and anything goes to achieve victory in that struggle. The only difference between Alt-Right and Alt-Lite is over who qualifies as "us." According to Spencer, for *Breitbart* and the Alt-Lite the role of "us" is played by "the people who occupy the current multiracial landmass known as the United States," but he is too charitable. Given *Breitbart*'s modus operandi of race-baiting, indulging in coarse ethnic humor, promoting xenophobia, and prejudicial stereotyping, its version of nationalism hardly qualifies as multiracial. The Alt-Lite's "us" is not the people of the United States but only *some* of the people of the United States. That favored few is what *VDARE* calls the "historic American Nation," that is, WASPs, the descendants of the older wave of European immigrants, and those African Americans and Jews willing to be good sports.

But the deeper objection to Bannon, *Breitbart*, and rightist "alt" ideologies generally goes beyond their lack of inclusiveness. The more fundamental problem is that raising the us/them or friend/foe distinction to an axiom of political philosophy is fatal to liberal democracy. The essence of liberal democracy includes unalienable rights and the rule of law, which means that there are some things that we can never do to anyone, not even to apparent enemies. José Ortega y Gasset—hardly a softhearted progressive—was correct when he wrote: "Liberal democracy . . . announces the determination to share existence with the enemy. . . . Govern with the opposition! Is not such a form of tenderness beginning to seem incomprehensible?"[44] The corrosive scorn dished out hardly less by *Breitbart* than by the Alt-Right represents just such incomprehension of the tenderness, or more exactly tolerance, that is essential to liberal democracy. The transgressive rhetoric of Bannon's outlet implies that transgressions against "them" are just fine, and indeed are not transgressions at all because there are no limits on what may be perpetrated against the enemy. With that assumption made, the difference between the Alt-Right and Alt-Lite becomes a matter of prudence rather than principle. How much can one get away with against a given enemy? Perhaps one wing of "our" forces ought to merely harass enemy forces that for the moment are too well entrenched to make all-out assault prudent. Then another, more expendable wing with less to lose can launch a really vicious attack on another front. In the forces of reaction, the Alt-Lite and *Breitbart* represent the harassers, while the Alt-Right constitutes the shock troops.

Since Bannon has said he's not Alt-Right, what, then, is objectionable about his connection to *Breitbart*? The site's penchant for shocking, "politically incorrect" rhetoric is clear and especially biting. Former *Breitbart* senior editor Milo Yiannopoulos wrote a guide to the Alt-Right that appeared on the site in March 2016. In the guide, he posited that the outlet's propensity for hyperbole could be defended as "a subset of the alt-right." At that time, Bannon was still the *Breitbart News* executive chairman, before leaving to join the Trump presidential campaign. According to a *Breitbart* press release, Bannon did not take a leave of absence to join the Trump campaign until August 17, 2016. Yiannopoulos, with Bannon still his superior, wrote of the millennial followers of the Alt-Right:

> These young rebels . . . aren't drawn to it because of an intellectual awakening, or because they're instinctively conservative. Ironically, they're drawn to the alt-right for the same reason that young Baby Boomers were drawn to the New Left in the 1960s: because it promises fun, transgression, and a challenge to social norms they just don't understand. . . . Are they actually bigots? No more than death metal devotees in the 80s were actually Satanists. For them, it's simply a means to fluster their grandparents.[45]

The Alt-Right can indeed be usefully compared to the New Left of the 1960s, but doing so does not provide the Alt-Right with much of a defense. Some young New Leftists offered critiques of the American regime that—whatever one finally thought of them—were serious and addressed legitimate concerns. The Port Huron Statement is an example. But there were other expressions of New Leftism—by Yippies such as Jerry Rubin and Abbie Hoffman—who used Guevarist and Maoist rhetoric but were primarily interested in hellraising stunts.

If the Alt-Right might be very loosely analogized to New Leftist theoreticians (the Port Huron Statement was vastly more responsible than Alt-Right extremism), *Breitbart News* and other outlets of the Alt-Lite play the role of the Yippies. But what is the value of doing so? Few sensible people found extreme New Leftist transgressions, such as the call to "Off the pigs," very funny. Indeed, after not too long the New Left itself recoiled at such jejune shock tactics. By the early 1970s Herbert Marcuse was calling on the movement to "overcome its Oedipus complex" and abandon its "standardized use of 'pig language.'" "In the society at large," Marcuse observed, "pubertarian rebellion has a short-lived effect; it often seems childish and clownish."[46]

Much the same thing can be said of the Alt-Lite. What real concerns it raises are entirely obscured by its coarseness and vulgarity. *Breitbart* and Bannon are masters of rough-hewn, attention-grabbing rhetoric. Perhaps we ought to take some comfort in the fact that the biggest Alt-Lite outlet is much less radical and much less serious than the hard-core Alt-Right. On the other hand, Jerry Rubin and Abbie Hoffman never did a stint as senior White House advisers.

Trump and the Alt-Lite

Bannon's brief and unhappy but striking tenure in the White House implies there is another major Alt-Lite outlet this chapter has not yet discussed: Donald Trump's Oval Office. It may not be correct to think of Trump as a serious exponent of Alt-Lite ideology, or indeed of any consistent pattern of ideas at all. Nonetheless, his affinities with that mode of thought are striking. Trump's remarkable choice of Bannon as a major spokesman and adviser has already been noted. Trump's policy agenda—which is anti-immigrant, antiglobalist, protectionist, populist,

Russophilic, nationalistic, and so forth—is identical with *Breitbart*'s. Also like *Breitbart*, Trump passes on Alt-Right material—such as tweets and memes from white nationalist sources—to a wider audience.[47] Trump's mean-spirited rhetoric is very much in the vein of Bannon's former outlet. And Trump has discovered the same means for disseminating without consequences such once taboo material: he relies on digital media, especially Twitter, to end-run the gatekeepers who used to filter out vulgar transgressions.

But the most striking affinity between Trump and the alt movements generally is that they both openly reject the principle that all men are created equal. That is, before he became president, Trump used to openly reject Jefferson's principle. Trump expressed that position many times. Here is the fullest version, made during an interview with the art critic Deborah Solomon:

> DONALD: They say all men are created equal. It doesn't get any more famous, but is it really true?
>
> DEBORAH: What do you think?
>
> DONALD: It's not true. Some people are born very smart. Some people are born not so smart. Some people are born very beautiful and some people are not so you can't say they are all created equal.
>
> DEBORAH: They're entitled to equal treatment under the law. I think that's what the statement means. It doesn't mean everybody has the same endowments.
>
> DONALD: That's correct. The phrase is used often so much and it's a very confusing phrase to a lot of people.[48]

It is the interviewer, not Trump, who makes the essential point that Jefferson's words obviously mean not that "everybody has the same endowments" but that "they're entitled to equal treatment under the law." Trump then perfunctorily agrees, but immediately adds, "it's a very confusing phrase to a lot of people." But as was discussed in chapter 6, virtually no one is confused by Jefferson's words. Trump does not cite anyone who thinks Jefferson was referring to equal endowments because no reasonable person has ever seriously said something so absurd. On none of the other occasions, before he was president, that Trump denied Jeffersonian equality did he spontaneously acknowledge the Declaration is referring to rights rather than factual endowments. In other words, Trump defaults to the same deliberately obtuse position Alt-Rightists deploy when they are muddying the waters as a preface to undermining Jeffersonian political equality altogether.

Trump's embarrassing statements received media attention during his presidential campaign. After the election Trump, as is his wont, reversed himself, now saying "We are a nation founded on the truth that all of us are created equal. We are equal in the eyes of our creator. We are equal under the law. And we are equal under our constitution." If anyone can be found who takes him seriously that will indeed be dispositive proof that all people do not have equal endowments.[49]

The forty-fifth American president's affinities with alt ideologies are intelligible when we realize that the phenomenon of Trumpism was predicted and endorsed very early by the intellectual progenitors of those movements. But back then the man who was to become Putin's favored presidential candidate was not yet on the political stage, and so proto-Alt-Rightists wrote not of Trumpism but of Caesarism. As early as 1982 Samuel Francis argued that the proto-revolutionary force of the Middle American Radicals (MARs) could overthrow the entrenched soft managerial oligarchy only if, like earlier rising subelites, it could "make alliances with charismatic leaders exercising autocratic power"[50]:

> Out of the structural interests and residual values of the MARs and similar forces in the Sunbelt . . . the New Right can construct a formula or ideology. . . . As a radical movement, representing rising social forces against an ossified elite, the New Right . . . should make use of the presidency as its own spearhead against the entrenched elite and should dwell on the fact that the intermediary bodies—Congress, the courts, the bureaucracy, the media, etc.—are the main supports of the elite. The adoption of the Caesarist tactic by the New Right would reflect the historical pattern by which rising classes ally with an executive power to displace the oligarchy that is entrenched in the intermediate bodies. . . . Only the presidency . . . has the visibility and resources to cut through the intractable establishment of bureaucracy and media to reach the MAR social base directly. Only the presidency is capable of dismantling or restructuring the bureaucratic-managerial apparatus that now strangles the latent dynamism of the MAR-Sunbelt social forces. The key to this Caesarist strategy is that the New Right does not now represent an elite but a subelite, that

it must acquire real social power and not preserve it in its current distribution. The intermediate institutions of contemporary America . . . are not allies of the New Right. . . . Hence, the New Right should not defend these structures but should expose them as the power preserves of the entrenched elite whose values and interests are hostile to the traditional American ethos and as parasitical tumors on the body of Middle America. These structures should be levelled or at least radically reformed, and only the presidency has the power and the resources to begin the process and to mobilize popular support for it. . . . Viewed in this sociopolitical perspective, the New Right is not a conservative force but a radical or revolutionary one.[51]

But there are at least two problems with this case for Caesarism, the first being that it is not a case at all. Francis offers no positive argument for Caesarism over republicanism. He merely wants victory for his party, the MARs, and supports Caesarism if Caesar is on their side but not otherwise. After his endorsement of Caesarism during the early Reagan years, Francis would become very critical of presidential power, but he denied there was any real change in his position:

> While my earlier support for a strong executive was predicated on the assumption that the presidency would represent MAR interests, would work aggressively on behalf of such interests, and, using a "Caesarist" tactic, would challenge the entrenched elite that predominated in the intermediary institutions, my later criticism of the apologists for an imperial presidency was based on the view that these apologists entertained no such purposes. . . . An authentic Middle American Radical view of the presidency would be supportive of a strong executive if the executive served MAR interests, but it would oppose an "imperial presidency" if the executive merely continues, as it did under Reagan and Bush, to express the interests of the incumbent managerial and bureaucratic elites in the executive branch.[52]

So Francis has no interest in Caesarism in itself, but only in MAR rule, Caesar or no Caesar, by hook or by crook. But as chapter 3 showed, Francis makes no case for the hard regime of the MARs except to note that it will be much harsher than the soft managerial regime. Those who do not share his unusual taste will likely reject MAR rule and Caesarism both.

Another problem with Caesarism is that everything depends on who will be Caesar. Will the proposed *Homo maximus* turn out to be Napoleon or Napoleon III? How does Trump measure up by this standard? A suitable comparison might be to another charismatic, populist president who is sometimes thought of as a Caesar figure, is widely admired by the Alt-Right, and is often praised by Trump: Andrew Jackson. Before being elected president in 1828 Jackson had been the victorious general in the Battle of New Orleans, military governor of Florida, a congressman and senator, and winner of a plurality of both the popular and electoral vote in the presidential election of 1824. Whatever else might be said of Jackson, as a Caesar he cut a plausible figure. Trump, with not a single day of public service to his credit before he became president, is less than convincing in the role.

Nonetheless, during the 2016 election, Francis's epigone quickly promoted Trump as the American Caesar their forefather had envisioned. Dugin's embrace of Trump as an American strongman has already been noted. Similarly, one contributor to ALTRIGHT.com asserted, "The success of the Alt-Right will come when ambitious and somewhat ruthless people pick up its ideas and use them to serve their ambition. Such a person is Donald Trump, who represents the ideas of nationalism and populism."[53] And James Kirkpatrick, a longtime regular contributor to *VDARE*, noted the connection between the ruthless Trump and Francis the theoretician of white identity politics:

> With the Sarah Palin/Donald Trump alliance, implicit white identity politics is now a real force in American politics. But the intellectual backing for such a project can only be found in the Alternative (John Derbyshire prefers "Dissident") Right. And more than any other figure, Sam Francis provided the vocabulary, analysis and strategy for dismantling the current order.
>
> If Trump can achieve a political triumph, it will surely speed Francis's postmortem intellectual one.[54]

Of course, Trump won the 2016 presidential election. It remains to be seen whether he, or the alt ideologies he makes use of, can achieve a lasting political triumph.

10
Conclusion
The Alt-Right and the Future of American Democratic Discourse

Is there, then, nothing to be said for the ideology of the Alt-Right? A key finding of this book is that given the defining theses of its ideology—a rejection of liberal democracy and advocacy of racialism, anti-Semitism, and anti-Americanism—the Alt-Right contributes nothing positive to the stock of ideas available to American political discourse.

This is not to say that the political concerns and policy suggestions the Alt-Right advances deserve no consideration. Immigration restrictions, protectionism, a nationalist foreign policy, and welfare state populism are all legitimate topics of debate, whatever one finally concludes about them. What is problematic is when these or any other proposals are presented as part of an ideology that values authoritarianism over democracy, substitutes the interest of one race for the general interest as the goal of political activity, and intemperately rejects the legitimacy of the country overall, lock, stock, and barrel.

But why is it problematic to think about politics in terms of one ideology rather than another? Isn't Alt-Rightism, like the various stripes of conservatism and progressivism, just one of many ideologies people may use to think about politics? Why should some ideologies be thought problematic and others not? For example, why should the right-wing extremism of the late 1950s and early 1960s and the Alt-Rightism of today be branded irresponsible and disreputable while mainstream conservatism, whatever one thinks of it, is not? What made the old anarchist, Leninist, Maoist, and Guevarist left-wing extremisms objectionable in a way that garden-variety progressivism, however much one may disagree with it, is not?

To answer this question, some basic terms must be defined. Let us say political philosophies are sets of debates about what social outcomes are desirable and what political arrangements can achieve them. Constitutional orders are broad generalizations about the results of those debates that polities provisionally take for granted and institutionalize in their regular processes of political decisionmaking. Ideologies are sets of ideas about politics that assume a particular constitutional order and the political philosophies behind them.

Conservatism and progressivism are ideologies derived from the political philosophy of liberal democracy, while the rightist and leftist ideologies mentioned above are not. Leninism and so forth are derived from communism, while Alt-Rightism is a twenty-first-century hodgepodge of fascism and other reactionary philosophies. The problem with these antidemocratic ideologies is not that they are "extreme" in some absolute sense. "Extreme" is a relative term, and whether it should be taken pejoratively depends on what the reference point or baseline is. As Barry Goldwater somewhat incoherently tried to express, that virtue is an extreme relative to vice is no reflection on virtue. What, then, is the reference point or baseline against which we can judge whether a particular ideology is problematic or not?

The question is vital because all thinking about politics—or anything else—must start from some baseline, that is, a set of ideas that are provisionally taken for granted. C. S. Peirce and the other pragmatists were correct in saying that all thinking can set out from only one point, "namely, the very state of mind in which you actually find yourself at the time you do 'set out' . . . laden with an immense mass of cognition already formed."[1] No person starts thinking from a blank slate, and no group of politically associated people, no polity, can begin a discourse, thinking together, about politics except from a baseline of political assumptions that is its starting point.

For historical reasons, different polities start from different baselines. Such a baseline set of general ideas about what political life should be like and how it should operate is a constitutional order. What constitutional order a polity starts its political deliberations from has an impact on where it ends up, certainly in the short and medium terms and perhaps for quite a long time. A polity that starts by assuming the divine right of kings has many issues to resolve before it can think through the desirability of a welfare state. From a constitutional order of Islamic theocracy, religious tolerance and separation of church and state are long treks. Of course, sometimes polities make revolutionary changes in their constitutional order. But even when a polity makes such a change, where it ends up often depends on its starting point. The Glorious Revolution and the French Revolution were both fundamental breaks with the constitutional orders of their days. But those orders were very different, with that of England prefiguring separation of power, while in France an absolute monarchy was the departure point. The different starting points partly explain the dramatically different results of those two great revolutions. So in a certain sense, no polity can make an absolutely fundamental break with its constitutional order, since even after a revolution the nature of the old order influences the new order. Then the new order influences what the next order will be. Where a polity can get to and how it can get there depends importantly on its starting point. A polity is lucky if its constitutional order is conducive to desirable social outcomes and makes the path toward still better outcomes relatively short and easy to traverse.

How we judge a constitutional order depends on the social outcomes, very broadly defined, achieved under it. Of course, what social outcomes are desirable is a deep question and always subject to hot debate. What is the goal of political life? "To engender a certain character in the citizens and to make them good and disposed to perform noble actions," as Aristotle had it?[2] To achieve the greatest good for the greatest number? To increase the power of man over nature and abolish the power of man over man?[3] To protect the unalienable rights of all people? This philosophical debate can never be resolved once and for all. However, at least we know *un*desirable social outcomes when we see them, assuming, that is, we take a wide enough view. No one now openly makes the case for death camps or chattel slavery, not even the Alt-Right, though it spreads falsehoods about Nazi Germany and the antebellum American South. Nor do communists now defend show trials, gulags, and terror famines. There is, then, some agreement, within very broad parameters, about what social outcomes we do not want, and so the philosophical debate about the goals of political life is not futile. Nor is the debate about what constitutional orders are most conducive to positive social outcomes futile for it has as its ground all of the political experience available to members of the polity.

Over time, the many point/counterpoints of these ongoing debates come to be well known and organized into distinct political philosophies. Political philosophies are nothing more than sets of very broad generalizations about what social outcomes are positive and what constitutional orders are conducive to them. The political philosophies that had the most influence on the developments of constitutional orders over the last century are liberal democracy, communism, fascism, Islamic theocracy, and various stripes of authoritarianism, of which perhaps the most significant at the moment is the quasi-capitalist authoritarianism of contemporary China.

The constitutional order of the United States is its unique variation on liberal democracy. Is that a good order to start from? In the recent past there was a near universal consensus that constitutional orders based on liberal democracy were indeed better than all available alternatives. In *The End of History and the Last Man*, Francis Fukuyama famously argued that liberal democracy was the only political philosophy for which a reasonable case could now be made. From the publication of Fukuyama's original essay in 1989 up to the turn of the millennium, his thesis was widely though not universally accepted, and among some supporters of liberal democratic constitutional orders a sense of triumphalism set in. So it is accurate to say that in the West during the late twentieth century there was a very widely shared conviction that constitutional orders based on liberal democracy were the best starting points for political practice and discourse.

After the attacks of 9/11 that conviction was shaken, and it received further blows from the series of political and social shocks that made the early twenty-first century a long-drawn-out version of the crisis year of 1968. Some commentators concluded that Fukuyama's thesis had been naïve all along.[4] Among them was Steven Sailer, then and now a regular contributor to the Alt-Right website *VDARE*. In 2003 Sailer wrote:

Francis Fukuyama famously announced at the end of the Cold War that humanity had reached "the end of history." Unfortunately, he forgot to tell history not to bother coming to work.

Easy as it is to make fun of Fukuyama, where exactly did he go wrong?

Fukuyama's conception was formed by his expensive miseducation in the works of Hegel and other 19th Century German philosophers. History consists of the struggle to determine the proper ideology. Now there are no plausible alternatives to capitalist democracy. History, therefore, must be finished.

Lenin held a more realistic theory of what history is about: not ideology, but "Who? Whom?" (You can insert your own transitive verb between the two words.) History continues because the struggle to determine who will be the *who* rather than the *whom* will never end.[5]

Sailer's argument is that the events of 9/11 shattered the presumption in favor of liberal democracy and vindicated a central tenet of Leninism, namely, that politics boils down entirely to the question, "Who? Whom?" It is interesting to note that conservatives used to think the Who? Whom? thesis was anathema. Hayek devoted an entire chapter of *The Road to Serfdom* to rejecting the idea.[6] Yet in literally scores of contributions to *VDARE* over the past fifteen years Sailer has repeatedly affirmed the centrality of Who? Whom? to his political vision. For example, in a 2017 article, Sailer asks, "Who Said 'Who? Whom?' Lenin, Trotsky, or Stalin?," and answers, "It was Lenin, Trotsky, and Stalin, with Stalin stripping away the semi-euphemistic facade to make clear the underlying meaning." Sailer illuminatingly offers his own interpretation of that underlying meaning: "I've long argued that the underlying trend in the modern world is the long downfall from the belief in objective principles for determining winners and losers to the subjective belief that all that matters is that there are Good Guys and Bad Guys . . . and that the Good Guys must win, by hook or by crook."[7] This, in a nutshell, is the political philosophy with which the Alt-Right would replace liberal democracy: the "Good Guys," as defined by the subjective belief of someone unspecified, must win by hook or by crook, that is, by any means necessary.

Now we can clarify the question of whether liberal democracy is a good political philosophy on which to base a constitutional order. That answer involves asking, what is the proposed alternative? In Sailer's case that alternative is Leninism, or more exactly an isolated tenet of Leninism. Leninism is an ideology derived from Marxist political philosophy, which Lenin interpreted as requiring the dictatorship of the Communist Party and a purely instrumental ethics. As Sailer notes in his article, Lenin relied on Marxism to prove, supposedly objectively, that the Communist Party was the Good Guys. That proof was theoretically subject to rational argument. In contrast, Sailer explicitly states that the Good Guys are to be determined not by reason but by someone's "subjective belief." That is, Sailer's proposed alternative to liberal democracy is Leninism minus Marxism. The political morality that results is well expressed by the advertising slogan for a recent Hollywood action movie: "It's not a crime if you're doing it for the Good Guys."

Other figures influential on the Alt-Right may embrace some form of Leninism. An example comes from an article by Ronald Radosh, noted scholar of the history of American communism, that appeared in August 2016 in the *Daily Beast*. It quotes Steve Bannon, who Radosh says told him in 2013—three years before he became involved in Trump's presidential campaign—"I'm a Leninist. . . . Lenin . . . wanted to destroy the state, and that's my goal too. I want to bring everything crashing down, and destroy all of today's establishment."[8] When Radosh asked Bannon in 2016 about using Bannon's words in the article, Bannon told him that he could not recollect having made the statement. Bannon has said separately that he is "virulently anti-establishment." And Richard Spencer presents Lenin (and Gramsci) as "the Left we can learn from" because their "strategic and tactical insights are useful, due, in part, to the fact that they existed in similar social positions as rightists find themselves in today."[9]

Further, nearly all Alt-Right thinkers embrace some variation of the Who? Whom? thesis, usually a racialized variation. The racialist component of Alt-Right ideology guarantees that once Lenin's thesis is accepted, the "who" in question will turn out to be the white race. For Samuel Francis and other populist extremists, the "who" is not the entire white race but only the Middle American Radicals, that is, the alienated white working-class postbourgeoisie that will dominate the hard managerial regime of the future. For the somewhat less radical elements of the Alt-Right and for the Alt-Lite as represented by *Breitbart News*, the "who" will be the "historic American nation," that is, a United States—if there is one after secessionist movements have played out—in which post-1960 immigrants and their descendants, and the "treason lobby" that supports them, are deported or marginalized.

Adding racialism to the Who? Whom? thesis clarifies Sailer's formulation, which fails to specify who will be Who. He leaves that all-important decision to the "subjective belief" of apparently just anyone, which means that any entity that subjectively believes it is the Good Guys may employ whatever means it deems necessary to "win" in some sense.

Undoubtedly other groups will have their own, contrary, subjective beliefs on the matter, and thus the war of all against all returns. Racialism stipulates that the white race is the Good Guys, who get to be the terror of the earth. The obvious rejoinder is to ask why whites are so privileged. If the response is merely that whites believe they are the Good Guys, we are embracing the "subjective belief" criterion and the state of nature it implies. If the response is that science supports white privilege, then one question is how convincing that science is.[10] Lenin and the rest of the Bolsheviks were convinced that, as Engels said, Marx was the Darwin of social science[11] and had scientifically demonstrated that the proletariat was the privileged class of world history. Today Darwin is again invoked to privilege a particular class, this time by the Alt-Right to support white supremacy. Is the Alt-Right's application—or misapplication—of Darwinian science to politics any more convincing today than the Marxists' application of it was in the early twentieth century? Of course, the social and biological sciences have greatly progressed since Lenin's time. But suppose we compare early twentieth-century Marxism with early twenty-first-century scientific racialism on such matters as the stature of the minds behind them, the breadth and depth of the research in their support, and the degree of agreement they have received from qualified experts. By these standards the Marxist case for the proletariat appeared to have much more weight than the Alt-Right's case for white supremacy—which, of course, is not to say the Marxists were right. The consequences of their mistaken conviction, we now know, were disastrous, and they should have been held to a vastly higher standard of proof.

The question, then, is what standard of proof a polity should apply in deciding whether it should shift from a constitutional order derived from one political philosophy to a new order based on another. America has such a standard in the justification of revolution provided in the Declaration of Independence:

Prudence, indeed, will dictate that Governments long established should not be changed for light and transient causes; and accordingly all experience hath shewn, that mankind are more disposed to suffer, while evils are sufferable, than to right themselves by abolishing the forms to which they are accustomed. But when a long train of abuses and usurpations, pursuing invariably the same Object evinces a design to reduce them under absolute Despotism, it is their right, it is their duty, to throw off such Government, and to provide new Guards for their future security.

As was discussed in chapter 6, in this passage Jefferson is merely paraphrasing the justification for revolution that Locke gives in chapter 19, paragraph 225, of *The Second Treatise of Government*. So the burden of proof for proposed revolutionary change is, though not insurmountable, very high in the liberal democratic tradition.

But the Alt-Right rejects the Declaration and liberal democratic thought, so to find a justification for revolutionary change its followers would accept we have to look to other political philosophies. What philosophers would the Alt-Right accept as authorities on this matter? Several sources suggest that Hobbes, Machiavelli, and Schmitt make up a canon of "illiberal political philosophy" that the Alt-Right would accept.[12] But these thinkers hold potential revolutionaries to even higher standards of proof than does the liberal democratic tradition, which developed partly in the course of justifying the Glorious Revolution and the American Revolution. So it is quite fair to require proponents of revolutionary change to provide at least as much evidence as Locke and Jefferson demand.[13] For the purposes of this book we can simply say that a polity should be very reluctant to make a revolutionary change in its constitutional order.

How reluctant depends on several considerations. One is our evaluation of the social consequences achieved under the status quo order. Another consideration is to what proposed order the status quo should be compared. A further consideration is the costs of maintaining the status quo and of making various sorts of revolutionary and nonrevolutionary changes to it. And finally, we must consider how certain we are of these calculations, especially those involving speculation about what might be. Developing these concerns into a full ethics of revolutionary change is far beyond the scope of this book.[14] But some back-of-the-envelope evaluations are possible here.

First, it may be bold to say so, but probably few readers of this book will dispute that the social consequences of liberal democratic constitutional orders, on balance, have compared quite favorably with those of other historical political baselines, for a very long time now—since, let's say, the beginning of that tradition with the Glorious Revolution of 1688, which is thought, somewhat inaccurately, to have inspired Locke's political philosophy. Of course, this is not to say that liberal democracy is a theoretical limit beyond which humanity can never pass and still less that any particular liberal democracy is perfect.

Second, the social consequences of the constitutional orders that the Alt-Right looks to as models compare very unfavorably, to say the least, with those produced by liberal democratic orders. In this regard, the example of Nazi Germany speaks for itself. Nor does much need to be said about the antebellum American South. Italy under Mussolini and Spain under Franco do not fare well in this comparison, especially if one considers how well these countries did once they left fascism behind and established liberal democratic orders. Jared Taylor and Hunter Wallace are nostalgic for the Jim Crow era, but the segregated South was in most respects a stagnant backwater compared to the liberal North and then took off dramatically after the civil rights movement.

Third, honest speculation about what life would be like in a "white ethnostate on the North American continent," in a secessionist American Federal Republic, or in any other Alt-Right fantasy regime is not encouraging. It is pure utopianism—or dystopianism—to imagine that such a regime could be achieved through "a well-planned, orderly, and humane process of ethnic cleansing," as Greg Johnson claims.[15] The most relevant historical parallel, our own bloody Civil War, suggests otherwise. And in the event such a pure-white state came into existence, it is unlikely that a population accustomed to traditional American political culture would long be happy under an Alt-Right authoritarian government. Further, the breakup of the continental American market would likely have dire economic consequences, and the patchwork of petty states that replaced it would be hard-pressed to provide for their common defense and to avoid making war on each other.

No doubt the above discussion merely lays out in detail the grounds for a conclusion that to most readers was obvious at the start: Trading in our liberal democratic constitutional order for one based on the reactionary philosophies embraced by the Alt-Right is a terrible idea. Indeed, trading in a liberal democratic order for one derived from any illiberal political philosophy is a terrible idea. In general, in our political deliberations, though a liberal democratic order cannot be dogmatically assumed, the presumption in favor of it should be very great.

But is it practically possible to maintain a strong presumption for a liberal democratic order without falling into mere dogmatism? A good case can be made that participants in democratic discourse must hold democratic liberalism at a critical distance if their thinking is to be of any value at all. John Mitchell has argued that "paradoxically . . . the survival of democracy requires . . . critical distance from the popular will. . . . [To] inculcate democratic values, the most important of those values is a profound and persistent ambivalence toward democracy."[16]

Mitchell makes a good point. For all citizens, critical distance, understood as the ability to think dispassionately and review evidence objectively, is essential to fairly evaluate democracy or anything else. This is especially true for public intellectuals, that is, those citizens whose profession it is to know and evaluate politics. (By the way, public intellectuals and all citizens should maintain a critical distance not only on democracy but on *all* political ideas.) But critical distance so defined is not inconsistent with a rebuttable presumption in favor of a liberal democratic order when evaluating proposed revolutionary, antidemocratic change. What is being suggested here is an informal standard of proof to be applied in certain types of discourse that assumes the participants retain their ability to think critically. Criminal trials show that such a standard of proof is not incompatible with critical distance. Criminal defendants receive a presumption of innocence absent proof beyond a reasonable doubt, which in no way conflicts with jurors' responsibility to think clearly, examine evidence objectively, and put aside irrelevant considerations. Critical distance is required in jury deliberations and in all practical matters. Since conviction is so consequential, critical thinkers ought to apply a very high standard of proof before they convict. Revolutionary change in a liberal democratic order can be at least as consequential as a criminal conviction. So in thinking critically about such a proposal, a similarly high standard is appropriate.

Nor does a presumption in favor of liberal democracy mean that public intellectuals or anyone else must ceaselessly celebrate liberal democracy and elevate that philosophy into what the proto-Alt-Rightist Paul Gottfried calls a "god term."[17] The argument is only that a very great deal of historical evidence suggests that, however one feels about liberal democracy, one ought to be extremely reluctant to overturn a liberal democratic order for an antidemocratic one. Whether one chooses to celebrate, bemoan, or simply acknowledge this state of affairs is a matter of temperament.

A strong but nondogmatic presumption in favor of liberal democracy—that is, the political philosophy developed in the second paragraph of the Declaration of Independence, updated in light of ongoing political experience—is the sine qua non of all healthy political discourse in America. *Everything* else merits, not necessarily a presumption of innocence, but at least tolerance. The questions now are how exactly speakers who reject the Declaration's principles should be dealt with, how to deal with speakers who accept those principles but who make other claims that are highly objectionable, and what different political discourse communities—ideological networks—can do to implement tolerance.

In saying that speakers who accept the principles of the Declaration merit a degree of tolerance that should not be accorded to speakers who reject those principles, I do not mean to say that speakers who dissent from the Declaration should be harassed, persecuted, censored, or criminalized in any way for what they say. I advocate at least initial tolerance of any speaker who accepts the Declaration's principles, but not active intolerance of those who do not. I simply mean that acceptance of the Declaration represents the outer limits of responsible political discourse in a democracy and that speakers who cross that Rubicon deserve the label "antidemocratic" and all the pejorative connotations that go with it.

However, it is vital to insist that a strong but theoretically rebuttable presumption in favor of liberal democracy does not mean we should reject out of hand any idea derived from a competitor political philosophy, such as communism, fascism, or whatever. To do so would deprive us of the insights of some of the great minds of political thought, including Plato, Machiavelli, Hobbes, and Marx, to say nothing of such considerably smaller fry as the elite theorists, Schmitt, and Marcuse.

For liberal democratic discourse has to some degree incorporated into its stock of useful ideas several concepts from Marxism, for example, historical materialism and an appreciation for the possibilities of social engineering. Marxist ideas that turned out to be less fruitful—the dictatorship of the proletariat, centralized economic planning, the cult of revolution—have also gotten a hearing. Separating the wheat from the chaff required great effort, took a long time, and involved making considerable adjustments to the Marxist ideas that were finally judged worthwhile. But the point is that liberal democracy can learn something from other political philosophies. We can insist on the presumption in favor of liberal democracy when the alternative is an antidemocratic revolutionary change. But that presumption must be based on historical experience and cannot be dogmatic. Liberal democrats, therefore, need not and should not simply stop listening to criticism based on other political philosophies.

Listening, however, does not necessarily imply accepting. Liberal democrats listened to Marxism and, after due consideration, cherry-picked its best ideas, modified them as seemed appropriate, and rejected the rest. The same can be done with right-wing, nondemocratic political philosophies. Obviously, great caution and much skepticism are in order. But dogmatic rejection has its disadvantages too.

I have listened to Alt-Right ideologues, waiting, without much hope, to hear something worthwhile. The wait has been entirely disappointing. One of the less obvious weaknesses of the Alt-Right intellectuals is that their extremism is such that even when they spy a potentially useful idea hidden in the illiberal canon they cannot make effective use of it. Borrowing insights from nondemocratic thinkers can be fruitful but requires caution. A good example of how not to conduct such borrowing is the Alt-Right's use of the elite theorists' critique of democracy as disguised oligarchy.

Chapter 3 documented the centrality of elite theory as it has been interpreted by Samuel Francis and others to Alt-Right ideology. One expression of the essence of elite theory is Michels's iron law of oligarchy, which Francis's mentor, James Burnham, sums up as follows:

> Social life cannot dispense with organization. The mechanical, technical, psychological, and cultural conditions of organization require leadership, and guarantee that the leaders rather than the masses shall exercise control. The autocratic tendencies are neither arbitrary nor accidental nor temporary, but inherent in the nature of organization. This . . . *the iron law of oligarchy* . . . would seem to hold for all social movements and all forms of society. The law shows that the democratic ideal of self-government is impossible.[18]

But Michels's iron law is only one way of expressing the claim that the imperatives of organization make democracy impossible. As Francis acknowledged in his account of Burnham's thought, Pareto's "elite" and Mosca's "ruling class" are the same concept as Michels's "oligarchy."[19]

Chapter 4 also showed how, in the hands of Francis and other proto-Alt-Right thinkers, elite theory has been used to argue that in contemporary democracies, a set of interlocking elites has established an oligarchical regime so thoroughgoing as to be totalitarian. This exceedingly grim analysis leads to the conclusion that the only hope of the nonelite is a near apocalypse followed by a hard authoritarian regime (Francis), or a populist-Caesarist putsch followed by Latin-style fascism (Gottfried), or national disintegration followed by a crazy quilt of racially pure ethnostates on the North American continent (Spencer, Wallace, Johnson). But these nightmarish fantasies are the result of an uncritical application of elite theory and the resulting dramatic misunderstanding of certain real political challenges the United States now faces.

A good sense of how far off track the Alt-Right's use of elite theory has gone comes from Kevin MacDonald's discussion of recent political science research on political inequality in America. MacDonald made the following comments concerning a study by Martin Gilens and Benjamin I. Page that the BBC and other media outlets widely reported as finding "US is an oligarchy, not a democracy":

> The idea that Western societies are democracies is an illusion. In fact, an oligarchic model fits U.S. politics much better than a democratic model (see Martin Gilens and Benjamin Page in *Perspectives on Politics*, Sept. 2014, "Testing Theories of American Politics: Elites, Interest Groups, and Average Citizens").[20]

> An elite group like American Jews pursue their interests in the MSM [Mainstream Media], the legislative process, and the judicial system—top-down influence that is far more compatible with oligarchy than democracy. (An oligarchic model fits U.S. politics much better than a democratic model—see Martin Gilens and Benjamin Page in *Perspectives on Politics*, September 2014, *Testing Theories of American Politics: Elites, Interest Groups, and Average Citizens*).[21]

So MacDonald cites a legitimate study in an effort to back up his claim that Jews are an elite group, indeed a "hostile elite," operating within an oligarchy. But, on examination, Gilens and Page's research not only does not support any of these charges—nothing at all is said about Jewish political influence—but it completely undermines the Alt-Right's conception of oligarchy, as does the general thrust of recent serious research on political inequality in America.

First of all, Gilens has noted "oligarchy" is "not a term that we used in the paper. It's just a dramatic sort of overstatement of our findings."[22] Other scholars of political inequality, including Page in other work, do refer to America as an oligarchy but explicitly deny that their use of the term has anything to do with the elite theory made use of by the Alt-Right. In a 2009 article Page and his co-author, Jeffrey A. Winters, explain that Michels's "famous 'iron law' muddles the most important aspects of oligarchy by focusing on organizational complexity rather than power." The authors explain:

> Contrary to elite theory (and to a range of writings on oligarchy that are confused versions of elite theory), we argue that the concept of oligarchy properly refers to a specific kind of minority power that is fundamentally material in character. In the US context, as elsewhere, the central question is whether and how the wealthiest citizens deploy unique and concentrated power resources to defend their unique minority interests.[23]

In other words, oligarchy, as political analysts now use the term, has nothing to do with the "mechanical, technical, psychological, and cultural conditions of organization" that require leadership and frustrate democratic control as Burnham and his Alt-Right progeny believe. Oligarchs do *not* wield influence by dint of mastering managerial skills that allow them to run large organizations and that can then be employed to manage society as a whole. Oligarchic power is, quite simply, a matter of money. According to Winters and Page:

> Oligarchs are actors who personally command or control massive concentrations of wealth—a material form of power that is distinct from all other power resources, and which can be readily deployed for political purposes. . . . Scholars such as Gaetano Mosca, Vilfredo Pareto, and Robert Michels stretched the analysis of oligarchy to include power resources other than wealth. The concept of oligarchy then lost clarity and explanatory value by being blended with notions of elite power. . . . Recent attempts to define

oligarchs and oligarchy, particularly in the US context, have foundered for a variety of reasons—the most important being that oligarchy has mistakenly been construed as incompatible, both conceptually and functionally, with democracy. We argue that oligarchy limits democracy but does not render it a sham.[24]

That is, the problem of oligarchy in America is not a matter of the organizational imperatives of modern society that make democracy impossible. The problem, rather, is that the extremely rich just have too much political influence. And the very wealthy assert that influence through such ordinary techniques as "lobbying, electoral impact, and opinion shaping,"[25] which, while all too effective, fall well short of a Gramscian cultural hegemony pervading every facet of consciousness or a scientistic social managerialism strangling every source of opposition. Nor does this undue power of the very wealthy reduce liberal democracy to a fraud no better than hard tyranny.

A correct diagnosis is much simpler: American politics is unduly influenced by the very rich, who are entirely different from the managerial oligarchy described by Francis. Francis's managers derive their power not from money but from their indispensable skills and training, with which they stifle all significant political challenges. Also, the managers of various sectors all supposedly share the same interests and therefore interlock to form an unchallengeable totalitarian oligarchy. In fact, the political power of the rich is based not on managerial skills but on wealth, which comes from different sources, and therefore the rich are not so monolithic. Further, the potential oligarchs of America's superwealthy are much fewer in number than the many millions of managers to be found in all spheres of social organization. It is the oligarchic potential of "the top tenth of 1 percent of the wealthiest households"—about 300,000 people—that should primarily concern us, according to Winter and Page. This group "is much smaller than a Marxian class" and "has a much more distinct character than a broadly defined 'elite.'"[26]

That is, the scholarship of Gilens, Page, Winters, and other serious researchers shows that the exaggerations served up by the Alt-Right are, at best, precisely the "confused versions of elite theory" that obscure the truth of the situation America now faces. The daunting task of taming the power of the extremely wealthy requires real-world political action.

Undermining the dominant cultural hegemony by shooting dirty words, vulgar images, hyperbolic rhetoric, and offensive proposals out into cyberspace will accomplish nothing. Despairing of democratic solutions and fantasizing about revolutionary cataclysms is, to use an Alt-Right term, "LARPing," that is, live action role playing.

Alt-Right thinkers, owing to their extremism and lack of intellectual depth, botch the task of making good use of the elite theorists' account of oligarchy. That task is accomplished by the academic researchers of the sort the Alt-Right despises. Reducing the role of money in politics would improve democratic accountability and make the system more responsive to nonelite groups in general, including the Middle American Radicals with whom the Alt-Right is sympathetic. That challenging reform, and not cataclysmic revolution, authoritarian Caesarism, or secession, whether literal or psychological, is the real challenge facing American politics.

The point is, studying and borrowing from thinkers outside the liberal democratic tradition is not only legitimate, it is vital if we are not to retreat into dogmatism and the social stagnation and eventual decay it would foster. But prudence and caution, two virtues the Alt-Right notably lacks, are necessary.

In short, antidemocrats, simply because of their antidemocratic ideology, are necessarily the political adversaries—*not*, as I will show, the enemies—of any discourse community that does accept the principles of the Declaration regardless of any other positions those two groups may or may not share.

The discourse communities of most concern to this book are web political magazines whose editors and contributors represent a relatively small and elite group. (Social media such as Twitter, Facebook, and 4chan, where the contributors do not pass through a screening process, are another matter.) What would it mean for such platforms to regard antidemocrats as adversaries but not to censor or persecute them in any way? It would mean doing just what the *National Review* did with the right-wing extremists of the late 1950s and early 1960s. Buckley simply refused to publish such people in his magazine, explicitly criticized them, and so did not acknowledge them as legitimate members of the movement he was leading. That policy, so hated by the Alt-Right, is, in fact, perhaps the single most creditable thing Buckley and the mainstream conservative movement he helped craft ever did. It was not censorship since the rejected writers were free to publish elsewhere if they could. It represented not only good manners and a shrewd long-term strategy but good public morals. It was the right's most striking contribution to the health of American democratic discourse. The only pity is that Buckley did not implement the policy sooner, thus allowing some infamous pro-segregationist sentiments to creep into his magazine early on.

Of course, this book has documented that with the shift in communications technology from print to the internet, ostracism from the respectable right has fewer consequences for right-wing, antidemocratic extremists than it used to have and less impact on their ability to reach a large audience. That is, the internet has weakened the sanctions available to gatekeepers, which makes their role *more* important than it used to be, not less. The gatekeepers of the mainstream right are less able than they once were to limit the audience reached by extremists. If readers now have access to potentially dangerous goods, it is more important that those goods be, in effect, labeled by the gatekeepers so that readers at least know what they are getting and so have help in deciding whether they really want what is being offered. Another way of putting the matter is that gatekeepers of the mainstream right have to deny antidemocratic extremists the credentials they would achieve if they were allowed to participate in respectable discourse. If readers can't be stopped from participating in potentially dangerous forums, at least they should not be misled by the imprimatur that gatekeepers' approval would provide.

Chapter 4 documented how a perfect storm of social and technological change undermined the position of gatekeepers and produced, in the internet, a discursive state of nature where, as one Alt-Right website editor put it, "everyone's voice is as loud as they are able to make it" and "the mob is the movement."[27] Thus we have provided some empirical evidence that gatekeepers are necessary for healthy democratic discourse and advanced one standard that gatekeepers ought to apply, a presumption in favor of liberal democracy. So the case in favor of gatekeepers has been sketched out. But detailed accounts of the institutional and technological arrangements necessary to reinforce the position of gatekeepers are far beyond the scope of this book. Such arrangements are very important but are secondary considerations compared to acknowledging the necessity of some sort of gatekeepers and understanding what they should do. Just as in the end, no formal system of constitutional restraints can preserve a liberal democratic order absent the determination of the citizens to do so, no technology or legislation can keep democratic discourse healthy without the public's willing cooperation. In an unfortunately overlooked essay from 1954, "The Ethics of Controversy," Sidney Hook correctly observed, "In the last analysis, only self-discipline can prevent the level of public discussion from sinking below the safety-line of democratic health. The restraints entailed by good form in discussion are, therefore, more than a matter of good manners: They are a matter of good public morals."[28]

But what else, besides working with a presumption in favor of liberal democracy, should gatekeepers to political discourse on the internet do? Hook's essay provides certain "ground rules of controversy in a democracy" that are worth considering.[29] They are:

1. Nothing and no one is immune from criticism.
2. Everyone involved in a controversy has an intellectual responsibility to inform himself of the available facts.
3. Criticism should be directed first to policies, and against persons only when they are responsible for policies, and against their motives or purposes only when there is some independent evidence of their character.
4. Because certain words are legally permissible, they are not therefore morally permissible.
5. *Before* impugning an opponent's motives, even when they legitimately may be impugned, answer his arguments.
6. Do not treat an opponent of a policy as if he were therefore a personal enemy or an enemy of the country or a concealed enemy of democracy.
7. Since a good cause may be defended by bad arguments, after answering the bad arguments for another's position, present positive evidence for your own.
8. Do not hesitate to admit lack of knowledge or to suspend judgment if evidence is not decisive either way.
9. Only in pure logic and mathematics, not in human affairs, can one demonstrate that something is strictly impossible. Because something is logically possible, it is not therefore probable. "It is not impossible" is a preface to an irrelevant statement about human affairs. The question is always one of the balance of probabilities. And the evidence for probabilities must include more than abstract possibilities.

10. The cardinal sin, when we are looking for truth of fact or wisdom of policy, is refusal to discuss, or action which blocks discussion.[30]

Hook's second ground rule, the intellectual responsibility of all participants to inform themselves of available (and relevant) facts, is extremely important. In fact, it addresses a fundamental weakness in the way political discourse on the internet is often thought about. As we saw in chapter 4, the concept of an "ideal speech situation" as developed by Habermas has been applied in evaluating the level of political discourse on the internet. To recapitulate, here are the features of an ideal speech situation as specified by Habermas:

(3.1) Every subject with the competence to speak and act is allowed to take part in a discourse.

(3.2) a. Everyone is allowed to question any assertion whatever.

   b. Everyone is allowed to introduce any assertion whatever into the discourse.

   c. Everyone is allowed to express his or her attitudes, desires and needs.

(3.3) No speaker can be prevented, by internal or external coercion, from exercising his rights as laid down in 3.1 and 3.2.[31]

The weakness of the ideal speech situation concept is that it focuses entirely on preventing abuses of power and considers not at all the problem of evidence. Habermas wants to eliminate the possibility that participants in a discussion can be coerced by power, and so guarantee that they are moved only by good arguments. His concern, as one commentator wrote, is that a false consensus will result when "the presence of power relations between the parties casts doubt on whether they were motivated by the force of the better argument alone."[32] Therefore the ideal speech situation demands that no speaker have any power whatsoever over any other. Everyone has absolute freedom to speak, and no one can be told to hold their peace for any reason.

But what if some speakers know what they are talking about and others do not? This is sure to be the case, no matter what the point at issue, because, as Will Rogers said, "Everybody is ignorant, only on different subjects." If the people who know something and those who do not all have equal and absolute freedom to question, assert, and express themselves, then even those who turn out to be uninformed cannot be asked to be quiet until the discussion shifts to something they do know about. But, to paraphrase a quip attributed to Winston Churchill, sometimes people have to stand up and speak and sometimes they have to sit down and listen. Shouldn't the people who know more on a given point speak, while those who know less stop talking and listen for the moment? If that does not happen, how will a given speech situation have any result at all, ideal or otherwise? Habermas's formulation does not recognize that an ideal speech situation has to be an ideal listening situation too.

Habermas has acknowledged his failure to adequately take into account the "evidential dimension" of ideal speech.[33] Hook's ground rules of controversy are an improvement in that regard as, among other things, they impose on all parties the intellectual responsibility to inform themselves of the available facts and to present positive evidence for their positions. In other words, it is irresponsible to speak when you do not know what you are talking about or cannot present positive evidence for claims you make. And so it is the gatekeepers' responsibility to make sure that those who speak know what they are talking about while others listen—which is merely to say that gatekeepers, such as editors of political websites, ought to exclude contributors who do not know what they are writing about.

That potential contributors to a political web magazine who do not know anything should be edited out is, of course, obvious. But the question then is, how can gatekeepers make sure that their contributors are in the know? Those in possession of relevant knowledge are experts. Of course, they are not necessarily experts in a professional, technical, or educational sense, although they might be. Everyone is an expert about her or his own affairs, regardless of formal training or credentials. Sometimes knowledge of one's own affairs is highly relevant to a given political discussion. If the point under discussion is policies that affect a particular group of individuals—women, minorities, MARs—then what members of that community know about their affairs is relevant, even if they are not experts in a formal sense. In that case, the feminist observation that the personal is political is correct. It does not follow, however, that personal experience should consistently trump formal expertise or that formal expertise is necessarily suspect. We might agree with the pragmatists that what counts as real knowledge as opposed to falsehood is in the end determined by the scientific community, very broadly defined as everyone who rationally seeks the truth. There is much more to the scientific community thus understood than just formal experts, and it is theoretically possible for a community of formal experts to go radically off track and be in need of correction by people who lack credentials but have access to knowledge the formal experts have overlooked. American intellectual culture bends over backward to avoid such a situation and is therefore skeptical about the importance of formal expertise. And since the credentials of formal expertise are generally obtained from academic institutions, American intellectual culture is often skeptical toward the academy.

In right-wing intellectual circles especially this skepticism toward academic institutions and experts has become absolutely pathological. Academia's internal safeguards against corruption, such as tenure, peer review, and institutional independence, are seen as failures by the Alt-Right, whence it is concluded those safeguards can be dispensed with. The movement has built up a parallel universe of irresponsible think tanks, research centers, and publications that has achieved credibility among its audience in large part because it is counter-academia. But the best-quality work in the social sciences comes out of traditional academia, and almost all real experts have to maintain some kind of relation with that sector if they are to stay informed. So gatekeepers of discourse communities of all ideological orientations have to maintain a working relationship with academic institutions and draw significantly, though not exclusively, from their experts. Gatekeepers to conservative networks especially have to rely vastly more on academic contributors and vastly less on the pseudo-experts of the conservative counter-academia if they are going to meet their responsibility to give platforms only to people who know what they are writing about.

The third, fourth, and sixth of Hook's ground rules address another weakness with the ideal speech situation posited by Habermas. Is it really ideal that "everyone is allowed to introduce *any assertion whatever* into the discourse" (emphasis added) and "express his or her attitudes, desires and needs" whatever they may be? What about assertions and attitudes that block discussion? Hook's fourth ground rule implies the obvious point that at a minimum, fighting words and hate speech should be excluded. Also implied is the less obvious and now often disregarded point that vulgarity, too, should be excluded.

Hook's sixth ground rule, which prohibits labeling participants enemies merely because they oppose a particular policy, gets at a deeper point. Calling a speaker an enemy is the ultimate block to discussion. It amounts to saying that the time for discussion has passed and the time for war has come.

The idea that identifying someone as an enemy is the essence of politics is, of course, central to Carl Schmitt's political philosophy and fully embraced by the Alt-Right. According to Schmitt, "The specific political distinction to which political actions and motives can be reduced is that between friend and enemy."[34] One article in the Alt-Right web magazine *Dissident Right* explained how that movement's acceptance of Schmitt distinguishes it from mainstream conservatism:

> Conservatives have traded Schmitt for Locke. . . . The Alt-Right is an inherently Schmittian movement. We have not bought into the premises of the Left on most issues, and we are keenly aware of how important group interests are as the representation for our distinct way of life. As a result, we fight far more skillfully and with far greater passion. Why? Because we understand the zero-sum nature of the coming identity confrontation, and we choose to legitimize ourselves on the level of the political by recognizing that those who name us as the enemy are also *our* enemy.[35]

It is well understood that Schmitt's philosophy is antithetical to liberal democracy. Less obvious is that it is an utterly unrealistic understanding of politics, and unrealistic on exactly the point where it is supposedly so hard-headed, that is, in its idea of the "enemy." Schmitt tells us, rather vaguely, that the relation between enemies is one of "the most intense and extreme antagonism."[36] He is a bit clearer when he writes, "An enemy exists only when, at least potentially, one fighting collectivity of people confronts a similar collectivity."[37] But two fighting collectivities of people confronting each other is, quite simply, war. Another German theorist, Carl von Clausewitz, is the true realist when he bluntly states: "War is thus an act of force to compel our enemy to do our will."[38] In other words, an enemy is no one other than someone who makes real war, violent war, against you. To paraphrase a line from a recent Hollywood action movie, you can tell who your enemies are because they are the ones who are shooting at you. Interestingly, the Declaration of Independence also assumes that only those who make literal war against a polity are enemies when, on the brink of the revolution, it states America will hold the British "as we hold the rest of mankind, Enemies in War, in Peace Friends." Anyone who is not literally at war with you is not your enemy, however much antagonism there otherwise is between you. If, therefore, it is agreed that nonviolent activities such as organizing, debating, campaigning, voting, legislating, implementing, and so forth are all part of political life, then to define politics as a confrontation between enemies, that is, as war, far from being hard-headed realism, is a highly romantic and highly dangerous rhetorical device.[39]

Thus, among the discussion-blocking assertions that gatekeepers ought to screen out of a community of democratic discourse are any that cast other speakers as enemies of any sort merely because of their opposition to a particular policy decision, however wrongheaded that policy may be. Of course, anyone who really is making literal war on the polity is accurately described as an enemy. (Note, however, that if the enemy is so defined, then Schmitt is quite right when he writes that the "enemy need not be morally evil or aesthetically ugly."[40] Further, enemy status will end with the coming of peace.) Alt-Right outlets, as they themselves sometimes admit, routinely violate this ground rule of controversy, often by casting themselves and non-Alt-Rightists as racial enemies. The *Dissident Right* article quoted above acknowledges that "one need only spend a few hours at *VDARE*, *The Right Stuff*, *Radix*, *American Renaissance*, or even *Breitbart* to see the racial awareness and animus of those who form the 'enemy' collective."[41]

At other times, adversaries are classified as enemies through being branded traitors. For example, *VDARE* editor Peter Brimelow has written, "What the immigration enthusiasts are doing is, in the last analysis, treason," though he immediately noted, "Well, I don't literally mean they should be arrested and tried," which is a step in the right direction but does not change the fact that calling someone a traitor is branding him an enemy who makes war against the country.[42] For, according to the Constitution, "Treason against the United States shall consist only in levying War against them, or in adhering to their Enemies, giving them Aid and Comfort." The logical implication of Brimelow's charge is that immigration enthusiasts are enemies making war on the United States or helping other enemies do so. When he denies the necessary thrust of his charge by inaccurately citing a Supreme Court case, Brimelow only makes things worse.[43]

To sum up: our experience with the internet shows that establishing a right for all participants to speak by itself hardly guarantees an ideal, or even decent, speech situation. Enforcing responsibilities to be informed, to abstain from discussion-blocking rhetorical strategies, and to give liberal democratic ideas a rebuttable benefit of a doubt is essential to any healthy community of democratic discourse. Gatekeepers should be empowered to do that enforcement, which means that not all power relations, only discussion-blocking ones, are to be avoided. The task facing democratic polities now is devising technologies and institutions that re-empower the gatekeepers whose position has recently been undercut without lapsing into mere censorship.

How important is this task? About as important as the recognition that all people are created equal.

Notes

Chapter 1

1. Sarah Posner, "How Donald Trump's New Campaign Chief Created an Online Haven for White Nationalists," *Mother Jones*, August 22, 2016 (www.motherjones.com/politics/2016/08/stephen-bannon-donald-trump-alt-right-breitbart-news).

2. Paige Lavender, "Read the Full Text of Hillary Clinton's Speech on the Alt-Right," *Huffington Post*, August 25, 2016 (www.huffingtonpost.com/entry/hillary-clinton-speech-text_us_57bf4575e4b02673444f2307).

3. Google Trends (www.google.com/trends/explore?date=today%2012-m&q=alt%20right&hl=en-US&tz=240&s=1).

4. Email correspondence from James Kirkpatrick, October 19, 2016.

5. Jared Taylor, "What Is the Alt Right?," *American Renaissance*, October 11, 2016 (www.amren.com/news/2016/10/what-is-the-alt-right-jared-taylor/).

6. Hateful Heretic, "Cuckservatism: The Alt-Right," *The Right Stuff*, July 7, 2015 (archive.is/zUoYg).

7. Interview with Richard Spencer, September 29, 2016.

8. Interview with Kevin MacDonald, February 7, 2017.

9. Interview with Mike Enoch, February 22, 2017.

10. Greg Johnson, "The Alt Right Means White Nationalism . . . or Nothing at All," *Counter-Currents Publishing*, August 30, 2016 (www.counter-currents.com/2016/08/the-alt-right-means-white-nationalism/).

11. Andrew Anglin, "A Normie's Guide to the Alt-Right," *Daily Stormer*, August 31, 2016 (www.dailystormer.com/a-normies-guide-to-the-alt-right/).

12. Hunter Wallace [Brad Griffin], "What Is the Alt-Right?," *Occidental Dissent*, August 25, 2016 (www.occidentaldissent.com/2016/08/25/what-is-the-alt-right/).

13. Peter Brimelow, "Emotion at Reason," *VDARE*, December 18, 2003, (www.vdare.com/articles/emotion-at-reason).

14. Interview with Peter Brimelow, October 14, 2016.

15. Peter Brimelow, "Stop the Witch's Hunt! Hillary Clinton vs. Alt Right," *VDARE*, August 24, 2016 (www.vdare.com/posts/vdare-com-and-hillary-clintons-alt-right-witch-hunt).

16. Jared Taylor, "An Open Letter to Cuckservatives," *American Renaissance*, July 30, 2015 (www.amren.com/news/2015/07/an-open-letter-to-cuckservatives/).

17. Michael Wines and Stephanie Saul, "White Supremacists Extend Their Reach through Websites," *New York Times*, July 5, 2015.

Chapter 2

1. Hrafnkell Haraldsson, "Bill O'Reilly Says 'White Power Movement' Is a 'Storyline That Simply Doesn't Exist,'" *PoliticusUSA*, November 29, 2016 (www.politicususa.com/2016/11/29/bill-oreilly-white-power-movement-storyline-doesnt-exist.html).

2. Andrew Anglin, "A Normie's Guide to the Alt-Right," *Daily Stormer*, August 31, 2016 (www.dailystormer.com/a-normies-guide-to-the-alt-right/).

3. Hunter Wallace [Brad Griffin], "The Economist: Alt-Right Q & A," *Occidental Dissent*, September 15, 2016 (www.occidentaldissent.com/2016/09/15/the-economist-alt-right-brad-griffin-q-a/).

4. Greg Johnson, "Dennis Fetcho Interviews Greg Johnson," *Counter-Currents Publishing*, December 29, 2014 (www.counter-currents.com/2014/12/dennis-fetcho-interviews-greg-johnson/).

5. Quoted in Joakim Anderson, "Liberalism's Time Is Up," ALTRIGHT .com, November 3, 2015 (altright.com/2015/11/03/liberalisms-time-is-up/).

6. Richard Spencer, "What It Means to Be Alt-Right," ALTRIGHT.com, August 11, 2017 (altright.com/2017/08/11/what-it-means-to-be-alt-right/).

7. Quoted in Marin Cogan, "The Alt-Right Gives a Press Conference," *New York*, September 11, 2016.

8. The list of Alt-Right sites was posted on Reddit on April 5, 2016, and last viewed by me on November 10, 2016 (www.reddit.com/r/altright/comments/4dgf5j/list_of_alt_right_websites/). The subreddit has since been banned and the list is no longer accessible.

9. "About," *MBFC News* (mediabiasfactcheck.com/about/). *MBFC News* discusses its methodology at mediabiasfactcheck.com/methodology/.

10. Email correspondence with Dave Van Zandt, owner-editor of *Media Bias/Fact Check*, October 19, 2017.

11. In distinguishing web magazines from other websites evaluated by MBFC, I used the following definition from Wikipedia: "An online magazine shares some features with a blog and also with online newspapers, but can usually be distinguished by its approach to editorial control. Magazines typically have editors or editorial boards who review submissions and perform a quality control function to ensure that all material meets the expectations of the publishers (those investing time or money in its production) and the readership" (*Wikipedia*, s.v. "Online Magazine" [en.wikipedia.org/wiki/Online_magazine], last accessed by me on March 3, 2017). On the basis of this definition I eliminated all sites that did not identify an editor or have either an editorial board or an "About" section that discussed editorial criteria. Aggregation sites that provided no original content and sites of organizations that were obviously not magazines or were not mainly political were excluded.

12. Visits to *Alternative Right* and *Radix Journal* for October 2017 were counted at 5,000. Data were available for ALTRIGHT.com starting in January 2017. Calculations for the Alt-Right category before that month were based on a total of nine sites. From January 2017 on, calculations were based on a total of 10 Alt-right sites.

13. Talia Lavin, "The Neo-Nazis of the Daily Stormer Wander the Digital Wilderness," *New Yorker*, January 7, 2018.

14. Thus, Hunter Wallace (Brad Griffin) writes in *Occidental Dissent*, "By the Alt-Lite, I am referring to Breitbart, the Milo [Yiannopoulous] phenomenon, Paul Joseph Watson and Infowars, [Mike] Cernovich and a few other people. . . . Breitbart, however, is the Wal-Mart of nationalism. It is the premier Alt-Lite conservative clickbait website run by some Jews out of Los Angeles." Hunter Wallace [Brad Griffin], "Alt-Right vs. Alt-Lite," *Occidental Dissent*, November 23, 2016 (www.occidentaldissent.com/2016/11/23/alt-right-vs-alt-lite/).

Chapter 3

1. William F. Buckley; "Why the South Must Prevail," *National Review*, August 24, 1957, pp. 148–49 (adamgomez.files.wordpress.com/2012/03/whythesouthmustprevail-1957.pdf).

2. Jonathan Chait, "Why Conservatives Got Segregation Wrong a Second Time in South Africa," *New York Magazine*; December 6, 2013 (nymag.com/daily/intelligencer/2013/12/mandela-and-conservative-racial-blindness.html).

3. Alvin Felzenberg, "How William F. Buckley, Jr., Changed His Mind on Civil Rights," *Politico*, May 13, 2017 (www.politico.com/magazine/story/2017/05/13/william-f-buckley-civil-rights-215129).

4. Gleaves Whitney, "Stephen Tonsor: A Professor of Rigor and Variety,"

Imaginative Conservative, February 8, 2014 (www.theimaginativeconservative.org/2014/02/observations-stephen-tonsor-interview-gleaves-whitney.html).

5. Hubert Collins, *"Leviathan and Its Enemies*: The Alt-Right's *Das Kapital*," *Social Matter*, October 3, 2016 (www.socialmatter.net/2016/10/03/alt-rights-das-kapital/).

6. Samuel T. Francis, *Leviathan & Its Enemies* (Arlington, Va.: Washington Summit Publishers, 2016), p. 674.

7. Albert O. Hirschman, *The Rhetoric of Reaction: Perversity, Futility, Jeopardy* (Harvard University Press, 1991).

8. Robert Michels, *Political Parties: A Sociological Study of the Oligarchical Tendencies of Modern Democracy* (New York: Hearst's International Library, 1915), p. 21.

9. Ibid. Emphasis in the original.

10. Ibid., p. 390.

11. James Burnham, "Part II. Machiavelli: The Science of Power," in *The Machiavellians: Defenders of Freedom* (New York: John Day Co., 1943), pp. 29–77.

12. According to Burnham, the science of power developed by the elite theorists had established the following main principles:

> The primary subject-matter of political science is the struggle for social power in its diverse open and concealed forms. . . .
>
> The laws of political life cannot be discovered by an analysis which takes men's words and beliefs, spoken or written, at their face value. Words, programs, declarations, constitutions, laws, theories, philosophies, must be related to the whole complex of social facts in order to understand their real political and historical meaning. . . .
>
> Historical and political science is above all the study of the elite, its composition, its structure, and the mode of its relation to the non-elite. . . .
>
> The primary object of every elite or ruling class, is to maintain its own power and privilege. . . .
>
> The rule of the elite is based upon force and fraud. The force may, to be sure, be hidden or only threatened; and the fraud may not entail any conscious deception. . . .
>
> The social structure as a whole is integrated and sustained by political formula, which is usually correlated with a generally accepted religion, ideology, or myth. . . .
>
> There occur periodically very rapid shifts in the composition and structure of elites: that is, social revolutions. . . .
>
> Burnham, *The Machiavellians*, pp. 223–25

13. Ibid, p. 236.

14. Thus Burnham writes: "With the help of centralized state direction, managed currency, state foreign-trade monopoly, compulsory labor, and prices and wages controlled independently of any free market competition, branches

of the economy or the whole economy can be directed toward aims other than profit. . . . In [a] managerial economy, the regulation of production will not be left to the 'automatic' functioning of the market but will be carried out deliberately and consciously by groups of men, by the appropriate institutions of the managerial state." James Burnham, *The Managerial Revolution: What Is Happening in the World* (Westport, Conn.: Greenwood Press, 1972), pp. 130–32.

15. Ibid., p. 73.

16. As Leszek Kolakowski points out in his authoritative account, *Main Currents of Marxism*, "The rulers of post-Revolutionary Russia were and are not the industrial managers but the political bureaucracy. . . . The key decisions, including those on industrial investment, imports, and exports are political and are taken by the political oligarchy. It is very implausible to suggest that the October Revolution is a special case of the transference of power to managers as a result of progress in technology and work organization." Leszek Kolakowski, *Main Currents of Marxism. 3. The Breakdown* (Oxford University Press, 1978), p. 165.

17. Thus Burnham writes: "Nevertheless, though it now seems possible, it [a democratic transition to a managerial society] it is the less likely variant. . . . Revolutionary mass movements, terror, purges, are the usual phases of a major social transition. Societies do not seem willing merely to change the old. At some stages they seem to want to smash it, at least symbolically. It is more likely than not that these more strenuous features, also, will be included in the United States way." Burnham, *The Managerial Revolution*, pp. 271–72.

18. Francis writes: "The conservatism of managerial liberalism was thus entirely distinct from the bourgeois conservatism of the Old Right. The former sought merely to conserve, rationalize, and legitimize the new managerial establishment in state, corporations, and mass media and cultural institutions. The Old Right conservatives sought to conserve and restore at least the principles and values if not the actual institutions of the premanagerial bourgeois order and the social, moral, and religious traditions that formed the substratum of bourgeois society. The two 'conservatisms' were, in fact, incompatible." Samuel Francis, *Beautiful Losers: Essays on the Failure of American Conservatism* (University of Missouri Press, 1993), p. 105. Originally published in *The World & I* 1, no. 9 (September 1986), pp. 547–63.

19. Francis, *Beautiful Losers*, pp. 110–11.

20. Francis, *Leviathan & Its Enemies*, pp. 261–63.

21. Francis writes: "Manipulation as a mode of power may very generally be defined as the elicitation of obedience by means of inculcating an apparently spontaneous disposition to obey, as opposed to gaining obedience from those not so disposed through coercion or intimidation." He specifies that "manipulation does not always involve deception," and that it includes "most forms of persuasion . . . inducement by means of rewards, and negotiations . . . and verbal and communicational skills" (*Leviathan & Its Enemies*, p. 273, note 15). Therefore, manipulation in this sense does not necessarily imply brainwashing

or involuntary conditioning of the sort presented in *Brave New World*, or the mendacious propaganda in *1984*. Garden-variety persuasion, communication, negotiation, and positive incentives are all manipulation by this account. Apparently, any form of nonviolent suasion exercised by a soft managerial regime is manipulation.

22. Samuel Francis, "Roosevelt's Big Government Legacy Nothing to Celebrate," *Human Events* 51, no. 20 (May 26, 1995), p. 16.

23. Francis, *Leviathan & Its Enemies*, p. 304.

24. Ibid., pp. 329–31.

25. Ibid., pp. 662–63.

26. Ibid., p. 674.

27. Ibid., pp. 667–70.

28. Burnham at the end of *The Machiavellians* and Michels in the final chapter of *Political Parties* claim that while democracy is impossible, the worst aspects of oligarchy can be mitigated if various would-be elite groups are played off against each other. In this way these authors back off from the most pessimistic conclusions of elite theory and anticipate the American pluralists.

29. Samuel Francis, "The Other Side of Modernism: James Burnham and His Legacy," in Samuel Francis, *Beautiful Losers: Essays on the Failure of American Conservatism* (University of Missouri Press, 1993), pp. 135–36. Originally published in *The World &I* 2, no. 10 (October 1987), pp. 675–82.

30. Francis, *Leviathan & Its Enemies*, p. 162.

31. Marcuse writes: "However, underneath the conservative popular base is the substratum of the outcasts and outsiders, the exploited and persecuted of other races and other colors, the unemployed and unemployable. They exist outside the democratic process; their life is the most intimate and most real need for ending intolerable conditions and institutions. Their opposition is revolutionary even when their consciousness is not. Their opposition hits the system from without and is therefore not deflected by the system; it is an elementary force which violates the rules of the game and, in so doing, reveals it as a rigged game. . . . The fact that they start refusing to play the game may be the fact which marks the beginning of the end of a period." Herbert Marcuse, *One-Dimensional Man* (Boston: Beacon Press, 1964), pp. 256–57.

32. Francis, *Leviathan & Its Enemies*, pp. 570–71.

33. Ibid., p. 599.

34. Ibid., p. 726.

35. Francis specifies that postbourgeois workers are "protected by the paternalistic regulatory policies of the mass state . . . including the provision of social security, unemployment compensation, workers' rights, job benefits, and legal protection of labor organization [which] are in in contradiction to . . . bourgeois conservative ideology" (*Leviathan & Its Enemies*, p. 726). Therefore it seems that the economic security desired by a postbourgeois political party is to be provided by a distinctly nonconservative welfare state.

36. George Orwell, "Second Thoughts on James Burnham" (orwell.ru/lib rary/reviews/burnham/english/e_burnh.html).

37. Burnham writes, "The primary object of every elite or ruling class, is to maintain its own power and privilege," and thus in effect claims that the elite want power in order to keep power, which perhaps is not exactly circular but is certainly unilluminating. For if power has no object beyond power itself, how is one to know who has power? According to Hobbes's famous definition, "The power of a man, to take it universally, is his present means to obtain some future apparent good" (Thomas Hobbes, *Leviathan*, p. 73 [scholarsbank.uoregon.edu/ xmlui/bitstream/handle/1794/748/leviathan.pdf]). Thus defined, power is the ability to achieve some desired end. If the apparent good or desired end is not specified, how can we know if someone who is perhaps powerful has achieved or can achieve that end or good and therefore is indeed powerful? To say the elite desires power to maintain its power only puts the question off a step. The problem persists if we use more contemporary definitions of power. For example, the American political scientist Steven Kelman defines power as "the ability to affect the content of political choices, to change the course of government decisions from what it otherwise would have been" (*Making Public Policy*, p. 31.) Here again, if the nature of the desired choices or changes is not specified, it is not possible to know who has power and who does not. Orwell in *1984* fills in this blank left by Burnham by having O'Brien, the spokesman for Oceania's ruling elite, specify that the purpose of power is "inflicting pain and humiliation." Francis approaches this position but for obvious reasons must be more circumspect.

38. According to Burnham, "The term, 'residue,' then, means simply the stable, common element which we may discover in social actions, the nucleus which is 'left over' (hence, perhaps, Pareto's choice of the word 'residue') when the variable elements are stripped away. . . . A residue corresponds to some fairly permanent human impulse or instinct or, as Pareto more often calls it, 'sentiment.'" Burnham, *The Machiavellians*, p. 185.

39. Francis, *Leviathan & Its Enemies*, p. 266.

40. Ibid., p. 267.

41. S. E. Finer, "Introduction," in Vilfredo Pareto, *Sociological Writings* (New York: Praeger, 1966), p. 39, quoted in Francis, *Leviathan & Its Enemies*, p. 270.

42. Francis, *Leviathan & Its Enemies*, p. 727.

43. Ibid., p. 727.

44. Ibid., p. 204.

45. Ibid., p. 728.

46. Ibid., p. 731.

47. Ibid., p. 728.

48. Ibid., p. 691.

49. Paul Gottfried, "Afterword," in *Leviathan & Its Enemies*, p. 745.

50. Marcuse, *One-Dimensional Man*, p. 257.

51. Samuel Francis, "Message from MARs: The Social Politics of the New Right," in *Beautiful Losers: Essays on the Failure of American Conservatism* (University of Missouri Press, 1993), p. 68. Originally published in *The New Right Papers*, edited by Robert W. Whitaker (New York: St. Martin's Press, 1982), pp. 64–83. Emphasis added.

52. Ibid. Emphasis added.

53. Paul Gottfried, "The Marcuse Factor," *Modern Age*, Spring 2005, pp. 113–20.

54. Daniel J. Flynn, "Conservative Crackup Redux," *American Spectator*, September 2, 2016 (spectator.org/conservative-crackup-redux/).

55. According to Gottfried, "When in 1987 neocons denounced me to the authorities at Catholic University of America" their argument was "flagrantly illogical. . . . Nevertheless, I still lost a graduate professorship" that the faculty had selected him for. See Paul Gottfried; "Attack of the Pod Person I: Amnesty to Remake GOP," *VDARE*, January 12, 2004 (www.vdare.com/articles/attack -of-the-pod-person-i-amnesty-to-remake-gop); and Paul Gottfried, "The Interminable Goldberg," LewRockwell.com, n.d. (www.lewrockwell.com/1970 /01/paul-gottfried/the-interminable-goldberg/). Francis was fired from his position as an editorial writer at the *Washington Times* when an account of a speech ("Race and American Culture") he gave at a 1994 *American Renaissance* conference was published in the *Washington Post*. Francis described his firing as a "hit job" perpetrated by "the self-appointed neoconservative Thought Patrol" and a result of "the permeation of the minds of the paper's top editors by neoconservative right-think." Samuel Francis, "The Rise and Fall of a Paleoconservative at the *Washington Times* (Part II)," *Chronicles*, May 1996, pp. 43–44 (www.unz.org/Pub/Chronicles-1996may-00043?View=PDF).

56. Gottfried, "Afterword," in *Leviathan & Its Enemies*, p. 745.

57. Ibid., pp. 738–39.

58. Ibid.

59. Paul Gottfried; "Sam and I," LewRockwell.com, August 18, 2003 (www. lewrockwell.com/1970/01/paul-gottfried/sam-and-i/).

60. Paul Gottfried, "A Sea of Bile," *Unz Review*, August 7, 2003.

61. Gottfried, "Sam and I."

62. Ibid.

63. Paul Gottfried, *Conservatism in America: Making Sense of the American Right* (New York: Palgrave Macmillan, 2007), p. xiii

64. Paul Gottfried, "John Derbyshire vs. Sam Tanenhaus: A Tale of Two 'Conservatisms,'" *Unz Review*, September 15, 2009 (www.unz.com/pgottfried /john-derbyshire-vs-sam-tanenhaus-a-tale-of-two-conservatisms/?high light=race). Here Gottfried sharply distinguishes "the real Right, as opposed to the happy-talk-mongers who multiply whenever the GOP is riding high."

65. Gottfried, *Conservatism in America*, p. xvii.

66. Ibid., p. 88.

67. Ibid., p. 86.

68. Paul E. Gottfried, *Fascism: The Career of a Concept* (Northern Illinois University Press, 2016), p. 152.

69. It is worth noting that in *Chaplinsky v. New Hampshire* (315 U.S. 568 (1942)), the Supreme Court decision that established the "fighting words" exception to the First Amendment's guarantee of free speech, one of the phrases held to be unprotected was "damned fascist." Later court decisions greatly narrowed the fighting words doctrine. See *Street v. New York* (1969), *Cohen v. California* (1971), *Gooding v. Wilson* (1972), *Lewis v. New Orleans* (1974), *R.A.V. v. City of St. Paul* (1992), and *Snyder v. Phelps* (2011).

70. Gottfried, *Fascism*, p. 139.

71. Ibid., p. 151.

72. Ibid., p. 155.

73. Paul Gottfried; "Who Isn't Fascist?," *American Conservative*, March/April 2015, pp. 8–10.

74. Gidi Weitz; "Signs of Fascism in Israel Reached New Peak during Gaza Op, Says Renowned Scholar," *Haaretz*, August 13, 2014 (www.haaretz.com/israel-news/.premium-1.610368).

75. In his article "Who Isn't Fascist?," Gottfried writes that "Sternhell introduces a sober thought when he reminds us that 'there are worse things than fascism,'" and then quotes Sternhell again about Mussolini's regime murdering "no more than a few dozen" opponents. So we are led to believe that Sternhell thinks fascism in general and Italian fascism in particular are not so bad. But when we read the *Haaretz* interview with Sternhell in full, we learn otherwise. There Sternhell clarifies that one of the things worse than fascism is Nazism, but this is hardly meant as any positive reflection on fascism. He further explains: "Let me put it in no uncertain terms: Fascism is a war against enlightenment and against universal values; Nazism was a war against the human race." Whatever one makes of Sternhell's scholarship, he is not here mitigating or qualifying the horrors of fascism. He thinks fascism is not a war against the human race, but neither were the regimes of Idi Amin Dada, Muammar Gaddafi, and Vlad the Impaler. Instead, Sternhell believes, fascism makes war against Enlightenment and universal values, which is about as negative a judgment as could be made against any regime. What Gottfried has done here is dipped into the work of a true scholar, snipped a few words out of context, and deployed them in an apologia for fascism.

76. Michael R. Ebner, *Ordinary Violence in Mussolini's Italy* (Cambridge University Press, 2016).

77. This paragraph is based on correspondence from Michael R. Ebner, May 31, 2017.

78. Gottfried; "Who Isn't Fascist?"

79. Jack Kerwick, "Paul Gottfried's 'Fascism: The Career of a Concept' Explains Why Elites Believe Trump Is a Fascist," *VDARE*, May 27, 2016 (www.vdare.com/articles/paul-gottfrieds-fascism-the-career-of-a-concept-explains-why-elites-believe-trump-is-a-fascist).

80. Paul Gottfried, "From Fascism to the Managerial State," *Telos*, April 1996, pp. 196–200.

81. Paul Gottfried, "After Liberalism?," *Telos*, September 1994, pp. 169–72.

82. Ibid.

83. Paul Gottfried, "The Name That Must Not Be Mentioned," *Unz Review*, September 8, 2009 (www.unz.com/article/the-name-that-must-not-be-mentioned/).

84. Ibid.

85. Paul Gottfried, "What Is Liberal Democracy? Exploring a Problematic Term," *Nomocracy in Politics*, April 16, 2014 (nomocracyinpolitics.com/20 14/04/16/what-is-liberal-democracy-exploring-a-problematic-term-by-paul-gottfried/). This article can also be found at thenomocracyproject.wordpress .com/2014/04/16/what-is-liberal-democracy-exploring-a-problematic-term-by-paul-gottfried/.

86. Ibid.

87. Ibid. Gottfried considers defenses of liberal democracy offered by James W. Ceaser of the University of Virginia, who is "another professionally successful Straussian complaining about his uncooperative colleagues," and John Fonte of the Hudson Institute, whose argument "made its appearance to the resounding cheers of the American Enterprise Institute (AEI) and other neoconservative foundations." That is to say, both these authors are associated with the Straussian/neoconservative bloc that allegedly heads the pseudoconservative movement and provides protective coloration for the managerial elite, so their arguments do not deserve real consideration.

88. Ibid.

89. Gottfried, *Fascism*, p. 158.

90. Ibid.

91. In an article for the online magazine *Tablet*, Jacob Siegel reported, "I spoke with Richard Spencer by telephone a few days after the first Trump-Clinton debate in late September. . . . Spencer claims that he's the one who actually invented the name 'alternative right.' He says he came up with it as a headline for Gottfried's speech, which never uses the words, when he published it in *Taki's Magazine*, where he worked as an editor. Gottfried insists they 'co-created' the name." Jacob Siegel, "The Alt-Right's Jewish Godfather," *Tablet*, November 29, 2016 (www.tabletmag.com/jewish-news-and-politics/218712/spencer-gottfried-alt-right).

92. Interview with Richard Spencer, September 29, 2016. The article Spencer referenced is Paul Gottfried, "A Paleo Epitaph," *Taki's Magazine*, April 7, 2008 (takimag.com/article/a_paleo_epitaph/print#axzz4yjJSQZY1).

93. Siegel, "The Alt-Right's Jewish Godfather."

94. Paul Gottfried, "The Decline and Rise of the Alternative Right," *Taki's Magazine*, December 1, 2008 (takimag.com/article/the_decline_and_rise_of_the_alternative_right/print#axzz4qQig0spH).

95. Ibid.

96. Gottfried, "John Derbyshire vs. Sam Tanenhaus."

97. Samuel Francis, "Why the American Ruling Class Betrays Its Race and Civilization," in *Race and the American Prospect: Essays on the Racial Realities of Our Nation and Our Time*, edited by Samuel Francis (Mt. Airy, Md.: Occidental Press, 2005), pp. 395–96; posted on *Radix Journal*, August 25, 2015 (www.radixjournal.com/journal/2015/8/25/why-the-american-ruling-class-betrays-its-race-and-civilization).

98. Ibid., p. 397. Emphasis added.

99. Heidi Beirich and Mark Potok; "40 to Watch: Leaders of the Radical Right," *Intelligence Report*, Fall 2003 (Southern Poverty Law Center, November 12, 2003) (www.splcenter.org/fighting-hate/intelligence-report/2003/40-watch-leaders-radical-right).

100. "VNN versus Sam Francis," *Vanguard News Network*, September 2, 2008 (www.vnnforum.com/showthread.php?t=76517).

101. Samuel T. Francis, "The Roots of the White Man," *Radix Journal*, February 15, 2015 (www.radixjournal.com/journal/2015/2/14/the-roots-of-the-white-man).

102. Ibid.

103. See the review of MacDonald's book, *The Culture of Critique*, by John Derbyshire, "The Marx of the Anti-Semites," *American Conservative*, March 10, 2003 (www.theamericanconservative.com/articles/the-marx-of-the-anti-semites/). According to Derbyshire, the title of the review was chosen not by him but by the editors of the magazine in which it appeared.

104. Anti-Defamation League archive, "Pat Buchanan in His Own Words" (archive.adl.org/special_reports/buchanan_own_words/print.html).

105. Kevin Mac Donald, *A People That Shall Dwell Alone: Judaism as a Group Evolutionary Strategy, with Diaspora People* (San Jose, Calif.: Writers' Club Press, 2002), pp. 276, 288, 297.

106. Kevin MacDonald, *Separation and Its Discontents: Toward an Evolutionary Theory of Anti-Semitism* (1st Books, 2004), p. xxxv.

107. George Michael; "Professor Kevin MacDonald's Critique of Judaism: Legitimate Scholarship or the Intellectualization of Anti-Semitism?," *Journal of Church & State* 48, no. 4 (Autumn 2006), pp. 779–806.

108. Kevin MacDonald, *The Culture of Critique: An Evolutionary Analysis of Jewish Involvement in Twentieth-Century Intellectual and Political Movements* (1st Books, 2002), pp. lxv–lxviii.

109. Ibid., p. v.

110. Kevin MacDonald, "Understanding Jewish Influence: III. Neoconservatism as a Jewish Movement," *Occidental Quarterly* 4, no. 2 (Summer 2004), p. 58 (www.toqonline.com/archives/v4n2/TOQv4n2MacDonald.pdf).

111. MacDonald, *The Culture of Critique*, p. 18.

112. Ibid., p. 230.

113. MacDonald, *Separation and Its Discontents*, p. xxxvi.

114. MacDonald, *The Culture of Critique*, pp. 209–10.

115. Ibid., p. 236.

116. Ibid., pp. 235, 224, 238.

117. Ibid., p. 234.

118. Karl R. Popper, *The Open Society and Its Enemies, Volume II; The High Tide of Prophecy: Hegel, Marx and the Aftermath* (Princeton University Press, 1962), pp. 94–5.

119. MacDonald, *The Culture of Critique*, p.v.

120. Ibid., p. lxix.

121. Max Hocutt, "The Rationale for Racial Preference: A Review of Michael Levin, 'Why Race Matters: Race Differences and What They Mean,'" *Behavior and Philosophy* 27 (1999), pp. 165–72.

122. Michael Levin, *Why Race Matters: Race Differences and What They Mean* (Westport, Conn.: Praeger, 1997), p. 213. Emphasis added.

123. "What's Wrong with Civil Rights?," *American Opinion* (Belmont, Mass.), (birchwatcher.files.wordpress.com/2015/03/whats_wrong_with_civil_rights .png).

124. Michael Levin, *Why Race Matters: Race Differences and What They Mean* (Oakton, Virginia: New Century Foundation, 2005), pp.298-99, italics in the original. The suggestions concerning subway cars and curfews are from Levin's paper "White Fear of Black Crime," which was distributed to the philosophy faculty at Long Island University and presented by him at a conference sponsored by the department on May 2, 1990. A student protest of Levin's talk resulted in minor injuries to five police officers and nine students arrested for disorderly conduct. Levin skipped the remarks quoted here when he spoke. In a paper published in 1991 Levin again raised the idea of segregated subway cars, asked if the practice would be justified, and concluded, "Certainly more research is needed. . . ." See Alexis Jetter, "Offending Speeches Spark Protests: Campus violence erupts in B'klyn over racist speech," *Newsday*, City Edition, May 3, 1990; and Michael Levin, "Race Differences: An Overview," *The Journal of Social, Political, and Economic Studies*, Summer 1991, 16, 2; Periodicals Archive Online, pg. 213.

125. John C. Loehlin, Gardner Lindzey, and J. N. Spuhler, *Race Differences in Intelligence* (San Francisco: W. H. Freeman, 1975), pp. 238–39.

126. Hirschman, *The Rhetoric of Reaction*, p. 80.

127. Samuel Francis, "From Household to Nation: The Middle American Populism of Pat Buchanan," *Chronicles*, March 1996, p. 16 (www.chroniclesmag-azine.org/1996/March/20/3/magazine/article/10838366/).

Chapter 4

1. Mark H. Moore, "What Sort of Ideas Become Public Ideas?," in *The Power of Public Ideas*, edited by Robert B. Reich (Harvard University Press, 1988), p. 79.

2. Marc K. Landy and Martin A. Levin, eds., *The New Politics of Public Policy* (Johns Hopkins University Press, 1995), and Martin A. Levin, Marc K. Landy, and Martin Shapiro, eds., *Seeking the Center: Politics and Policymaking at the New Century* (Georgetown University Press, 2001).

3. See Landy and Levin, eds., *The New Politics of Public Policy*, chaps. 5, 8, 2, and 3, for accounts of public ideas originating in tax, environmental, special education, and immigration policy, respectively. See M. Anne Hill and Thomas J. Main, *Is Welfare Working? The Massachusetts Reforms Three Years Later* (Boston: Pioneer Institute for Public Policy Research), chap. 3, for a similar account of the welfare reforms of 1996.

4. F. A. Hayek, "The Intellectuals and Socialism," *University of Chicago Law Review* 16, no. 3 (1949), article 7 (chicagounbound.uchicago.edu/uclrev/vol16/iss3/7).

5. Ibid.

6. Peter H. Schuck, "The Politics of Rapid Legal Change: Immigration Policy in the 1980s," in Landry and Levin, eds., *The New Politics of Public Policy*, p. 82.

7. David M. Ricci, *The Transformation of American Politics: The New Washington and the Rise of Think Tanks* (Yale University Press, 1993), p. 103.

8. Ibid., p. 217.

9. Michael G. Davis, "Impetus for Immigration Reform: Asian Refugees and the Cold War," *Journal of American-East Asian Relations* 7, nos. 3/4 (Fall-Winter 1998), p. 139.

10. Daniel J. Tichenor, "The Politics of Immigration Reform in the United States, 1981–1990," *Polity* 26, no. 3 (Spring 1994), p. 341. Tichenor suggests that the New Deal, entrance into World War II, and opposition to Jim Crow and to the National Origins system all gained support from the "imperatives of the Cold War."

11. Pew Research Center, "U.S. Politics & Policy," moving average of polls October 6, 2001, and October 4, 2015 (www.people-press.org/2017/05/03/public-trust-in-government-1958-2017/).

12. Steve Sailer, "The Gods of the Copybook Headings with Terror and Slaughter Return," *VDARE*, September 14, 2001 (www.vdare.com/articles/the-gods-of-the-copybook-headings-with-terror-and-slaughter-return).

13. On how paleoconservatives and others on the far right "regarded the September 11 attacks as a predictable response to the United States' own brutal crimes overseas . . . [and] portrayed the September 11 attackers as rational enemies, not evil nihilists," see Matthew N. Lyons, "Fragmented Nationalism: Right-Wing Responses to September 11 in Historical Context," *Pennsylvania Magazine of History and Biography* 127, no. 4 (October 2003), p. 402.

14. Sailer, "The Gods of the Copybook Headings with Terror and Slaughter Return."

15. Jerry Berman and Daniel J. Weitzner, "Technology and Democracy," *Social Research* 64, no. 3 (Fall 1997), pp. 1313–19.

16. Jeffrey M. Ayres, "From the Streets to the Internet: The Cyber-Diffusion of Contention," *Annals of the American Academy of Political and Social Science* 566, special issue: *The Social Diffusion of Ideas and Things* (November 1999), pp. 132–43.

17. Ibid., p. 135.

18. Steven Livingston; "Clarifying the CNN Effect: An Examination of Media Effects According to the Type of Military Intervention," Joan Shorenstein Center on Press, Politics, and Public Policy Research Paper R-18 (Cambridge, Mass.: Harvard Kennedy School of Government, June 1997), p. 3.

19. Ayres, "From the Streets to the Internet," pp. 141–42.

20. Ibid., p. 141.

21. Barbara Perry, "'Button-Down Terror': The Metamorphosis of the Hate Movement," *Sociological Focus* 3, no. 2 (May 2000), p. 121; Carol M. Swain, *The New White Nationalism in America: Its Challenge to Integration* (Cambridge University Press, 2002), pp. 6, 31.

22. Val Burris, Emery Smith, and Ann Strahm, "White Supremacist Networks on the Internet," *Sociological Focus* 3, no. 2 (May 2000), p. 216.

23. Robert Futrell and Pete Simi, "Free Spaces, Collective Identity, and the Persistence of U.S. White Power Activism," *Social Problems* 51, no. 1 (February 2004), pp. 16–42.

24. Ibid.

25. Jared Taylor, "Special announcement to all subscribers from editor Jared Taylor," *American Renaissance* 23, no. 1 (January 2012) (www.amren.com /archives/back-issues/january-2012/).

26. Andrew Anglin, "A Normie's Guide to the Alt-Right," *Daily Stormer*, August 31, 2016 (www.dailystormer.com/a-normies-guide-to-the-alt-right/).

27. Jürgen Habermas, "Discourse Ethics: Notes on a Program of Philosophical Justification," in *The Communicative Ethics Controversy*, edited by Seyla Benhabib and Fred Dallmayr (MIT Press, 1990), pp. 85–86. Habermas notes that here he is presenting "rules of discourse" for an "ideal speech situation" suggested by R. Alexy "following my analysis." These rules are cited in John Branstetter, "The (Broken?) Promise of Digital Democracy: An Early Assessment," *International Journal of Technology, Knowledge and Society* 7, no. 3 (2011), p. 154.

28. Branstetter, "The (Broken?) Promise of Digital Democracy," pp. 151, 156.

29. Ibid., p. 157.

30. Ibid.

31. Ibid., p. 152.

32. James Madison, *Federalist* No. 10, *The Federalist Papers* (www.congress.gov/resources/display/content/The+Federalist+Papers#TheFederalist Papers-10).

33. Hunter Wallace [Brad Griffin], "My Alt-Right Biography," *Occidental Dissent*, December 15, 2016 (www.occidentaldissent.com/2016/12/15/my-alt-right-biography/). The immediately following quotations are all from this source.

34. Ibid.

35. Hunter Wallace [Brad Griffin], "My Worldview," *Occidental Dissent*, November 29, 2012 (www.occidentaldissent.com/2012/11/29/hunters-vision-goals-strategy-tactics/).

36. Hunter Wallace [Brad Griffin], "Response to Marc Ferguson," *Occidental Dissent*, March 20, 2012 (www.occidentaldissent.com/response-to-marc-ferguson/).

37. Ibid.

38. Allum Bokhari and Milo Yiannopoulos, "An Establishment Conservative's Guide to the Alt-Right," *Breitbart News*, March 29, 2016 (www.breitbart.com/tech/2016/03/29/an-establishment-conservatives-guide-to-the-alt-right/).

39. Interview with Richard Spencer, September 29, 2016.

40. Josh Harkinson, "The Trump Train to Lasting Power," *Mother Jones*, October 27, 2016.

41. Josh Dawsey and Eliana Johnson, "Trump's Got a New Favorite Steve," *Politico*, April 3, 2017 (www.politico.com/story/2017/04/stephen-miller-white-house-trump-237216).

42. Richard B. Spencer, "The Future of the AlternativeRight.com," *Radix Journal*, May 3, 2002 (archive.is/MKotX).

43. Ibid.

44. Alex Kurtagic, "Collapse Scenarios in the West and Their Implications," speech presented at a conference, Identitarian Ideas IV, Stockholm, July 28, 2012 (www.youtube.com/watch?v=0--TKIBPTOG, 31:50-32:28). For a poster of the event advertising Kurtagic as a scheduled speaker, see arktospublishing.tumblr.com/post/27262532181/the-fourth-conference-in-the-series-identitarian.

45. Colin Daileda, "The Alt-Right Is an Ideological Mixture of Racism, White Nationalism and Neo-Nazism," *Mashable*, August 27, 2016 (mashable.com/2016/08/27/alt-right-white-men-pillars-of-movement/#EYWwkXEpESqn).

46. Greg Johnson; "Greg Johnson Interviewed by Laura Raim about the Alt Right (Transcript)," *Counter-Currents Publishing*, September 28, 2016 (www.counter-currents.com/2016/09/greg-johnson-interviewed-by-laura-raim-about-the-alt-right-transcript/#more-66352).

47. Gregory Robert Johnson, "A Commentary on Kant's Dreams of a Spirit-Seer" (Ph.D. diss., Catholic University of America, 2001).

48. Greg Johnson, comment on Hunter Wallace, "TOO [*The Occidental Observer*] Holocaust Debate," *Occidental Dissent*, August 6, 2012 (www.occidentaldissent.com/2012/08/06/too-holocaust-debate/comment-page-3/#comments); Johnson comment posted August 7, 2012, at 1:47 a.m.

49. Ibid.

50. Greg Johnson; "Frequently Asked Questions, Part 2," *Counter-Currents Publishing*, June 8, 2012 (www.counter-currents.com/2012/06/frequently-asked -questions-part-2/).

51. Ibid.

52. Greg Johnson, comment on Greg Johnson, "New Right vs. Old Right," *Counter-Currents Publishing*, May 11, 2012 (www.counter-currents.com/new-right-vs-old-right/); comment posted May 11, 2012, at 11:08 p.m.

53. Greg Johnson; "The Shadow of Trump: Interview with *Il Primato Nazionale*," *Counter-Currents Publishing*, November 5, 2016 (www.counter-currents. com/2016/11/interview-with-il-primato-nazionale/); Greg Johnson; "Interview on White Nationalism *&* the Alt Right," *Counter-Currents Publishing*, October 19, 2016 (www.counter-currents.com/2016/10/interview-on-white-nationalism-and-the-alt-right/).

54. *Occidental Quarterly* is a publication of the far-right Charles Martel Society, named after the French warrior who defeated the Arab Moorish armies at Tours in 732.

55. Johnson, "The Shadow of Trump."

56. Greg Johnson; "Interview on White Nationalism *&* the Alt Right," *Counter-Currents Publishing*, October 19, 2016 (www.counter-currents.com/2016 /10/interview-on-white-nationalism-and-the-alt-right/).

57. Johnson; "Greg Johnson Interviewed by Laura Raim about the Alt Right (Transcript)."

58. Johnson; "The Shadow of Trump."

59. Alex Linder, "Notes/Comments on Johnson's 24m Radio Delivery on Old Right vs. New Right," *Vanguard News Network*, last edited August 26, 2012 (vnnforum.com/showpost.php?p=1428354&postcount=504).

60. Greg Johnson, comment on Greg Johnson, "New Right vs. Old Right," *Counter-Currents Publishing*, May 11, 2012 (www.counter-currents.com/new-right-vs-old-right/), comment posted May 12, 2012, at 1:59 p.m.

61. Greg Johnson, "Reframing the Jewish Question," *Counter-Currents Publishing*, October 27, 2015 (www.counter-currents.com/2015/10/reframing-the-jewish-question/).

Chapter 5

1. This argument is made in Charles Bloch, "*American Thinker* Disses 'White Nationalism'—A.K.A. American Patriotism," *VDARE*, July 12, 2011 (www.amren.com/news/2011/07/american_thinke); Peter Brimelow, "Trump's Immigration Patriotism, His High-Concept Campaign, Pascal's Wager: Peter Brimelow Talks to Alan Colmes," *VDARE*, September 4, 2016 (www.vdare. com/articles/trumps-immigration-patriotism-his-high-concept-campaign-pascals-wager-peter-brimelow-talks-to-alan-colmes); and Peter Brimelow,

"VDARE—Peter Brimelow on Unzism," *VDARE*, April 20, 2000 (www.vdare.com/articles/vdare-peter-brimelow-on-unzism).

2. Interview with Peter Brimelow, October 14, 2016.

3. Barack Obama, "Remarks by the President on Comprehensive Immigration Reform," press release, White House, Office of the Press Secretary, July 1, 2010 (obamawhitehouse.archives.gov/the-press-office/remarks-president-comprehensive-immigration-reform).

4. John Derbyshire, "Derb's Canceled Williams College Hate Address—'The National Question: Race, Ethnicity, and Identity in the 21st Century,'" *VDARE*, February 21, 2016 (www.vdare.com/articles/derbs-canceled-williams-college-hate-address-national-question-race-ethnicity-and-identity-in-the-21st-century).

5. Tnerb, "Behold, I Teach You the Amerikaner," *The Right Stuff*, June 16, 2016 (therightstuff.biz/2016/06/16/behold-i-teach-you-the-amerikaner/).

Chapter 6

1. In *The Uses of Argument* (1958), Stephen Toulmin proposed a model for good arguments. A simplified version of his model includes a claim, the merits of which must be established; evidence that supports the claim; a warrant that is accepted by both the speaker and the audience and that shows why the evidence is relevant to the claim; and qualifications that rebut obvious objections or limit the scope of the claim.

2. John Locke, *Two Treatises of Government*, rev. ed., edited by Peter Laslett (New York: New American Library, 1960), pp. 463–65 (chap. 19, paragraph 225).

3. The phrases "gauzy bunk" and "ceremonial language" are used by Jared Taylor and John Derbyshire respectively (citations appear later in the chapter). The terms "we-only-said-that-to-get-her-into-bed" and "drivel" are used by "VDARE.com Reader" in "A Reader Wonders about That 'Created Equal' Thing in the Declaration," *VDARE*, January 25, 2013 (www.vdare.com/letters/a-reader-wonders-about-that-created-equal-thing-in-the-declaration).

4. Samuel Francis; "Race and American Identity," *American Renaissance*, December 1998 (www.amren.com/news/2017/07/race-american-identity/).

5. The importance of the phrase "we hold" is pointed out by Robert Ginsberg in his useful article, "Suppose That Jefferson's Rough Draft of the Declaration of Independence Is a Work of Political Philosophy . . . ," *Eighteenth Century* 25, no. 1 (Winter 1984), p. 28.

6. Walter Isaacson, *Benjamin Franklin: An American Life* (New York: Simon & Schuster, 2003), p. 312.

7. Francis, "Race and the American Identity."

8. *A Dictionary of the English Language: A Digital Edition of the 1755 Classic by Samuel Johnson*, p. 1252 (johnsonsdictionaryonline.com/page-view/?i=1252).

9. There is debate over the relative influence of Locke versus that of other

thinkers on the Declaration of Independence. Gary Wills, in *Inventing America: Jefferson's Declaration of Independence* (New York: Doubleday, 1978), argues that the document is primarily influenced not by Locke but by the thinkers of the Scottish Enlightenment, especially Francis Hutcheson. Wills acknowledges only "verbal echoes of the *Treatise* in the Declaration" but "nothing distinctively Lockean" (pp. 172–73). He concludes, "Those who think Jefferson had to derive his natural right of revolution from Locke have no direct textual parallel to draw on. But the parallels within the Scottish school are everywhere" (pp. 170, 174, 238, cited by Ronald Hamowy, "Jefferson and the Scottish Enlightenment: A Critique of Garry Wills's *Inventing America*," *William and Mary Quarterly*, October 1979, pp. 503–23). But it is hard to imagine a more direct textual parallel than Jefferson's obvious and therefore probably calculated near plagiarism, in the Declaration's second paragraph, of paragraph 225 from the *Two Treatises*.

10. Interview with Richard Spencer, September 29, 2016.

11. Richard B. Spencer, "The Metapolitics of America," *Radix Journal*, July 4, 2014 (www.radixjournal.com/journal/2014/7/4/the-metapolitics-of-america?rq=Alexander%20Stephens). Emphasis added.

12. Alexander Stephens, Cornerstone speech, Savannah, Ga., March 21, 1861 (www.ucs.louisiana.edu/~ras2777/amgov/stephens.html).

13. Jared Taylor, "Miscegenation at Monticello?," *Taki's Magazine*, December 6, 2012 (takimag.com/article/miscegenation_at_monticello_jared_taylor#axzz 4VHo3gzeU).

14. Greg Johnson, "New Right vs. Old Right," *Counter-Currents Publishing*, May 11, 2012 (www.counter-currents.com/2012/05/new-right-vs-old-right/).

15. Hunter Wallace, "What Is the Alt-Right?," *Occidental Dissent*, August 25, 2016 (www.occidentaldissent.com/2016/08/25/what-is-the-alt-right/).

16. Gregory Hood, "The One-Way Conversation," *American Renaissance*, November 7, 2014 (www.amren.com/features/2014/11/the-one-way-conversation/).

17. Francis; "Race and the American Identity: Part I."

18. George Hawley, *Right-Wing Critics of American Conservatism* (University Press of Kansas, 2016), pp. 267–68.

19. "What's Wrong with Civil Rights?," *American Opinion* (Belmont, Mass.), 1965. Of course, the John Birch Society never lived up to its endorsement of political equality. The society opposed and spread lies about the civil rights movement.

20. Friedrich A. Hayek, *The Constitution of Liberty* (University of Chicago Press, 1960), p. 86. On the next page Hayek writes, "As a statement of fact, it is just not true that 'all men are born equal.'" But he immediately continues: "We may continue to use this hallowed phrase to express the idea that legally and morally all men ought to be treated alike."

21. Karl R. Popper, *The Open Society and Its Enemies* (Princeton University Press, 1962), p. 234.

22. Interview with Richard Spencer, September 29, 2016.

23. Interview with Mike Enoch, February 22, 2017.

24. Jefferson's use of the phrase "created equal" does not necessarily carry a theological implication. Robert Ginsberg suggests, "We may read 'created equal' as a normative commitment to the essential nature of human beings, which avoids the debatable language of factual description, such as 'all persons are born equal.'" That reading usefully reinforces the point that Jefferson is speaking of political equality, that is, an equality of rights, not about a factual or empirical equality of measurable traits. Robert Ginsberg, "Suppose That Jefferson's Rough Draft of the Declaration of Independence Is a Work of Political Philosophy . . . ," *Eighteenth Century* 25, no. 1 (Winter 1984), p. 28.

25. John C. Calhoun; *Disquisition on Government* and *A Discourse on the Constitution and Government of the United States*; edited by Richard K. Cralle (New York: D. Appleton and Co., 1853), pp. 55–57.

26. Personal correspondence from James Kirkpatrick, October 19, 2016. Emphasis added to Kirkpatrick's words.

27. It is sometimes argued that in replacing the word "property" in the supposedly Lockean triad of rights with "the pursuit of happiness," Jefferson is making a break with Locke and that therefore the Declaration is a less Lockean document than is sometimes suggested (Wills, *Inventing America*, pp. 229–30). But Jefferson's iconic phrase is in fact a better Lockeanism than what had been the more usual formulation, "life, liberty, and property." That exact phrase appears nowhere in Locke and in his terms would have been a redundancy. In the *Second Treatise*, sec. 123, Locke writes of "Lives, Liberties and Estates, which I call by the general Name, Property." Thus for Locke, property includes life and liberty, and therefore the phrase "life, liberty, and property" is in Lockean terms redundant. The phrase "pursuit of happiness" is taken from Locke, who, in *Essay Concerning Human Understanding*, book 2, chap. 20, sec. 2, chap. 21, secs. 47, 51–52, writes as follows: "pursuit of our happiness; . . . the highest perfection of intellectual nature lies in a careful and constant pursuit of true and solid happiness." Thus Jefferson's words, far from being a departure from Locke, are more thoroughly Lockean than the more common alternative of the day. Therefore Kirkpatrick's editing of the Declaration does not return us to the "true" meaning of its inspiration and is entirely arbitrary.

28. For a definitive account of this episode in Confederate history, see Charles B. Dew, *Apostles of Disunion: Southern Secession Commissioners and the Causes of the Civil War* (University of Virginia Press, 2001).

29. Ibid. The full text of Harris's address is provided on pp. 83–89.

30. Ibid. The full text of Hale's letter is provided on pp. 90–103.

31. Ibid., pp. 85–86. Emphasis added.

32. Ibid., pp. 91, 101. Emphasis added.

33. Steve Sailer; "Never End a Nation with a Proposition," *VDARE*, August 24, 2003 (www.vdare.com/articles/never-end-a-nation-with-a-proposition).

34. Steve Sailer; "Debugging the Declaration of Independence," *VDARE*, February 16, 2011 (www.vdare.com/posts/debugging-the-declaration-of-independence). Emphasis added.

35. Ibid.

36. Sailer; "Never End a Nation with a Proposition."

37. It is instructive to compare Sailer's analysis with that of Danielle Allen, who argues that owing to a mistake in typesetting of the Declaration, at one point a period was substituted for a comma. Unlike Sailer, Allen shows that earlier drafts of the Declaration did indeed specify a comma.

38. Pauline Maier, "Mr. Jefferson and His Editors," chap. 3 of *American Scripture: Making the Declaration of Independence* (New York: Vintage Books, 1997), pp. 98, 148.

39. Jared Taylor, *What the Founders Really Thought about Race: The White Consciousness of U.S. Statesmen* (Alexandria, Va.: National Policy Institute, February 17, 2012) (nationalpolicy.institute/2012/01/17/what-the-founders-really-thought-about-race/).

40. Ibid., pp. 3–4.

41. Library of Congress, "Declaring Independence: Drafting the Documents: Jefferson's "original Rough draught" of the Declaration of Independence" (www.loc.gov/exhibits/declara/ruffdrft.html).

42. Danielle Allen writes, "So when, in his [Jefferson's] second sentence, he writes that all men are created equal, he means all people—whatever their color, age, or status." Danielle Allen, *Our Declaration: A Reading of the Declaration of Independence in Defense of Equality* (New York: W. W. Norton, 2014), pp. 153–54.

43. Maier, "Mr. Jefferson and His Editors," pp. 146–47.

44. Eugene Gant, "On Independence Day, a Catholic Reflects on Race," *VDARE*, July 5, 2017 (www.vdare.com/articles/on-independence-day-a-catholic-reflects-on-race?content=truth%20will%20out).

45. Personal correspondence from James Kirkpatrick, October 19, 2016.

46. Dr. Ken Dombey, "Sam Francis: The Unfinished Book," *VDARE*, November 17, 2005 (www.vdare.com/articles/sam-francis-the-unfinished-book).

47. Interview with Peter Brimelow, October 14, 2016.

48. "When Thomas Jefferson wrote that memorable line—'All men are created equal'—he was not talking about an equality of rewards, but of rights with which men are endowed by their Creator. He was talking about an ideal." Patrick J. Buchanan, "The Equality Racket," *VDARE*, November 11, 2011 (www.vdare.com/articles/the-equality-racket). "Dear Heavenly Father . . . for 'All Men are Created Equal,' for 'Tear down this wall,' for 'Ask not what your country can do for you,' for 'Eternal vigilance is the price of liberty,' for 'I swear to uphold the laws and Constitution of the United States of America, against all enemies foreign and domestic,' we give thee praise." Michelle Malkin, "Thanksgiving Prayer 2002," *VDARE*, November 27, 2002 (www.vdare.com/articles/thanksgiving-prayer-2002).

49. Interview with Peter Brimelow, October 14, 2016.

50. In an interview I conducted with Derbyshire on October 4, 2016, he said, "I don't consider myself part of the alt right. . . . My twitter handle is dis-

sident right. I like dissident right. . . . I'm good friends with Jared. I worked for Peter Brimelow. I've had Richard Spencer for dinner, we're all friends. . . . [The] alt right is a youthful movement, it's a lot of fizzy young people going off in all sorts of wild directions. . . . But it's sometimes hard to engage with the younger generation, even when you're on approximately the same wave length, which I think we are."

51. Interview with John Derbyshire, October 4, 2016.

52. Interview with Richard Spencer, September 29, 2016.

53. Anthony Hilton, "Book Review: Might Is Right or the Survival of the Fittest, by Ragnar Redbeard," *Occidental Observer*, September 29, 2009 (www. theoccidentalobserver.net/2009/09/book-review-might-is-right-or-the-survival-of-the-fittest-by-ragnar-redbeard/).

54. Lysander Swooner, "Degenerate Electorate," *The Right Stuff*, November 9, 2014 (therightstuff.biz/2014/11/09/degenerate-electorate/).

55. Lawrence Murray, "The Fight for the Alt-Right: The Rising Tide of Ideological Autism against Big-Tent Supremacy," *The Right Stuff*, March 6, 2016 (therightstuff.biz/2016/03/06/big-tentism/).

56. Angus; "The Problems of Democracy and Its Impact on Family Structure," *The Right Stuff*, September 16, 2015 (therightstuff.biz/2015/09/16/problems-of-democracy/).

57. Darth Stirner, "Fascist Libertarianism: For a Better World," *The Right Stuff*, January 23, 2013 (therightstuff.biz/2013/01/23/fascist-libertarianism-for-a-better-world/).

58. Jared Taylor, "The Myth of Diversity," *American Renaissance* 8, nos. 7/8 (July–August 1997), pp. 4–5.

59. Francis, "Race and the American Identity."

60. Taylor, *What the Founders Really Thought about Race*, p. 5.

61. Peter Brimelow, "Proposition Nation—First Sighting, by Peter Brimelow," *VDARE*, February 17, 2000 (www.vdare.com/articles/vdare-proposition-nation-first-sighting-by-peter-brimelow); Steve Sailer, "L.A. Times on The Alt Right: America Is Anti-American," *VDARE*, August 27, 2016 (www.vdare.com/posts/l-a-times-on-the-alt-right-america-is-anti-american); and Tom Tancredo, "Is America A 'Proposition Nation'?," *VDARE*, October 6, 2011 (www.vdare.com/articles/is-america-a-proposition-nation).

62. Martin Diamond, "The Federalist," in *History of Political Philosophy*, 3rd ed., edited by Leo Strauss and Joseph Cropsey (University of Chicago Press, 1987), p. 660.

63. See John Jay to Dr. Benjamin Rush; March 24, 1785, Jay ID 9450; linked at Jake Sudderth, "Jay and Slavery," *The Papers of John Jay* (www.columbia.edu/cu/libraries/inside/dev/jay/JaySlavery.html). Emphasis added.

64. Publius and Sanford Levinson, "Federalist No. 2," *Slate*, November 24, 2015 (www.slate.com/articles/news_and_politics/history/2015/11/the_federalist_papers_federalist_no_2_and_the_immigration_debate.html).

65. James Madison, *Federalist* No. 42, *Federalist Papers* (www.gutenberg.org/files/1404/1404-h/1404-h.htm#link2H_4_0042).

66. James Madison, *Federalist* No. 54, *Federalist Papers* (www.gutenberg.org/files/1404/1404-h/1404-h.htm#link2H_4_0054).

67. Alexander Hamilton to John Jay, 14 Mar. 1779, *Papers 2:17–18*; *The Founders' Constitution*, vol. 1, chap. 15, doc. 24.

68. Nathan Damigo, "Paper Worship," *Radix Journal*, February 29, 2016 (www.radixjournal.com/2016/02/2016-6-29-paper-worship/).

69. Hunter Wallace [Brad Griffin], "The Constitution Cargo Cult," *Occidental Dissent*, March 27, 2016 (www.occidentaldissent.com/2016/03/27/the-constitution-cargo-cult/).

70. Joe Fallon, "The Dangerous Myth of American Exceptionalism," *VDARE*, December 21, 2001 (www.vdare.com/articles/the-dangerous-myth-of-american-exceptionalism).

71. "An Alt-Right Defense of the U.S. Constitution," Foundation for the Marketplace of Ideas, December 26, 2016 (www.freedomfront.org/news/2016/12/26/an-alt-right-defense-of-the-us-constitution).

72. See the discussion of "(((Echoes)))" in Andrew Anglin, "A Normie's Guide to the Alt-Right," *Daily Stormer*, August 31, 2016 (www.dailystormer.com/a-normies-guide-to-the-alt-right/).

73. The Constitution of the United States, National Archives, Archives.gov (www.archives.gov/founding-docs/constitution).

74. Greg Johnson, "Is White Nationalism Un-American?," *Counter-Currents Publishing*, April 17, 2017 (www.counter-currents.com/2017/04/is-white-nationalism-un-american/).

75. Christian Miller, "White American Identity Politics," *Counter-Currents Publishing*, February 9, 2011 (www.counter-currents.com/2011/02/white-american-identity-politics/).

76. Gregory Hood, "For Others *&* Their Prosperity," *Counter-Currents Publishing*, May 2, 2014 (www.counter-currents.com/2014/05/for-others-and-their-prosperity/#more-46905). The relevant phrase from the Preamble reads "to ourselves and our Posterity," not, as Hood has it, "for Ourselves and Our Posterity."

77. Tancredo, "Is America A 'Proposition Nation'?"

78. Steve Sailer; "Proposition Nation v. Preposition Nation," *VDARE*, December 15, 2012 (www.vdare.com/posts/proposition-nation-v-preposition-nation).

79. Hood, "For Others *&* Their Prosperity."

80. According to Marcin, "It is generally acknowledged that the individual author of the Committee of Style's new Preamble (the one that we see today in the Constitution) was Gouverneur Morris of Pennsylvania." Raymond B. Marcin, "'Posterity' in the Preamble and a Positivist Pro-Life Position," *American Journal of Jurisprudence* 38, no. 273 (1993) p. 285.

81. Ibid., p. 34

82. Ibid., pp. 85–86.

83. Marcin provides a detailed account of "the Legislative History of the Preamble" that documents no reference to race. The debate was mostly about the absence of any mention of individual states in the Preamble and the possible impact of the Preamble on the states' declarations and bills or rights. Marcin, "'Posterity' in the Preamble and a Positivist Pro-Life Position," pp. 284–91.

84. Peter Brimelow, "Peter Brimelow in The Daily Caller: 'The Media's Steve King Meltdown,'" *VDARE*, March 15, 2017 (www.vdare.com/articles/peter-brimelow-in-the-daily-caller-the-medias-steve-king-meltdown-2).

85. I once had the good fortune to date a woman who could trace her ancestry directly back to George Washington. According to Brimelow's reasoning, the Constitution and the Union were formed for her and other physical descendants of Washington, Madison, Hamilton, Franklin, and so forth, but not for anyone else. By this standard, even the majority of the Daughters of the American Revolution would not qualify as posterity, for most of them trace their origins back to "an ancestor who aided in American independence" but not to Washington or other founders themselves.

86. Nachman writes, "The purpose of the United States is to benefit its citizens (recall the passage in our Constitution's preamble '. . . to . . . secure the Blessings of Liberty to ourselves and . . .')." Nachman, "John Higham and 'Nativism'—Sometimes the Nativists Were Right," *VDARE*, October 9, 2015 (www.vdare.com/posts/john-higham-and-nativism-sometimes-the-nativists-were-right).

87. *Dred Scott v. Sandford*, 60 U.S. (19 How.) 393, 410–11 (1857).

88. The relevant passage is "one of the declared objects of the Constitution was to secure the blessings of liberty to all under the sovereign jurisdiction and authority of the United States." Justice Harlan; *Jacobson v. Massachusetts*, 197 U.S. 11, 22 (1905).

89. Joseph Story, *Commentaries on the Constitution of the United States* (abridged ed. 1833), p. 189.

90. Frederick Douglass, "The Constitution of the United States: Is it Pro-Slavery or Anti-Slavery?," Speech delivered in Glasgow, Scotland, March 26, 1860.

91. *A Dictionary of the English Language: A Digital Edition of the 1755 Classic by Samuel Johnson*, p. 1540 (johnsondictionary.com/page-view/?i=1540).

92. Charles L. Black Jr., "And Our Posterity," *Yale Law Journal* 102, no. 7 (May 1993), pp. 1527–32 (www.jstor.org/stable/796825).

93. Even scholars who give a narrower account of the intentions of the founders than the one taken here admit that the debate is moot and that today only a quite universalistic reading of the Preamble is possible. Thus Forkosch writes that his "conclusion is that 'the People' in the Preamble today includes not only women, Negroes, servants, and all who come within amendments such as the 13th, 15th, 19th, and 24th, but also all who have rights under the due process and equal protection clauses of the 14th." Morris D. Forkosch, "Who Are the

People in the Preamble to the Constitution?," *Case Western Reserve Law Review* 19, no. 644 (1968) (scholarlycommons.law.case.edu/caselrev/vol19/iss3/8).

94. Joe Fallon, "Lincoln and the Death of the Old Republic," *VDARE*, January 5, 2003(www.vdare.com/articles/lincoln-and-the-death-of-the-old-republic).

95. Paul Craig Roberts, "Lincoln and the War on Terror: A Conservative Reappraisal," *VDARE*, March 19, 2002 (www.vdare.com/articles/lincoln-and-the-war-on-terror-a-conservative-reappraisal).

96. Hunter Wallace [Brad Griffin], "Happy John Wilkes Booth Day!," *Occidental Dissent*, April 26, 2012 (www.occidentaldissent.com/2012/04/26/happy-john-wilkes-booth-day/).

97. Derbyshire further writes: "You may disagree with Lincoln's reading of the Founders, but there is no doubt he revered them and interpreted them sincerely, to the best of his ability . . . and so on." John Derbyshire, "Lowry on Lincoln: A Safe Whiggish Pep Talk for GOP Loyalists—Useless on the Real Issues," *VDARE*, August 22, 2013 (www.vdare.com/articles/lowry-on-lincoln-a-safe-whiggish-pep-talk-for-gop-loyalists-useless-on-the-real-issues).

98. Taylor; *What the Founders Really Thought about Race*, p. 10. Taylor is here quoting Lincoln in his fourth debate with Stephen Douglas. See "Lincoln-Douglas Debates 4th Debate Part I, Charleston, Illinois, September 18, 1858," TeachingAmericanHistory.org (teachingamericanhistory.org/library/document/the-lincoln-douglas-debates-4th-debate-part-i/).

99. "Abraham Lincoln: What They Won't Teach You in School," *Daily Stormer*, April 8, 2014 (www.dailystormer.com/abraham-lincoln-what-they-wont-teach-you-in-school/).

100. Abraham Lincoln, First Lincoln-Douglas debate, Ottawa, Ill., August 21, 1858; see *First Debate: Ottawa, Illinois—Lincoln Home National Historic Site*, National Park Service (www.nps.gov/liho/learn/historyculture/debate1.htm).

101. Taylor; *What the Founders Really Thought about Race*; p. 10.

102. Lincoln, First Lincoln-Douglas debate.

Chapter 7

1. *Oxford Living Dictionaries English* (en.oxforddictionaries.com/definition/racism).

2. "Prejudice Plus Power," *Wikipedia* (en.wikipedia.org/wiki/Prejudice_plus_power).

3. Özlem Sensoy and Robin DiAngelo, *Is Everyone Really Equal? An Introduction to Key Concepts in Social Justice Education*, 2nd ed. (New York: Teachers College Press, 2017), p. 125.

4. Interestingly, an empirical study of how a multiracial, nationwide sample of 2,474 respondents evaluated two scenarios of race relations "raise[d] serious questions about the plausibility of a 'blacks cannot be racists' perspective being common among African-Americans." See George Yancey, " 'Blacks Cannot Be Racists': A Look at How European-Americans, African-Americans, Hispanic-

Americans and Asian-Americans Perceive Minority Racism," *Michigan Socio-logical Review* 19 (Fall 2005), p. 149.

5. Hunter Wallace [Brad Griffin], "Why Do You Hate America?," *Occidental Dissent*, November 22, 2011 (www.occidentaldissent.com/why-do-you-hate-america/).

6. Richard M. Weaver, *Ideas Have Consequences* (University of Chicago Press, 1948).

7. Interview with Greg Johnson, October 7, 2016.

8. Ibid.

9. Interview with Richard Spencer, September 29, 2016.

10. Zeiger, "Libertarianism and Marxism: The Twin Offspring of Liberalism," *The Right Stuff*, November 5, 2015 (therightstuff.biz/2015/11/05/libertarianism-and-marxism-two-sides-of-the-same-coin/).

11. Interview with Kevin MacDonald, February 7, 2017.

12. Ibid.

13. Michael Cushman, "Mike Enoch Interview with Dr. Thomas Main," *Occidental Dissent*, February 23, 2017 (www.occidentaldissent.com/2017/02/23/mike-enoch-interview-with-dr-thomas-main/).

14. Jared Taylor, "Spread the Message of White Consciousness," *American Renaissance*, January 26, 2017 (www.amren.com/commentary/2017/01/spread-message-white-consciousness/). See also "Printed Posters," *American Renaissance* (www.amren.com/printable-posters/).

15. Nathan Glazer and Daniel P. Moynihan, *Beyond the Melting Pot: The Negroes, Puerto Ricans, Jews, Italians and Irish of New York*, 2nd ed. (MIT Press, 1970), p. xxii.

16. Ibid., p. xxxix.

17. Black Lives Matter, "What We Believe," BlackLivesMatter.com (blacklivesmatter.com/about/what-we-believe/).

18. Interview with Mike Enoch, February 22, 2017.

19. "About Us," *American Renaissance* (www.amren.com/about/).

20. "Race: The Power of an Illusion," PBS, program transcript, 2003 (www.pbs.org/race/000_About/002_04-about-01-01.htm).

21. Jared Taylor, "Race Realism & the Alt Right," *Counter-Currents Publishing*, October 25, 2016 (www.counter-currents.com/2016/10/race-realism-and-the-alt-right/).

22. Alex Kurtagic, "Moral Barriers to White Survival," *American Renaissance*, November 2011 (www.amren.com/features/2012/11/moral-barriers-to-white-survival/). Also found at Chechar (WordPress.com/2013/02/19/Egalitarianism-Evil/).

23. John Derbyshire, "John Derbyshire on Why Race Realism Makes More Sense than 'Magic Dirt' Theory," *VDARE*, November 1, 2015 (www.vdare.com/articles/john-derbyshire-on-why-race-realism-makes-more-sense-than-magic-dirt-theory).

24. Michael Bell, "The Caste System of the Alt Right," *Counter-Currents*

Publishing, September 22, 2016 (www.counter-currents.com/2016/09/the-caste-system-of-the-alt-right/).

25. Interview with Hunter Wallace [Brad Griffin], February 7, 2017.

26. Taylor, "Race Realism *&* the Alt Right."

27. Sean Last, "Gavin McInnes, Race, and Cuckservatism," *The Right Stuff*, August 9, 2015 (www.therightstuff.biz/2015/08/09/gavin-mcinnes-race-and-cuckservatism/).

28. Steve Sailer, "'Climate Change,' 'Population Change,' and the Need for an Immigration Moratorium," *VDARE*, published December 3, 2009 (www.vdare.com/articles/climate-change-population-change-and-the-need-for-an-immigration-moratorium).

29. Philip Santoro, "What Does It Mean for Whites If Climate Change Is Real?," *American Renaissance*, September 10, 2017 (www.amren.com/news/2017/09/climate-change-mass-immigration-green-identity-politics/).

30. NASA, *Vital Signs of the Planet: Facts*, "Scientific Consensus: Earth's Climate Is Warming" (climate.nasa.gov/scientific-consensus/).

31. Introduction to Part III, "Metaphysics and Philosophy of Science," in *The Oxford Handbook of Philosophy and Race*, edited by Naomi Zack (Oxford University Press, 2017), p. 135.

32. John H. Relethford, "Biological Anthropology, Population Genetics, and Race," in Naomi Zack, ed., *The Oxford Handbook of Philosophy and Race*, p. 168.

33. Ulric Neisser et al., "Intelligence: Knowns and Unknowns," *American Psychologist* 51, no. 2 (February 1996), p. 77 (differentialclub.wdfiles.com/local-files/definitions-structure-and-measurement/Intelligence-Knowns-and-unknowns.pdf).

34. Ibid., p. 97.

35. Ibid., p. 90.

36. Robert Nozick, *Philosophical Explanations* (Harvard University Press, 1981), p. 325.

37. David Reich, "Race in the Age of Modern Genetics," *New York Times*, March 25, 2018.

38. Quintilian; "The Future Is White," *Counter-Currents Publishing*, August 28, 2017 (www.counter-currents.com/2017/08/the-future-is-white/).

39. Charles the Hammer, "Psychological Hurdles to the Right," *The Right Stuff*, June 5, 2015 (therightstuff.biz/2015/06/05/psychological-hurdles-to-the-right/).

40. F. Roger Devlin and Richard B. Spencer, "Race: Stalking the Wild Taboo," *Radix Journal*, July 6, 2016 (www.radixjournal.com/the-red-pill/2016/7/6/race).

41. Interview with Jared Taylor, September 27, 2016.

42. Ibid.

43. Jared Taylor, "*Why Race Matters:* A Philosopher's Elegant and Compelling Dissection of the Race Problem," *American Renaissance*, October 1997 (www.amren.com/news/2017/12/why-race-matters-michael-levin-iq-review-jared-taylor/).

44. Michael Levin, *Why Race Matters: Race Differences and What They Mean* (Westport, Conn: Praeger, 1997), p. 10.

45. Taylor, *"Why Race Matters."*

46. Jared Taylor, "The Racial Revolution," *American Renaissance* 10, no. 5 (May 1999) (www.amren.com/news/2008/09/the_racial_revo/). Emphasis added.

47. Ibid.

48. Jared Taylor, "Africa in Our Midst," *American Renaissance* 16, no. 10 (October 2005) (www.amren.com/archives/back-issues/october-2005/).

49. Jamie Hines, "Race Realist Jared Taylor Declares the 'Civil Rights Struggle Was Won Long Ago,'" *Washington Examiner*, July 20, 2010, reposted on *American Renaissance*, July 20, 2010 (www.amren.com/news/2010/07/race_realist_ja/).

50. Cited in Jared Taylor, "The Long Retreat on Race," *American Renaissance*, August 23, 2013 (www.amren.com/features/2013/08/the-long-retreat-on-race/).

51. Ibid.

52. Jared Taylor, "An Open Letter to Cuckservatives," *American Renaissance*, July 30, 2015 (www.amren.com/news/2015/07/an-open-letter-to-cuckservatives/).

53. Peter Brimelow, "Children of the Angry Apes: Salon and Its Stale Smear," *VDARE*, May 24, 2003 (www.vdare.com/articles/children-of-the-angry-apes-salon-and-its-stale-smear#right-wing); Jared Taylor, "Jared Taylor: Donald Trump, White Supremacism, and the Insanity of the WASHINGTON POST," January 14, 2016 (www.vdare.com/articles/jared-taylor-donald-trump-white-supremacism-and-the-insanity-of-the-washington-post). See also Jared Taylor and Peter Brimelow, "'A Public/Private Initiative to Curtail Debate'"—The Op-Ed the NYT Wouldn't Run," *VDARE*, September 9, 2017 (www.vdare.com/articles/a-publicprivate-initiative-to-curtail-debate-the-op-ed-the-nyt-wouldnt-run); VDARE.com Reader, "A Reader Asks 'Is VDARE.Com White Supremacist?' Peter Brimelow Replies," *VDARE*, April 20, 2004 (www.vdare.com/letters/a-reader-asks-is-vdarecom-white-supremacist-peter-brimelow-replies).

54. *Oxford Living Dictionaries English* (en.oxforddictionaries.com/definition/nigger; en.oxforddictionaries.com/definition/white supremacist), accessed March 3, 2018.

55. Throughout this book, the word "factual," when used in connection with equality or inequality, refers to personal traits or characteristics such as intelligence, temperament, strength, and so forth. Of course, inequalities of social resources such as income, employment, and wealth are matters of fact too. When it is said here that political equality does not depend on factual equality, what I mean is that people can be politically equal even if they are unequal in terms of important personal traits. Whether political equality depends on a certain amount of equality of social resources is a separate issue not for the most part taken up in this book.

56. Eugene Gant, "On Independence Day, a Catholic Reflects on Race," *VDARE*, July 5, 2017 (www.vdare.com/articles/on-independence-day-a-catholic-reflects-on-race).

57. Lindsay M. Howden and Julie A. Meyer, "2010 Census Briefs, Age and Sex Composition: 2010," U.S. Census Bureau; C2010BT-03; p. 2; Table 1. Population by Sex and Selected Age Groups: 2000 and 2010 (May 2011).

Chapter 8

1. Gregory Hood, *Waking Up from the American Dream* (San Francisco: Counter-Currents Publishing, 2016), p. 13.

2. Hunter Wallace, "The Southern Project: On Romanticizing Failed Republics," *Occidental Dissent*, January 17, 2015 (www.occidentaldissent.com/the-southern-project-on-romanticizing-failed-republics/).

3. Interview with Mike Enoch, February 22, 2017.

4. Peter Brimelow, "Dear Reader!," n.d. (www.vdare.com/vdare-quarterly). Bold in the original.

5. Peter Brimelow, "America, Anti-America, and the Role of VDARE.com," *VDARE*, September 18, 2012 (www.vdare.com/articles/america-anti-america-and-the-role-of-vdarecom-0).

6. Peter Brimelow, back cover copy to paperback edition of Michael Hart, *Restoring America* (Litchfield, Conn.: VDARE.com Books, 2015).

7. VDARE.com Reader, "An Irish Reader Is Puzzled about the 'Historic American Nation,'" February 1, 2017 (www.vdare.com/letters/an-irish-reader-is-puzzled-about-the-historic-american-nation).

8. Ibid.

9. Peter Brimelow, "Brimelow on Canada, US: 'We May See Boundaries Redrawn across North America,'" transcript of podcast, *VDARE*, March 15, 2017 (www.vdare.com/articles/brimelow-on-canada-us-we-may-see-boundaries-redrawn-across-north-america).

10. Brimelow, "America, Anti-America, and the Role of VDARE.com." Bold in the original.

11. Ibid. Emphasis added.

12. Albert Jackson, "A New Nation Is Finding It Can Speak," *Occidental Dissent*, April 10, 2010 (www.occidentaldissent.com/2010/04/10/a-new-nation-is-finding-it-can-speak/).

13. Hunter Wallace [Brad Griffin], "Why Do You Hate America?," *Occidental Dissent*, November 22, 2011 (www.occidentaldissent.com/why-do-you-hate-america/).

14. Michael Hart, *Restoring America* (Litchfield, Conn.: VDARE.com Books, 2015), p. 9. See also Michael Hart, "Michael Hart's RESTORING AMERICA—The Introduction," *VDARE*, September 26, 2015 (www.vdare.com/articles/michael-harts-restoring-america-the-introduction).

15. Samuel Francis, "An Infantile Disorder," *Chronicles*, January 1, 1998 (www. chroniclesmagazine.org/1998/February/22/2/magazine/article/10834562/).

16. Interview with Richard Spencer, September 29, 2016.

17. How Derbyshire squares his endorsement of Hart's book with the opposition to secession he expressed to me during an interview is not clear. Derbyshire said, "We have the USA. And it's not that bad, we've got issues but it's not that bad. Let's try to keep it working. So I'm not for secession" (interview with John Derbyshire; October 4, 2016).

18. John Derbyshire, Peter Brimelow, back cover copy to paperback edition of Michael Hart, *Restoring America*.

19. James Fulford, "Paul Gottfried on Michael Hart's *Restoring America*," *VDARE*, November 5, 2015 (www.vdare.com/posts/paul-gottfried-on-michael-harts-restoring-america). For the full version of Gottfried's review, see Paul Gottfried; "Secession Is Our Only Hope," *LewRockwell.com*, November 5, 2015 (www.lewrockwell.com/2015/11/paul-gottfried/secession-hope/).

20. James Fulford, "The Fulford File: Nothing Succeeds Like Secession—A VDARE.com Secession Roundup," *VDARE*, November 24, 2012 (www.vdare. com/articles/the-fulford-file-nothing-succeeds-like-secession-a-vdarecom-secession-roundup).

21. *Texas v. White*, 74 U.S. 700 (www.law.cornell.edu/supremecourt/text/74 /700).

22. Eric Turkewits, "Scalia: 'There Is No Right to Secede,'" *New York Personal Injury Law Blog*; February 16, 2010 (www.newyorkpersonalinjuryattorney-blog.com/2010/02/scalia-there-is-no-right-to-secede.html).

23. Alexander Hamilton, *Federalist* No. 9, *Federalist Papers* (www.gutenberg. org/files/1404/1404-h/1404-h.htm#link2H_4_0009).

24. Richard Spencer, "Facing the Future as a Minority," April 30, 2013 (Alexandria, Va.: National Policy Institute (www.npiamerica.org/the-national-policy-institute/blog/facing-the-future-as-a-minority).

25. Jared Taylor, "The Myth of Diversity," *American Renaissance* 8, nos. 7/8 (July–August 1997).

26. Interview with Jared Taylor, September 27, 2016.

27. Greg Johnson, "The Slow Cleanse," *Counter-Currents Publishing*, June 24, 2014 (www.counter-currents.com/2014/06/the-slow-cleanse/).

28. Interview with Greg Johnson, October 7, 2016.

29. William Z. Foster, *Toward Soviet America* (International Publishers, printed by Coward-McCann, New York, 1932), p. 304.

30. John W. van Zanten, "Communist Theory and the American Negro Question," *Review of Politics* 29, no. 4 (October 1967), p. 444.

31. Hart, *Restoring America*, p. 77.

32. Alexander Hamilton, *Federalist* No. 7, *Federalist Papers* (www.gutenberg. org/files/1404/1404-h/1404-h.htm#link2H_4_0007).

33. Interview with Mike Enoch, February 22, 2017.

34. Samuel T. Francis, *Leviathan & Its Enemies*, p. 722. The quotation regarding "a prison-house" is from Arnold J. Toynbee, *A Study of History*, 2 vols., abridged (Oxford University Press, 1946–57), vol. 1, p. 77.

Chapter 9

1. Glenn Thrush and Maggie Haberman, "Bannon Is Given Security Role Usually Held for Generals," *New York Times*, January 29, 2017.

2. Ben Shapiro, "I Know Trump's New Campaign Chairman, Steve Bannon: Here's What You Need to Know," *Daily Wire*, August 16, 2017, updated November 13, 2016 (www.dailywire.com/news/8441/i-know-trumps-new-campaign-chairman-steve-bannon-ben-shapiro).

3. Sarah Posner, "How Donald Trump's New Campaign Chief Created an Online Haven for White Nationalists," *Mother Jones*, August 22, 2016 (www.motherjones.com/politics/2016/08/stephen-bannon-donald-trump-alt-right-breitbart-news).

4. Kimberley A. Strassel, "Steve Bannon on Politics as War," *Wall Street Journal*, November 18, 2016.

5. Betsy Woodruff and Gideon Resnick, "Alt Right Rejoices at Donald Trump's Steve Bannon Hire," *Daily Beast*, August 17, 2016 (www.thedailybeast.com/articles/2016/08/17/alt-right-rejoices-at-trump-s-steve-bannon-hire.html).

6. Correspondence from Jared Taylor, November 20, 2016.

7. Correspondence from Greg Johnson, November 19, 2016.

8. Hunter Wallace [Brad Griffin], "The Truth about Steve Bannon," *Occidental Dissent*, November 20, 2016 (www.occidentaldissent.com/2016/11/20/the-truth-about-steve-bannon/#comment-3396676.).

9. Interview with Mike Enoch, February 22, 2017

10. Assemblyman Tim Donnelly, "Government, Not Racism, Is the Greatest Threat," *Breitbart News*, January 19, 2015 (www.breitbart.com/.../government-not-racism-is-the-greatest-threat/) ("Lincoln shrewdly chose the Declaration as his benchmark. The idea of 'all men created equal' was the most inspiring possible goal"). Another *Breitbart* article endorsing Jefferson's words is Joel B. Pollak, "Democrats Desecrate Martin Luther King, Jr.'s Legacy," *Breitbart News*, January 16, 2012 (www.breitbart.com/.../democrats-desecrate-martin-luther-king-jrs-legacy/) ("Americans celebrate Martin Luther King, Jr.'s birthday to honor his contributions to our Republic. His struggle against racial prejudice and discrimination brought the words of the Founders—'that all men are created equal'—to true fruition").

11. Gerald Warner, "Hoist It High and Proud: The Confederate Flag Proclaims Glorious Heritage," *Breitbart News*, July 1, 2015 (www.breitbart.com/.../hoist-it-high-and-proud-the-confederate-flag-proclaims-a-glorious-heritage/).

12. Anti-Defamation League, *Anti-Semitic Targeting of Journalists during the*

2016 Presidential Campaign: A Report from ADL's Task Force on Harassment and Journalism (New York, October 19, 2016), p. 6.

13. Mike Pesca, "The Alt-Right Is Using Trump: Ben Sapiro on How the Group Will Take Advantage of Its Newfound Prominence," *Slate*, November 23, 2016 (www.slate.com/articles/news_and_politics/gist/2016/11/ben_shapiro_on_steve_bannon_the_alt_right_and_why_the_left_needs_to_turn.html).

14. Strassel, "Steve Bannon on Politics as War."

15. John Hayward, "Immigration, Migration, and the Death of Democracy," *Breitbart News*, August 26, 2015 (www.breitbart.com/.../immigration-migration-and-the-death-of-democracy/).

16. Warner, "Hoist It High and Proud."

17. For a full transcript of Bannon's Vatican remarks, see Lester Feder, "This Is How Steve Bannon Sees the Entire World," *BuzzFeed News*, November 15, 2016, updated November 16, 2016 (www.buzzfeed.com/lesterfeder/this-is-how-steve-bannon-sees-the-entire-world?utm_term=.uvV01xWAk#.xxl2qEwRG). An unedited audio recording of these words can be found at soundcloud.com/buzzfeednews/steve-bannon-at-dhi.

18. Ibid.

19. Anton Shekhovtsov and Andreas Umland, "Is Aleksandr Dugin a Traditionalist? 'Neo-Eurasianism' and Perennial Philosophy," *Russian Review* 68, no. 4 (October 2009), p. 676.

20. Guido Stucco, "Translator's Preface," in Julius Evola, *Revolt against the Modern World* (Rochester, Vt.: Inner Traditions International, 1969), p. xxiii.

21. Edmund Burke; *Reflections on the Revolution in France and on the Proceedings in Certain Societies in London Relative to that Event* (New York: Penguin Books, 1968) p. 183.

22. Evola; *Revolt against the Modern World*, p. 55.

23. Guido Stucco, "The Legacy of a European Traditionalist: Julius Evola in Perspective," in *The Fourth Political Theory*, n.d. (www.4pt.su/bg/node/705).

24. Evola, *Revolt against the Modern World*, p. xxxi.

25. Ibid., p. 3.

26. Julius Evola, *Gli uomini e le rovine* (Rome: Edizioni Settimo Sigillo, 1990), p. 41. Quoted in Guido Stucco, "The Legacy of a European Traditionalist."

27. Evola, *Revolt against the Modern World*, p. 184.

28. Ibid., p. 167.

29. Ibid., p. 364.

30. Ibid.

31. Ibid., p. 365.

32. James D. Heiser; *"The American Empire Should Be Destroyed": Aleksander Dugin and the Perils of Immanentized Eschatology* (Malone, Tex.: Repristination Press, 2014), p. 41.

33. Alexander Dugin, *The Fourth Political Theory* (London: Arktos, 2012), pp. 51–52.

34. Ibid., p. 52.

35. Ibid., p. 53.

36. Ibid.

37. Mark Lilla provides a balanced account of Heidegger in chapter 1 of *The Reckless Mind: Intellectuals in Politics* (New York: New York Review Books, 2001). Lilla's summary of the literature on that philosopher's association with the Nazi party convincingly refutes "Heidegger's air-brushed account of this period" and notes that Heidegger at one point explained to a "former student how concepts in *Being and Time* had inspired his political commitment" (pp. 21–23).

38. When a humorous newspaper article made the "sarcastic suggestion to bring Alaska 'home' to Russia . . . Aleksandr Dugin, a prominent nationalist ideologist and proponent of Eurasianism, stressed, 'You meant this as a joke, but we did not get it. Let's sit and discuss the terms of the sale.'" See Andrei A. Znamenski; "History with an Attitude: Alaska in Modern Russian Patriotic Rhetoric," *Jahrbücher für Geschichte Osteuropas* (2009), pp. 346–73. Regarding Dugin's remarks on Ukraine, see Catherine A. Fitzpatrick, "Russia This Week: Dugin Dismissed from Moscow State University?" (23–29 June), *Interpreter*, June 27, 2014 (www.interpretermag.com/russia-this-week-what-will-be-twitters-fate-in-russia/).

39. "Alexander Dugin on Martin Heidegger, Interviewed by Michael Millerman, November 3, 2015," in Alexander Dugin, *The Fourth Political Theory*, vol. 2, *The Rise of the Fourth Political Theory* (London: Arktos, 2017), pp. 218–19.

40. Sohrab Ahmari; "How the Kremlin Sees Trump's Re-Reset with Moscow," *Wall Street Journal*, November 20, 2016.

41. Alexander Dugin; "Donald Trump: The Swamp and the Fire," *The Fourth Political Theory* (www.4pt.su/en/content/donald-trump-swamp-and-fire).

42. Thomas D. Williams, "Fake News! Newsweek Continues War on Steve Bannon by Inventing Russia 'Ties,'" *Breitbart News*, April 19, 2017 (www.breitbart.com/big-government/2017/04/19/newsweek-war-on-steve-bannon-inventing-russia-ties/).

43. Richard B. Spencer, "Clinton's Attack on the Alt Right," press release, National Policy Institute, August 25, 2016 (www.radixjournal.com/blog/).

44. José Ortega y Gasset, *The Revolt of the Masses* (New York: W. W. Norton, 1932), p. 76.

45. Allum Bokhari and Milo Yiannopoulos, "An Establishment Conservative's Guide to the Alt-Right," *Breitbart News*, March 29, 2016 (www.breitbart.com/tech/2016/03/29/an-establishment-conservatives-guide-to-the-alt-right/).

46. Herbert Marcuse, *Counterrevolution and Revolt* (Boston: Beacon Press, 1972), p. 51.

47. Caleb Howe, "Trump Retweets 'White Genocide' Account . . . Stop Me If You've Heard This One," *Red State*, February 10, 2016 (www.redstate.com/absentee/2016/02/10/trump-retweets-white-genocide-account-...-stop-youve-heard-one/).

48. Deborah Solomon, "Found a transcript of my '09 talk w/Trump for the @NYTimes. He says he doesn't get why 'all men are created equal,'" January 16, 2017, tweet quoting Donald Trump's words (twitter.com/deborahsolo/status/821048406550441984).

49. See *The Daily Beast*, "But it's not true. Because all people and all men aren't created equal," August 14, 2017, tweet quoting Donald Trump's words (twitter.com/thedailybeast/status/897233073821151232).

50. Samuel Francis, "Message from MARs: The Social Politics of the New Right," *Beautiful Losers: Essays on the Failure of American Conservatism* (University of Missouri Press, 1993), p. 67. Originally published in Robert W. Whitaker, ed., *The New Right Papers* (New York: St. Martin's Press, 1982), pp. 64–83.

51. Ibid., pp. 74–76.

52. Francis, *Beautiful Losers*, pp. 10–11.

53. Anton Stigermark, "James Burnham—Like Gramsci, Only Better," ALTRIGHT.com, June 4, 2016 (altright.com/2016/06/04/james-burnham-like-gramsci-only-better/).

54. James Kirkpatrick, "Donald Trump, Sam Francis and the Emergence of the Alternative ('Dissident') Right," *VDARE*, January 22, 2016 (www.vdare.com/articles/donald-trump-sam-francis-and-the-emergence-of-the-alternative-dissident-right).

Chapter 10

1. C. S. Peirce, "The Essentials of Pragmatism," in *Philosophical Writings of Peirce*, edited by Justus Buchler (New York: Dover Publications, 1955), p. 256.

2. Aristotle, *Nicomachean Ethics*, 1099b30.

3. Leon Trotsky, *Their Morals and Ours*, Marxists Internet Archive (www.marxists.org/archive/trotsky/1938/morals/morals.htm).

4. See, for example, Fareed Zakaria, "The End of the End of History," *Newsweek*; September 23, 2001; and George Will; "The End of Our Holiday from History," *Jewish World Review*, September 12, 2001. Francis Fukuyama responded to these and other critics in "History Is Still Going Our Way," *Wall Street Journal*, October 5, 2001

5. Steve Sailer, "Will U.S. Retain Its 'Market-Dominant Majority'?," *VDARE*, February 2, 2003 (www.vdare.com/articles/will-us-retain-its-market-dominant-majority).

6. Friedrich A. Hayek, "Who? Whom?," in *The Road to Serfdom* (University of Chicago Press, 1944, 1972), pp. 101–18.

7. Steve Sailer, "Who Said 'Who? Whom?' Lenin, Trotsky, or Stalin?," *VDARE*, June 19, 2017 (www.vdare.com/posts/who-said-who-whom-lenin-trotsky-or-stalin).

8. The historian Ronald Radosh reported that Bannon made this comment to him at a party in Washington, D.C., on November 12, 2013. The

fact-checking website *Snopes* concluded, "While the purported quote bears a resemblance to other comments that Bannon has made, we have marked it as 'Unproven' since we have been unable to turn up any other documentation of the conversation Bannon specifically said he does not recall. A request for comment from Bannon had not been responded to by publication time." The journalist Diana West found inconsistencies in Radosh's account that he later corrected. Radosh is an accomplished historian of American communism and Cold War politics who has no reason to lie on this matter. Ronald Radosh, "Steve Bannon, Trump's Top Guy, Told Me He Was 'a Leninist,'" *Daily Beast*, August 22, 2016 (www.thedailybeast.com/steve-bannon-trumps-top-guy-told-me-he-was-a-leninist); Dan Evon, "Did Steve Bannon Describe Himself as 'Leninist' Who Wants to Destroy the State?," *Snopes*, February 3, 2017 (www.snopes.com/bannon-leninist-destroy-state/); Diana West, re-posting, "After Fact-Checking, What's Left?," February 4, 2017.

9. Richard B. Spencer, "Canon Wars," *Radix Journal*, November 20, 2010 (www.radixjournal.com/altright-archive/altright-archive/main/blogs/untimely-observations/canon-wars?).

10. Another vital question is whether purely positive science can justify the normative decision to politically privilege whites. This issue is a matter of ethical theory and so beyond the scope of this book.

11. Friedrich Engels, "Speech at the Graveside of Karl Marx," in *The Marx-Engels Reader*, edited by Robert C. Tucker (New York: W. W. Norton, 1972), p. 603.

12. On July 4, 2017, the new website very recently established by Richard Spencer, ALTRIGHT.com, posted an article that answered its title's question in the affirmative: "Was Independence Day a Mistake?" In the article's comment section a poster using the anti-Semitic pseudonym Yehudah Finkelstein drew out the implication: "Locke was wrong. The Founders were wrong. . . . The Alt Right embraces Hobbes, Machiavelli, and Schmitt" (altright.com/2017/07/04/was-independence-day-a-mistake/). Interestingly, Richard Spencer also presents the latter three authors as his canon of "Illiberal Political Philosophy": Richard B. Spencer, "Canon Wars," *Radix Journal*, November 20, 2010 (www.radixjournal.com/altright-archive/altright-archive/main/blogs/untimely-observations/canon-wars?).

13. According to Hobbes, revolution is always unjustifiable unless the sovereign power is entirely unable to protect the physical well-being of the subjects (Hobbes, *Leviathan*, chap. 21, "Of the Liberty of Subjects," chap. 29, "Of Those Things That Weaken or Tend to the Dissolution of a Commonwealth"). Schmitt agrees entirely with Hobbes (Carl Schmitt, *The Concept of the Political*, expanded ed. [University of Chicago Press, 2007], p. 52). For Machiavelli, reordering a polity's constitution involves danger, peril, the possibility of ruin, and cannot be attempted unless necessity so demands (Machiavelli, *Discourses*, chap. 2, "Of the Kinds of Republics there are, and of which was the Roman Republic").

14. For a brief but useful account of the ethics of revolution, see Herbert Marcuse, "Ethics and Revolution," in *Ethics and Society: Original Essays on Contemporary Moral Problems*, edited by Richard T. DeGeorge (Garden City, N.Y.: Anchor Books, 1966), pp. 133–47. One scholar astutely commented that Marcuse's "doctrine is disarming in its simplicity: revolutions are justified provided that, first, the proposed new society represents a gain in freedom and would secure more liberty, of more kinds, to more people, and second, the revolutionary movement has a fair chance of achieving and maintaining the projected changes. The doctrine surprises not only by its simplicity but also by its moderation. Here is a notorious leftist speaking in the accents of John Locke. . . . Marcuse is no Leninist. Revolutions need to be justified because they involve coercion, violence, misery, and death, and there is no sacred class or movement whose revolutionary activities are exempt from moral appraisal." Keith Campbell, "Marcuse on the Justification of Revolution," *Politics* 4, no. 2 (1969), pp.161–67.

15. Greg Johnson, "The Slow Cleanse," *Counter-Currents Publishing*, June 24, 2014 (www.counter-currents.com/2014/06/the-slow-cleanse/)

16. John Michael, "Intellectuals and Democracy: Ambivalence, Sovereignty, Translation," in *The New Public Intellectual: Politics, Theory, and the Public Sphere*, edited by Jeffrey R. Di Leo and Peter Hitchcock (New York: Palgrave Macmillan, 2016), p. 100.

17. Michael writes, "The intellectual may have to stop celebrating democracy and acknowledge an ambivalence toward democratic communities" (ibid., p. 97). Gottfried says of liberal democracy, "No one but a fool could imagine that the term we are discussing is purely descriptive. It is a god term, on the altar of which the worshipper can never slay enough fattened calves. 'Liberal democratic' has been made to serve a number of political purposes, but the key thing is its invariably polemical character." Paul Gottfried, "What Is Liberal Democracy? Exploring a Problematic Term," *Nomocracy in Politics*, April 4, 2014 (nomocracyinpolitics.com/2014/04/16/what-is-liberal-democracy-exploring-a-problematic-term-by-paul-gottfried/). See also Paul Gottfried, "Strauss and the Straussians" (www.nhinet.org/gottfried18-1&2.pdf). Foolish as it may be, this book uses the term "liberal democracy" to describe a political philosophy that embraces political equality, human rights, the necessity of a limited state, the rule of law, electoral democracy, a political culture of tolerance, and the right of revolution against tyranny.

18. James Burnham, *The Machiavellians: Defenders of Freedom* (New York: John Day Co., 1943), p. 166.

19. Samuel Francis in *Power and History* sums up the central thesis of elite theory as follows. "Driven by insatiable appetites and irrational beliefs, men seek to dominate each other or to escape domination by others. This struggle inevitably results in a minority coming to power, monopolizing as much as possible political, economic, military, technical, and honorific resources and excluding and oppressing the majority. In this way there is formed an 'elite'

(Pareto), 'ruling class' (Mosca), or 'oligarchy' (Michels) that rules the majority and exploits it for its own benefit through force and fraud . . . The record of this unending rise and fall of ruling minorities is human history."

20. Kevin MacDonald, "I agree with Adelson: Democracy Is Not a Jewish Value (or a Reality in the U.S.)," *Occidental Observer*, November 17, 2014 (www. theoccidentalobserver.net/2014/11/17/i-agree-with-adelson-democracy-is-not-a-jewish-value-or-a-reality-in-the-u-s/).

21. Kevin MacDonald, "Why Do Jewish Organizations Want Anti-Israel Refugees?," *VDARE*, January 17, 2017 (www.vdare.com/articles/why-do-jewish-leaders-want-anti-israel-refugees).

22. Sahil Kapur, "Scholar behind Viral 'Oligarchy' Study Tells You What It Means," *Talking Points Memo*, April 22, 2014 (talkingpointsmemo.com/dc/princeton-scholar-demise-of-democracy-america-tpm-interview).

23. Jeffrey A. Winters and Benjamin I. Page, "Oligarchy in the United States?," *Perspectives on Politics* 7, no. 4 (December 2009), pp. 731–51.

24. Ibid.

25. Ibid., p. 740.

26. Ibid., p. 738.

27. Andrew Anglin, "A Normie's Guide to the Alt-Right," *Daily Stormer*, August 31, 2016 (www.dailystormer.com/a-normies-guide-to-the-alt-right/).

28. Sidney Hook, "The Ethics of Controversy," in *The Essential Essays: Sidney Hook on Pragmatism, Democracy, and Freedom*, edited by Robert B. Talisse and Robert Tempio (Amherst, N.Y.: Prometheus Books, 2002), pp. 290–91.

29. Ibid., p. 294.

30. Ibid., pp. 294–95.

31. Jürgen Habermas, "Discourse Ethics: Notes on a Program of Philosophical Justification," in *The Communicative Ethics Controversy*, edited by Seyla Benhabib and Fred Dallmayr (MIT Press, 1990), pp. 85–86. Habermas notes that here he is presenting "rules of discourse" for an "ideal speech situation" suggested by R. Alexy "following my analysis." These rules are cited in John Branstetter, "The (Broken?) Promise of Digital Democracy: An Early Assessment," *International Journal of Technology, Knowledge and Society* 7, no. 3 (2011), p. 154.

32. Seyla Benhabib, *Critique, Norm, and Utopia: A Study of the Foundations of Critical Theory* (Columbia University Press, 1986), p. 285.

33. In response to criticism from John B. Thompson, Habermas has written: "I regard as justified the admonition that I have hitherto not taken the 'evidential dimension' of the concept of truth adequately into account." Jürgen Habermas, "A Reply to My Critics," in *Habermas: Critical Debates*, edited by John B. Thompson and David Held (MIT Press, 1982), p. 274. Benhabib has also criticized Habermas's treatment of the evidential dimension (Benhabib, *Critique, Norm, and Utopia*, p. 286.)

34. Carl Schmitt, *The Concept of the Political*, expanded ed., translated by George Schwab (University of Chicago Press, 2007), p. 26.

35. aberrantharpooner; "Refusal to Name the Enemy: Schmittian Political Reality, Conservatism, & the Alt-Right," *Dissident Right*, August 31, 2016 (dissidentright.com/2016/08/31/refusal-to-name-the-enemy-carl-schmitt-political-reality-conservatism-and-the-alt-right/).

36. Schmitt; *The Concept of the Political*, p. 29.

37. Ibid., p. 28.

38. Carl von Clausewitz, *On War*, edited and translated by Michael Howard and Peter Paret (Princeton University Press, 1976), p. 75.

39. Of course, voting, campaigning, and so forth are impossible unless the law is enforced, and law enforcement is impossible unless, ultimately, the state can exercise a legitimate use of force. Will it be said on this basis that all apparently nonviolent political activities "potentially" involve a confrontation between fighting collectivities of people, which is war, and thus do in fact assume the friend/enemy distinction? This argument equates law enforcement with war making and so ignores Schmitt's insistence that "the friend and enemy concepts are to be understood in their concrete and existential sense, not as metaphors or symbols" (Schmitt, *The Concept of the Political*, p. 27).

40. Ibid., p. 27.

41. aberrantharpooner; "Refusal to Name the Enemy."

42. Peter Brimelow, "The Immigration Debate: Racism—or Treason?," *VDARE*; May 28, 2006 (www.vdare.com/articles/the-immigration-debate-racism-or-treason).

43. In this article, Brimelow writes: "But the Founders did not mean that only armed attack constituted treason. The Supreme Court, in *Cramer*, quoted a definition of treason as 'an act which weakens or tends to weaken the power of the [United States] . . .' Treason required an act and conscious intent; but not necessarily war." But Brimelow's quotation from *Cramer v. United States*, which reversed the treason conviction of an American citizen who had meetings with Nazi saboteurs, is grossly out of context. The relevant section of the case is as follows: "'Aid and comfort' was defined . . . with as much precision as the nature of the matter will permit: '. . . an act which strengthens or tends to strengthen the enemies of the King *in the conduct of a war* against the King, that is in law the giving of aid and comfort' and 'an act which weakens or tends to weaken the power of the King and of the country *to resist or to attack the enemies of the King and the country* . . . is . . . giving of aid and comfort'" (emphasis added). Brimelow's truncated quotation fails to show that the passage defines aid and comfort in the context of "the conduct of a war" or of resisting or attacking enemies. Thus treason *does* necessarily involve war. So to call immigration enthusiasts traitors is in fact to say they are making war on the United States. Whether Brimelow understands that or not is unclear, but he should.

Index

Adams, John, 138

Adorno, Theodor, 105

African Americans: and Alt-Lite, 224; and anti-Americanism, 198, 200–01, 205; and race consciousness, 168–76; and race realism, 176–81; and right-wing extremism, 33; and secession, 206; and Stalinism, 207. *See also* Racialism; Slavery

Allen, Danielle, 141

Alternative Right (website), 17, 105, 106, 107

Alt-Lite, 9, 210–30; and Alt-Right, 212–14; ideology of, 214–24; as New Yippies, 224–26; and Spencer, 105; and Trump, 226–30; website traffic analysis for, 27, 29

Alt-Right: and Alt-Lite, 212–14; anti-Americanism of, 195–209; emergence of, 3–10; on foundational principles of American politics, 123–65; as ideological vs. political

movement, 12–13, 28; ideology of, 9, 115–230; intellectual roots of, 9, 31–111; problem of, 3–30, 231–54; racialism ideology of, 166–94; size of, 8–9, 11–30

ALTRIGHT.com, 13, 17, 230

American Conservative (magazine), 105

American Enterprise Institute, 87

American Interest (website), 27

American Prospect (website), 27

American Psychological Association, 179

American Renaissance (website): and *Breitbart News*, 213–14; evolution from print magazine, 15, 96–97; on *Federalist Papers*, 149; and Griffin, 102; on race consciousness, 174; on race realism, 176, 178; on racialism, 185; website traffic analysis, 23, 27, 29; on white supremacy, 95

American Spectator (magazine), 54

Environmental Protection Agency (EPA), 87
Ethnicity, 121, 174–75
Euclid, 117–18
Eurasianism, 218, 222–23
European New Right (ENR), 12–13, 216, 221
Evola, Julius, 217–20; *Man among the Ruins*, 219; *Revolt against the Modern World*, 218, 219–20

Facebook, 246
Fairness doctrine, 88
Fallon, Joe, 154–55
Fanaticism, 81
Fascism, 39, 40, 57–62
Federalist Papers: Alt-Right attacks on, 9, 117, 119, 149–53; and liberal democracy, 100; and political egalitarianism, 159; and secessionism, 204, 207–08
Feminism, 4, 5
Foster, William Z.: *Toward Soviet America*, 206
Foucault, Michel, 102
Francis, Samuel, 35–53; Burnham's influence on, 37–40; critiques of, 47–52; on egalitarianism, 128–29; and elite theory, 37, 40–45, 81–82, 242–43, 245; on *Federalist Papers*, 149, 150; on free market capitalism, 216; Griffin on, 102; *Leviathan & Its Enemies*, 35–36, 41, 42, 44, 46, 47–48, 50, 51, 53, 65, 82, 208; on liberal democracy, 55; "Neoconservatism and the Managerial Revolution," 40–41; and *Occidental Quarterly*, 109; on political egalitarianism, 126; as postexpert, 101; *Power and History*, 36; and racialism, 65–66; on radical change, 45–47, 228–29, 236; "The Roots of the White Man," 67; on secession,

202, 208–09; on soft managerial regimes, 57–58
Franco, Francisco, 239
Frankfurt School, 53, 72, 75
Franklin, Benjamin, 138
French Revolution (1789), 233
Friberg, Daniel, 12–13
Friendly fascism, 44
Fugitive Slave Act of 1850, 137
Fukuyama, Francis, 91, 234–35; *The End of History and the Last Man*, 234
Fulford, James, 199–200, 203
Futility argument, 38, 81
Futrell, Robert, 95–96

Gatekeepers, 9, 90, 94, 97, 100, 111, 227, 247–54
Gender equality, 4, 5
Gerhard, Victor, 66
Germany: fascism in, 58–61; managerialism in, 49
Gilens, Martin, 243–44, 245
Gingrich, Newt, 87
Glazer, Nathan, 34, 41, 174–75; *Beyond the Melting Pot* (with Moynihan), 34, 174–75
Globalism, 4
Glorious Revolution (1688), 125, 233, 238, 239
Gnosticism, 7
Goldwater, Barry, 33, 232
Gottfried, Paul, 53–64; *Conservatism in America: Making Sense of the American Right*, 58; "The Decline and Rise of the Alternative Right," 63; and Dugin, 221; *Fascism: The Career of a Concept*, 58; and futility argument, 81, 82; liberal democracy critique, 35, 51, 53–57, 241, 243; as postexpert, 101; on radical vs. generic fascism, 57–62; on secession, 202–03; and

298

Index

IQ, 178–79
Iron law of oligarchy, 38, 242–44
Isolationism, 93
Italy, fascism in, 58–61, 239

Jackson, Andrew, 230
Jay, John, 149–51
Jefferson, Thomas: and Declaration
of Independence, 118, 125–26,
238; and egalitarianism, 127, 128,
138, 140–42, 144, 162; and race
consciousness, 174; Trump on,
227–28
Jeopardy argument, 36
Jews: and Alt-Lite ideology, 214–15,
224; and Alt-Right ideology, 5–6;
and conservatism, 68; and conspiracy theory, 76–77; and elite theory,
243–44; and fascism, 59; Francis
on, 66–67; Johnson on, 110; and
neoconservatism, 34, 77–78; and
political egalitarianism, 155–56.
See also Anti-Semitism
Jim Crow era, 187, 191, 239
John Birch Society, 33, 34, 78–79, 129
Johnson, Greg, 108–11; on Alt-Right,
5, 12; on anti-Americanism, 201;
on *Breitbart News*, 212; on Constitution, 157; on political egalitarianism, 128; on race consciousness,
168–69; on secession, 205–06, 239
Johnson, Lyndon, 89
Johnson, Samuel, 126, 160

Kansas-Nebraska Act of 1854, 163
Kant, Immanuel, 108
Kemp, Jack, 87
Kennedy, Robert, 89
Kilpatrick, James Jackson, Jr., 186–87
King, Martin Luther, Jr., 89, 214
Kirk, Russell, 56–57, 218
Kirkpatrick, James, 4, 131, 135–37,
143, 230

Kissinger, Henry, 69
Krauthammer, Charles, 68
Kristol, Irving, 29, 34
Kristol, William, 27, 29
Ku Klux Klan, 7, 15, 95
Kurtagic, Alex, 106–07, 176–77

Leninism, 39, 232, 235–36
Le Pen, Marine, 217
Levin, Michael, 35, 58, 68, 78–81,
184, 190; *Why Race Matters: Race
Differences and What They Mean*,
68, 78–79, 184
Levinson, Sanford, 151
Liberal democracy opposition, 8,
123–65; and Alt-Lite, 224; Alt-
Right as philosophical competitor
with, 8, 35–64; and constitutional
orders, 231–35; and Declaration
of Independence, 124–27; and
Dugin, 221; and electoral democracy, 147–64; and Evola, 219;
futility argument, 38; Gottfried's
critique, 53–57; intellectual roots
of, 34; jeopardy argument, 36;
perversity argument, 36; and
political rights, 127–46; problem
of, 240–42
Libertarianism, 58, 108
Lincoln, Abraham, 117, 161–64, 214
Lipset, Seymour, 41
Locke, John, 125–26, 127, 189, 238;
Second Treatise on Government,
125–26, 238
Lumpenproletariat, 45–46, 101

MacDonald, Kevin: on Alt-Right, 5;
and anti-Semitism, 35, 66, 68–78;
conspiracy theory methodology
of, 76–77; *Cultural Insurrections:
Essays on Western Civilization,
Jewish Influence, and Anti-Semitism*, 109; *The Culture of Critique:*